Eudora Welty
Revised Edition

Twayne's United States Authors Series

Warren French, Editor

University College of Swansea, Wales

TUSAS 15

EUDORA WELTY
1909–
Photograph by Jill Krementz

Eudora Welty
Revised Edition

By Ruth M. Vande Kieft

Queens College, City University of New York

Twayne Publishers
A Division of G. K. Hall & Co. • Boston

To my friend and mentor
Austin Warren
1899–1986

Austin Community College
Learning Resources Center

Eudora Welty, Revised Edition

Ruth M. Vande Kieft

Copyright © 1987 by G. K. Hall & Co.
All Rights Reserved
Published by Twayne Publishers
A Division of G. K. Hall & Co.
70 Lincoln Street, Boston, Massachusetts 02111

Copyediting supervised by Lewis DeSimone
Book production by Marne B. Sultz
Book design by Barbara Anderson

Typeset in 11 pt. Garamond
by P&M Typesetting, Inc.

Printed on permanent/durable acid-free paper
and bound in the United States of America

Library of Congress Cataloging in Publication Data

Vande Kieft, Ruth M.
    Eudora Welty.

    (Twayne's United States authors series; TUSAS 15)
    Bibliography: p. 203
    Includes index.
    1. Welty, Eudora, 1909–   —Criticism and
interpretation.   1. Title.   II. Series.
PS3545.E6Z9   1987   813'.52   86-25612
ISBN 0-8057-7487-4

Contents

About the Author

Ruth M. Vande Kieft is professor of English at Queens College, City University of New York. She was born in Holland, Michigan, spent most of her childhood and early youth in Paterson, New Jersey, and her college years in the South, where she received her B.A. from Meredith College in Raleigh, North Carolina. She received her M.A. and Ph.D. degrees from the University of Michigan, and also studied at Oxford University, the University of California at Berkeley, Stanford University, and the Breadloaf School of English, under such notable critic-scholars as Austin Warren, C. S. Lewis, Yvor Winters, Robert Heilman, and Henry Nash Smith. She has held teaching positions at the University of Michigan, Wellesley College, Calvin College, and Fairleigh Dickinson University. Her publications include *Thirteen Stories by Eudora Welty* (a collection that she selected and for which she wrote a critical introduction) and a number of articles and reviews, chiefly on Eudora Welty, but also on Dickens, Sir Thomas Browne, Faulkner, and Flannery O'Connor, and appearing in such publications as *Sewanee Review*, the *Southern Review*, *Nineteenth Century Fiction*, the *Georgia Review*, *Mississippi Quarterly*, and *Southern Quarterly*. The original edition of *Eudora Welty*, written with the aid of American Association of University Women and Yaddo fellowships, was published a quarter century ago. The first full-length study of Eudora Welty's work, it has been continuously in print, and widely regarded as the most influential critical work on the fiction of this world-famous modern American writer.

Preface to the Revised Edition

It is now over a half-century since Eudora Welty's first story was published, and a quarter-century since the original edition of this book (one of the earliest in the TUSAS series) appeared in 1962. The book was written in answer to the need for a comprehensive study of a small body of fiction as varied and demanding as it was alluring and beautiful. In writing it, I increased my own understanding of and delight in Eudora Welty's fiction, and have been pleased to know it has been helpful to many others through the years.

By now her reputation has seen a spectacular rise, not only because of the "best-selling" fiction and autobiography she has added to her work, but also because the merit and durability of her earlier fiction has been widely appreciated in this country and abroad. No longer does it seem necessary to draw her out from under the shadow of that mountain of a fellow Mississippian writer near her in place and time, for she stands clearly in the radiance of her own incomparable achievement. Because Eudora Welty's fiction attracted growing attention, especially after the appearance of *Losing Battles* and *The Optimist's Daughter*, I was asked some years ago to update the chronology and bibliography of the original edition of this study. I did so, and the resulting second edition of *Eudora Welty*, with a considerably expanded bibliography, appeared in 1973.

This present revised edition is the result of a five-year labor in which I set myself the impossible task of condensing the original text sufficiently to allow for the expansion necessary to include discussion of the works by Eudora Welty that have appeared since 1955. I could not condense radically without destroying my method, which was that of detailed explication with the free use of quotation. I believe now, as I did at first, that Eudora Welty's stories require the kind of patient and loving scrutiny we apply to poems, and that to treat them with dispatch would be to leave only a skeletal idea or concept which could not be faithful to their total meaning. I used my "close reading" chiefly as a way to convey the inner life of the stories and novels, and to demonstrate their great variety in form and content, as well as the patterns of their relationship to each other.

A few comments about my method seem required. I am aware that it is "dated," though only, I believe, insofar as I am countering the current agnosticism about "meaning"—that it *can* exist, for all its complexity and subjectivity, in a literary text, and come as close in the mind of a reader to the intent of a writer in creating a literary work as a matching of imaginations, through language, can hope for or envision. This is a faith I hold high with or without Eudora Welty's fiction, but higher because she holds it.

I know as well the dangers of the method: that explication may seem to become coercive or reductive, appear to provide "keys" or substitutes for the stories, which it absolutely can and does not. Yet it is as foolish, to me, to deny understanding as ignorance. I aspire to one and reject the other, hoping for further enlightenment, eager to share what I have seen.

Thanks to my sympathetic and far-sighted editor and publishers, who have allowed me to exceed the customary length of volumes in the TUSAS series, I have not had to abandon what readers have found most valuable in my original study. Hence, though the first, biographical chapter and a few sections on less important stories have been much revised and shortened, chapters two through four remain essentially unchanged. In them I explore the central themes of the early fiction (what I have called "The Mysteries of Eudora Welty"), the methods she uses to convey them, the varied and complex attitudes she shows in their presentation, her use of comedy and its related modes, and her projection of the world of dream and fantasy. The chapters on *Delta Wedding* and *The Golden Apples* are followed by a substantially revised chapter on *The Bride of the Innisfallen,* and in the succeeding three chapters I have added discussions of Eudora Welty's two stories of the Civil Rights era, *Losing Battles,* and *The Optimist's Daughter*. In the final chapter I do not attempt, as I did in the original edition, to clarify Eudora Welty's position in relation to Southern and other modern writers of fiction, or to "place" her achievement: all this has been much discussed and now seems largely self-evident. Instead, I have tried to show a few of the patterns relating her life to her fiction. Chief among these, made freshly visible in her autobiography, *One Writer's Beginnings,* is the pattern of lyricism in her fiction, present in various forms from its beginnings.

My hope for this revised edition of *Eudora Welty* is what it was twenty-six years ago: to help in leading the readers of Eudora Welty's stories firmly and happily into their heart.

Ruth M. Vande Kieft

Queens College,
City University of New York

Acknowledgments

For the original edition of this work I am greatly indebted to the American Association of University Women Educational Foundation, which granted me the Minnie Cummock Blodgett Fellowship, 1960–61, for the purpose of writing it, and to the Corporation of Yaddo for the privilege of working at Yaddo during the first two months of 1961. To my friend and mentor, Professor Austin Warren, and to Robert Garis, I am most indebted for all they taught me about reading and interpreting literature, and to Virginia Prettyman for her salutary comments and suggestions on the first edition. My chief debts in preparing this new revised edition are to my thoughtful and encouraging editor, Professor Warren French, and to Sylvia Berkman, whose discerning and thorough critical and editorial reading of this book at every crucial stage brought me always closer to my impossible goal of perfection.

My greatest debt is to the gentle lady who wrote the stories, chiefly for the supreme gift of writing and giving them to us, but also for the generous gift of her kindness and friendship. D. H. Lawrence once famously advised, "Never trust the artist. Trust the tale. The proper function of a critic is to save the tale from the artist who created it." This advice I have happily ignored; where trust flows so freely in all directions, the tale requires no "saving" from its creator, and trust and gratitude only deepen with time.

I wish to make further acknowledgments to the following:

To Russell & Volkening, Inc., literary representatives, for permission to quote from Eudora Welty's published work.

To Harcourt Brace Jovanovich, Inc., for permission to quote from *A Curtain of Green*, copyright 1936, 1937, 1938, 1939, 1941, © renewed 1965, 1966, 1967, 1969 by Eudora Welty; *The Robber Bridegroom*, copyright 1942, © renewed 1970 by Eudora Welty; *The Wide Net*, copyright 1943, © renewed 1971 by Eudora Welty; *Delta Wedding*, copyright 1945, 1946, © renewed 1973, 1974 by Eudora Welty; *The Golden Apples*, copyright 1947, 1948, 1949, © renewed 1975, 1977 by Eudora Welty; *The Ponder Heart*, copyright 1953, 1954, © renewed 1981, 1982 by Eudora Welty; *The Bride of the Innisfallen*, copyright 1949, 1951, 1952, 1954, © 1955, © renewed 1977, 1979, 1982, 1983 by Eudora Welty.

To Random House, Inc., for permission to quote from *Losing Battles,* © 1970 by Eudora Welty; *The Optimist's Daughter,* © 1969, 1972 by Eudora Welty; *The Eye of the Story,* copyright 1942,1943, 1944, 1949, © 1955, 1956, 1957, 1965, 1966, 1971, 1973, 1974, 1975, 1977, 1978 by Eudora Welty, © renewed 1970, 1971, 1972, 1977 by Eudora Welty.

To Harvard University Press for permission to quote from *One Writer's Beginnings,* © 1983, 1984 by Eudora Welty.

To Russell & Volkening, Inc., for permission to quote from "Where Is the Voice Coming From?" © 1963 by Eudora Welty, and "The Demonstrators," © 1966 by Eudora Welty. Both of these stories were originally published in the *New Yorker.*

To the *Georgia Review* for permission to use my article "The Mysteries of Eudora Welty" (September 1961).

To Harcourt Brace Jovanovich, Inc., for permission to use sections of my essay "Demonstrators in a Stricken Land," which appeared in *The Process of Fiction,* 1969, 1974.

To the *Mississippi Quarterly* for permission to use sections of my articles "The Vision of Eudora Welty" (Fall 1973) and "Eudora Welty Visited and Revisited" (Fall 1986).

Chronology

1909   Born April 13 in Jackson, Mississippi.[1]

1925   Graduates from Central High School, Jackson, Mississippi.

1925–1927   Attends Mississippi State College for Women, Columbus, Mississippi.

1929   B.A. University of Wisconsin, Madison, Wisconsin.

1930–1931   Studies advertising at Columbia University School of Business.

1931   Returns to Jackson; death of father.

1931–1933   Works for local radio station. Society correspondent for Memphis *Commercial Appeal*.

1933–1936   Does publicity work for W.P.A. throughout state of Mississippi.

1936   One-woman show of unposed studies of Mississippi black people in Lugene Gallery, New York City. "Death of a Traveling Salesman" published in June *Manuscript*.

1937   "A Memory" and "A Piece of News" published in the *Southern Review*.

1940   Diarmuid Russell becomes Welty's literary agent.

1941   Second prize, The O. Henry Awards for "A Worn Path." *A Curtain of Green and Other Stories*.

1942   *The Robber Bridegroom*. Guggenheim Fellowship. First prize, The O. Henry Awards for "The Wide Net."

1943   *The Wide Net and Other Stories*. First prize, The O. Henry Awards for "Livvie is Back."

1944 $1000 award from the American Academy of Arts and Letters. On staff of *New York Times Book Review* for six months.

1946   *Delta Wedding*.

1949   *The Golden Apples.* Guggenheim Fellowship renewed for travel to France, Italy, England, Ireland 1949–1950.

1952   Election to National Institute of Arts and Letters.

1954   *The Ponder Heart.* Modern Library edition of *Selected Stories.* Honorary LL.D. degree from the University of Wisconsin.

1955   *The Bride of the Innisfallen.* William Dean Howells Medal of the Academy of Arts and Letters for *The Ponder Heart.*

1956   *The Ponder Heart* dramatized on Broadway. Honorary LL.D. from Smith College.

1958   Lucy Donnelley Fellowship Award from Bryn Mawr College.

1958–1961   Honorary Consultant of the Library of Congress.

1964   *The Shoe Bird* (children's fiction).

1966   Creative Arts Medal for Fiction from Brandeis University. Death of mother.

1968   First prize, The O. Henry Awards for "The Demonstrators."

1970   *Losing Battles.* Receives Edward MacDowell Medal.

1971   *One Time, One Place* (photographs, with an introduction). Election to the American Academy of Arts and Letters.

1972   *The Optimist's Daughter.* Gold Medal for Fiction of the National Institute of Arts and Letters. Appointed to six-year term on National Council of the Arts.

1973   Pulitzer Prize for fiction awarded *The Optimist's Daughter.*

1978   *The Eye of the Story.*

1980   *The Collected Stories of Eudora Welty.*

1981   Awarded National Medal of Literature and Medal of Freedom.

1983   William E. Massey lecture series delivered at Harvard University in April.

1984   *One Writer's Beginnings.* Modern Language Association Commonwealth Award.

1985 American Association of University Women Achievement Award.

1986 Jackson Public Library named in honor of Eudora
Welty. National Medal of Arts.

Chapter One

Beginnings and Fruitions: The Literary Career of Eudora Welty

The literary career of Eudora Welty[1] has something in common with several of her best stories. Striking in either case is both the disarming simplicity of the external facts, the setting, basic actions, and style, and the richness and complexity of the inner reality inherent in that simplicity. For years she suggested that her life was lacking in excitement and drama in the way of the world; the idea of a biography discouraged her, not only because of her instinctive shyness and desire for privacy, but also because of her conviction that a writer's work should be paramount. Over the years she had shared some of her personal history with interviewers and in autobiographical sketches (particularly one titled "The Little Store").[2] But in 1983 she was invited to inaugurate the William E. Massey lecture series in the History of American Civilization at Harvard University, and following the suggestion that she speak about her own early experiences as a writer, she gave three autobiographical lectures to a warmly receptive, largely student audience. Revised and collected, with accompanying photographs of herself and her family, the lectures became *One Writer's Beginnings* (1984), an act of supremely generous self-disclosure. In recreating and interpreting her own early life in relation to her development as a writer, Eudora Welty serves as the best possible guide to the reading of her fiction.

The book is dedicated to her mother and father. Weaving family history at various time periods throughout her chapters on "Listening," "Learning to See," and "Finding a Voice," she shows us two parents as deeply cherished in her memory as she was cherished by them throughout their lives, providing the strong emotional source of all she has been, or done, or written.

Disparate in almost every respect save that both came from pre-Revolutionary families and were schoolteachers, her parents met one summer in the mountains of West Virginia when her father worked there in a lumber construction company. Mary Chestina ("Chessie") Andrews Welty, a Virginian by descent, was of English, Irish, Scottish, and French Huguenot stock. Her grandfather, Edward (Ned) Raboteau Andrews, had been a poor, adventuresome country lawyer of legendary fame; her grandmother, Eudora Carden Andrews, daughter of a pious Baptist preacher, had shared a life of pioneer ruggedness with him in a gray-weathered house on a mountaintop in West Virginia. As a girl of fifteen, Chessie had journeyed by river raft and train with her father when ill health forced him to seek medical care in Baltimore. It was too late; he died, and Chessie returned home alone. Adored by her five rambunctious brothers, a brave young teacher passionately devoted to books and learning, her mother passed that devotion on to the incipient writer together with a strong independence of spirit. The water Eudora drank as a child when, on visits to her grandmother and uncles, she dipped with a tin cup from a mountain stream, seemed to her a distillation of the pioneer mountain spirit that neither her mother nor she ever lost.

Christian Webb Welty was the only child of an Ohio farmer of German Swiss ancestry. His mother, a pious and sober woman, had died when he was a boy of seven years; a little keepsake book, discovered after his death, held all the memorabilia of that seemingly lonely and uneventful childhood. A quiet and gentle man like his father, Christian Welty had looked resolutely to the future, in contrast to his wife and her family, whose memories were laden with stories, anniversaries, the triumphs, joys, and griefs of the past. He called himself an optimist for what the future would bring, all portents being favorable. The products of science and modern technology fascinated him: clocks, victrolas, gadgets, train travel, and schedules. With his young wife he settled in Jackson, Mississippi, where he built up a highly successful business, became President of the Lamar Life Insurance Company, put up Jackson's first skyscraper (thirteen stories)—and for his family, a fine home in the Tudor style. Yet he was also protective, cautious, and conservative in his public as in his private life. He had the skyscraper designed in the Gothic style to harmonize with the beautiful little Gothic church that stood beside it and the handsome antebellum Governor's mansion across the street. His interests and talents passed on to his two sons: Edward, the older, was an architect and designer of several of Jackson's most successful buildings; Walter, the younger, was with the Standard Life Insurance Company.

To Eudora her father gave less obvious but equally valuable legacies. He provided a "frame of regularity" for the life of his impressionable daughter, and undoubtedly, with her mother, instilled in her an instinctive love of truth and a capacity for sacrifice and self-discipline that served her well as a writer. Some of her joy in craftsmanship was probably inherited from her father: she built stories as he saw to the building of the "skyscraper" or made a kite, doing it right, making it good, hoping to please.

In the Welty family, order rather than disorder had been the fruit of early sorrow. Her parents' devotion had come charged with the inner mandate of special care and protection. Early deaths had made them so—more than their shared loss of a parent. They had lost their first child, a boy, at his birth. Her father had always taken special precautions, such as scoring the soles of Eudora's new shoes to insure that she would not fall.

The supreme gift her parents gave her, however, was that of their own love for each other. From her earliest years a rapt listener to stories of all kinds, true or fictional, many regarded by her parents as being scandalous, untrue, or otherwise unfit for her ears, she was "in on" that best of open secrets they shared. Thus she acquired "the turn of mind, the nature of temperament, of a privileged observer" of "the loving kind."

Eudora Welty is at her descriptive best in *One Writer's Beginnings* in presenting what she calls her "sensory education." She evokes the outside world impressing itself on her absorbing, imaginatively hyperactive sensibility, caught up by her (at one point literally) "fast-beating heart." Each object, impression, learning process, event, she links to her development as a writer: the sound of ubiquitous clocks ticking in their house to the fiction writer's sense of time; her father's acute farmer's "weather sense" to her "meterological sensibility," merging inner and outer atmosphere. Her love of the letters of the alphabet as shapes fraught with the "wizardry of letter, initial, and word" she saw realized years later in the Book of Kells, as the gold of the illumination "seemed a part of the word's beauty and holiness." An awareness of movement not only in music, but in the sound of the human voice and words on a page—an inward voice "with cadences," listened to "inwardly"—informed her own stories later as she wrote. She recalls her first awareness of the moon's roundness as coming with a sound experienced tactually, filling her mouth "as though fed to me out of a silver spoon," round as "a Concord grape Grandpa took off his vine and gave me to suck out of its skin and swallow whole, in Ohio." While perceiving the roundness of the moon as part of its sound, then *tasting* it with the smooth, cool grape, the reader can also see, beyond the teller's saying it, the little girl's small mouth open and close lovingly about the *o* sounds, especially in *Ohio*. This is pure demonstration: the child is a *writer*, abandoned almost from the birth of self-consciousness to the ecstasies of pure sensation, to become synesthesia, alliteration, and assonance in the adult writer's prose.

Eudora Welty's childhood was packed with the large and small glories, excitements, and terrors that happen in the sensitive, happy child's real world, fantasies, play, and delighted exploration of the world of nature, human nature, and books. Encouraged by her mother, who informed the librarian that she could read any book except *Elsie Dinsmore,* she devoured everything she could lay her hands on, including fairy tales, legends, myth, the "Series Books," Mississippi history, and adult fiction. Like the little girls in "June Recital," she studied the piano; like the ones in "Moon Lake," she went to summer camp. She loved traveling—by car, on short excursions and on summer trips to visit her grandparents; by train, with her father to meet her mother after a visit to her family in West Virginia, and later, on trips to New York City. She viewed the outside world through window frames; regularly it composed itself into expected, imagined, or surprising scenes.

She loved entertainers: the organ grinder with his monkey, acrobats, magicians, musical comedy performers, musicians of all sorts, "live" or on the Victrola, "classical" or "popular." "Then as now," she says,"my imagination was magnetized toward transient artists—toward the transience as much as the artists."

She indulged her imagination by writing romantic stories, one with an exotic Parisian setting which began with the sentence, "Monsieur Boule deposited a delicate dagger in Mademoiselle's left side and departed with a poised immediacy." During her teens she was also instructed in drawing and painting locally and in college.

From 1921 to 1925 Eudora Welty attended Central High School in Jackson, and then for two years she attended Mississippi State College for Women, in Columbus. Encouraged by her parents, she transferred to the University of Wisconsin in 1927, where she became an English major and began a more serious and focused study of English literature under Ricardo Quintana and other professors. During these undergraduate years she was interested in the great Russian novelists and also began reading William Butler Yeats, Virginia Woolf, William Faulkner, and other modern writers.

After receiving her bachelor of arts degree in 1929, Eudora Welty decided to equip herself to earn a living. She entered the School of Business at Columbia University, studied advertising for a year, wrote and sold advertisements on the side, attended the theater, and enjoyed a pleasantly varied social life. She sought work in New York, but it was the Depression; she found nothing, and returned to Jackson in 1931. The same year her father died—a heavy loss to her and her family. During the next eight or nine years she held a number of jobs in advertising and publicity and did some free-lance writing. The first of these was a part-time job with radio station WJDX—the first in Mississippi and a venture initiated by her father's insurance company—at which she earned sixty-five dollars a month for writing scripts and being generally useful at assorted tasks (among which was cleaning the canary bird cage). She then did free-lance work for local papers, wrote the Sunday column of Jackson society for the Memphis *Commercial Appeal,* and worked briefly for an enterprising newspaperman, whose attempts at starting a paper were, however, unsuccessful.

At her next (and first full-time) job with the Works Progress Administration (W.P.A.) she had the official title of "Junior Publicity Agent." In this capacity she traveled by bus and car all over the state of Mississippi, writing newspaper copy and taking photographs of various "projects," such as the rebuilding of Tupelo, Mississippi, after it had been demolished by a tornado, studying juvenile delinquency, putting up booths in county fairs, interviewing everybody from farmers to the Key Brothers (aviators). The best thing about the job was the opportunity it gave her to meet and talk to all kinds of people and become familiar with the small towns and countryside of her home state. Her job ended suddenly, in 1936, with the defeat of the Democratic Party. Then for a year she worked for the Mississippi Advertising Commission, writing copy and taking photographs designed to attract industry and tourism to the state.

Odd jobs these, but with her habit of sensitive observation she was developing as an artist. She began serious writing in a solitary, intuitive way, in an attempt to capture the elusive, revealing actions, gestures, and words of the people she encountered, and the places which, more than mere settings, seemed to carry part of her characters' truth and mystery in their atmosphere. She had the stories ready for publication, but she tried first to sell her unposed photographs of mostly rural black people to New York publishing houses. Her hope was that the photographs might incline publishers to take her stories, "but they weren't decoyed." For three or four years she went on periodic trips to New York trying to sell the stories, without success, but not discouraged because she enjoyed writing them anyway. In 1936 a number of her unposed studies of Mississippi blacks were displayed for a month in a one-man show in a small New York camera shop named the Lugene Gallery.

The importance of the photographs to her development as a writer is evident from her introduction to a collection of them published, in 1971, under the title *One Time, One Place: A Family Album.* Here she speaks of her ignorance and innocence, in coming from a stable, sheltered, and comfortable home, with the advantages of a good education, seeing now the lives and settings of Mississippi country people during the Depression. Using the camera's eye as the natural defense of a shy person, she soon learned to wait for the right, *revealing* moment to snap the shutter. Often fascinated, troubled, or horrified by what she saw and photographed, she would develop her own prints in the kitchen at night and study them. Then slowly they yielded to her their deep meanings of the tragedy, joy, and nobility of the lives of the people she had photographed. "I learned from my own pictures, one by one, and had to," she wrote, "for I think we are the breakers of our own hearts." She learned also, however, that what she wanted to find out about people "had to be sought for through another way, through writing stories."

In June 1936 her first published story "Death of a Traveling Salesman," appeared in a small magazine called *Manuscript,* edited by John Rood. During the next two years Robert Penn Warren and Albert Erskine, editors of the then influential *Southern Review,* published six of her stories, including "A Memory," "A Piece of News," "A Curtain of Green," and "Petrified Man." In 1940 Diarmuid Russell (son of the Irish poet George Russell—"AE") became her friend and literary agent, and sold such stories as "Why I Live at the P.O." and "A Worn Path" to the *Atlantic* and other nationally known magazines. With the added championship of John Woodburn, an editor of Doubleday, Doran & Company, *A Curtain of Green,* was published in 1941.

The book was a collection of these stories, well received; and with her literary career safely launched, Eudora Welty was able to give up odd jobs and devote herself more fully to writing. She spent a summer at Yaddo in Saratoga Springs, New York, where her friend Katherine Anne Porter was working at the same time. A short novel, *The Robber Bridegroom,* was published in 1942, and her second collection of short stories, *The Wide Net,* in 1943. A full-length novel, *Delta Wedding,* appeared in 1946; a collection of related stories titled *The Golden Apples* in 1949; *The Ponder Heart,* a long story which had originally appeared in the *New Yorker,* was published in 1954; and the same year saw the publication of a Modern Library edition of *A Curtain of Green* and *The Wide Net.*

Her next collection of stories, *The Bride of the Innisfallen,* appeared in 1955. During the next fifteen years, no longer works by Eudora Welty appeared, though she did publish several essays and reviews, and two stories, "Where Is the Voice Coming From?" (1963) and "The Demonstrators" (1966), both in the *New Yorker.* During all these years there was in the making, however, a fiction that grew in length and complexity as she worked on it. Originally conceived as a novella, it was finally published as her longest novel, *Losing Battles* (1970); it became her first work to appear on the best-seller lists. A long private ordeal, which ended with her mother's death and soon after that of a brother, led to a somewhat autobiographical novel, *The Optimist's Daughter* (1972), in which she made use of scenes, events, and recollections from her mother's youth in West Virginia. In 1978 she published a collection of her essays and reviews, *The Eye of the Story,* and in 1980, her *Collected Stories.* In 1984 her autobiography, *One Writer's Beginnings,* for months on the best-seller list, brought her the kind of general fame she had not yet experienced.

In the fifty or more years of her writing career Eudora Welty has won many honors and awards. In 1942 and 1943 she received first prize in the O. Henry Awards series for "The Wide Net" and "Livvie Is Back"; she also held a Guggenheim Fellowship for two years and won the William Dean Howells medal for "the most distinguished work of American fiction" of 1950–1955 for *The Ponder Heart.* She was elected to the National Institute of Arts and Letters in 1952, and from 1958 to 1961 served as an Honorary Consultant of the Library of Congress. In 1956 *The Ponder Heart* was dramatized by Jerome Chodorov and Joseph Fields, and produced on Broadway; "Why I Live at the P.O.," *The Robber Bridegroom,* and other works have been adapted for the theater, musical comedy, and television. Her works have been widely anthologized, have appeared in many British editions and have been translated into several foreign languages.

In the last fifteen years, with the success of her last two novels, the

Collected Stories, and *One Writer's Beginnings,* Eudora Welty's reputation has taken a quantum leap. By now she has received every major honor and award we bestow upon our greatest American writers: election to the American Academy of Arts and Letters (1971) and the Academy's Gold Medal for Literature (1972), a Pulitzer Prize for *The Optimist's Daughter* (1973), the Presidential Medal of Freedom (1980), and the Modern Language Association Commonwealth Award (1984). Honorary degrees have been bestowed on her by many of the leading colleges and universities of the country; she has been writer-in-residence at a great variety of academic institutions, including Oxford and Cambridge Universities. Her work has been the subject of a number of symposia, which she sometimes graces with her presence, contributing most often a reading, with occasionally a lecture or appearance on a panel. She has been honored by her state through the proclamation by Governor William L. Waller of 2 May 1973 as Eudora Welty Day—an occasion celebrated in the chamber of the House of Representatives of the old state capitol and attended by a throng of persons famous and unknown, all capitivated by her reading from *Losing Battles.* Her photographs have been exhibited in New York, at the state capitol in Jackson, and elsewhere.

On her seventy-fifth birthday, 13 April 1984, Eudora Welty was honored by a celebration featuring a variety of lectures, readings, and receptions at Millsaps College, another assembly in the House of Representatives, and an exhibition of her family photographs in the rotunda of the old state capitol. She has appeared for readings or interviews on a wide spectrum of occasions, from nationwide television programs to the scholarly Modern Language Association to small church and school groups in Jackson and elsewhere. Many new readers have been drawn to her fiction for the first time because of exposure to the wit, courtesy, and unsentimental human warmth so palpable in all her public appearances, as well as in her autobiography. There is an ideal quality to this career that makes it unique and purely pleasurable to contemplate: never, one imagines, has public celebration and adulation of an author been so justly and joyfully given, and so graciously and modestly received.

In *One Writer's Beginnings* and elsewhere Eudora Welty has provided her readers with much information about the sources and processes of fiction writing—her own and others'. She has long stressed the importance of place[3] as a prime resource of a writer in providing roots, "testing his truth," giving the reader the "pleasing illusion" that what he views is indeed the world's reality instead of the author's. She early discovered the Natchez Trace as a treasured place for her fiction. Originally carved by animals in the wilderness floor, it was used by Indians, outlaws, riverboatmen, mail carriers, evangelists, and settlers. Having passed through more than two centuries of Mississippi history and beside small country homes and villages, it provided the setting for many of her early fictional works. She reached back into history—the pioneer days when the Trace was still wilderness—for such stories as "A Still Moment" and *The Robber Bridegroom;* but the same country, in the thirties, was the setting for "Livvie" and "At the Landing." She has not often strayed from the Mississippi settings of her stories: the Jackson area; the Yazoo Delta cotton country; the red clay farms and hill country in the north and northeast; the forests, the Mississippi river bottoms; and the Natchez Trace. And when she has shifted to other settings, as in "Music from Spain" or "The Bride of the Innisfallen," she has continued to use place to define the feelings conveyed. She believes that the validity of great fiction depends on its being placed exactly where it is because of the accumulated feelings that are associated with places and because characters are made actual and credible when they are fixed by and in their settings. "It seems plain," she says, "that the art that speaks most clearly, explicitly, directly, and passionately from its place of origin will remain the longest understood."

Place also affects language. To be a Southern writer she regards as a special "endowment" because of the richness of local speech, and she has often expressed gratitude for the Southern delight in talking, listening, remembering. Southern talk tends to be narrative—adventure tales, tall tales, folk tales, or local legends; but most commonly it centers on families and their history. The continuity and stability of family and community life in Southern culture has provided Eudora Welty with a natural source of many of her stories and all of her novels.

For all of her attachment to Mississippi, Eudora Welty has also shown a detachment, a broadness of perspective, that comes from both her personal history and her temperament. Since her father might be called an "immigrant" from the North, and her mother came from a border state, she lacked the sprawling "extended family" characteristic of southern clans. Her ancestors were not part of the landed, aristocratic South, or small farmers, or politicians, or any-

thing else that might have given her that strong sense of a blood in-
heritance which is to be found in many distinguished modern
southern writers, most notably, Faulkner.

The pattern that made for detachment and perspective was enforced
by her experiences in advertising and publicity. She was neither totally immersed in this work, nor strongly rebellious against it. Her
father, whom she has described as being "of the gentlest possible
character," was a cautious and successful businessman; it was he who
urged her to take the advertising course at Columbia. The period was
mid-Depression; her flair for painting and writing, which her adventurous mother always encouraged, could be put to practical uses in
the writing of publicity and advertising copy, and in commercial pho-
tography. That she should have done this work at all is amusingly
ironic, considering that several of her classmates must have joined the
race that flourishes on Madison Avenue, with its techniques and goals
so alien to those of art.

She didn't take to advertising but she never expressed disillusion-
ment or revulsion against any of the odd jobs she held, nor against
anything in American culture generally. As an artist, she does not
seem to have felt any deep personal alienation from her culture, made
no strong protests about the encroachments of industrialism or the
passing of the old order. If she has preferred the South, it is not that
she has condemned the North and does not enjoy her frequent trips
to New York City and elsewhere. She has seemed matter-of-factly at
home both in her Mississippian and her native American culture, and
just as matter-of-factly distanced from them. She has displayed in her
fiction no strong partisanship of any specific social or political cause.

Temperamentally, her shyness and deep respect for her own and
others' privacy has made her approach her fictional subjects from the
outside, as an observer, detached, sometimes cautious, but always
growing toward the understanding that comes from empathy. The utmost in distance and objectivity and the utmost in intimacy are made
possible by the "outside" and "inside" kinds of narrative she employs;
in her care for external detail, she is always strongly in pursuit of
meaning, of essences, inner reality.

The pattern of detachment and independence is also apparent in
Eudora Welty's formal and informal literary life. Though she was a
member of a group of aspiring Mississippi journalists in the 1930s
and 1940s, they had no formative literary influence on her. She has
been a solitary, self-taught writer, and has never been attached to any

literary group such as the Nashville Fugitives or the Agrarians. She met certain members of those groups, many of whom became widely known as creative writers and "new critics" after a nucleus of them had settled at the University of Louisiana in Baton Rouge and used the *Southern Review* as the vehicle for their distinguished criticism, stories, and poems. Robert Penn Warren and Cleanth Brooks were serving as editors for the review, and Katherine Anne Porter, who also lived in Baton Rouge at the time, was a frequent contributor. Most warmly, they gave Eudora Welty their friendship along with their encouragement. Without doubt Katherine Anne Porter's introduction to *A Curtain of Green* and Brooks's and Warren's inclusion of "A Piece of News" and "Old Mr. Marblehall" in the first edition (1943) of their influential critical anthology, *Understanding Fiction,* did much to stimulate interest in Eudora Welty's fiction among discerning readers. But before meeting any important literary friends, she had developed independently as a writer; she has never consciously been a member of any literary, political, or philosophical "school."

In happy possession of a supple, clear, and sympathetic mind and sensibility, Eudora Welty has found the germs of her fiction in the living world around her. The inspiration of a story, she has said, is like "a pull on the line," "some outside signal" that has "startled or moved the story-writing mind to complicity: some certain irresistible, alarming (pleasurable or disturbing), magnetic person, place or thing."[4] The pull of "Powerhouse" on the line of her imagination must have been strong and insistent, for she wrote that story rapidly just after going to a dance where the black jazz musician, Fats Waller, played with his band. Sometimes a vivid impression was made on her mind and heart by a few words and gestures of a person, and out of this simple human encounter a story developed. The sight of a solitary old black woman walking "at middle distance, in the winter country landscape," an invented errand as the reason for her journey, brought old Phoenix Jackson into fictional being in one of Eudora Welty's best-loved stories, "The Worn Path." "Death of a Traveling Salesman" began with an intriguing remark: "I had to go borry some fire."[5] "Why I Live at the P.O." was sparked by her seeing, from a train window, a lady ironing in the small backroom of a post office, though "a lifelong listening to tales" was the enabling cause.[6]

The stories that Eudora Welty has written "by ear," as she calls it, are most easily set down. In these stories, such as "Petrified Man," she surrenders to the sound of her characters' speaking voices, while consciously selecting and shaping what they will say. Most of her stories have not, however, been quickly written, especially not in the later stages of her career. They "hang around" in her mind for a long time and in the writing undergo countless revisions. Because of its length and the many years during which she worked on it, *Losing Battles* probably "hung around" in her mind longer than any of her other works and underwent the most extensive revision. The sheer comic zest of the work seems to have spawned a variety of hilarious incidents and exchanges that later had to be cut by their exacting author.

Since the creative process has worked in such widely differing ways for Eudora Welty, she has always found it difficult to generalize about how she writes. But she feels that all stories spring from one source within a writer, the lyrical impulse "to praise, to love, to call up into view." What is praised, loved, evoked in her fiction is the life around her that presents itself as real, irresistible.

Although she has never claimed special privileges for herself as an artist, preserving always a natural modesty and dignity in everything pertaining to her own work and person, she has made great claims for the powers and fruits of the imagination, especially as they are perceived and enjoyed in the work of some of her favorite writers. Imagination, she believes, acts upon raw experience which is without significant meaning until it is interpreted. Out of deep and often unconscious patterns drawn from his or her own life experience, out from the seeming chaos of ordinary life, the artist creates the patterns and order of fiction. To this work of the artistic imagination, this truth, Eudora Welty has dedicated herself with patience, passion, and joy. No "intolerable wrestle with words" for this writer, and not because there hasn't been struggle, adventure, risk-taking. But the discipline of writing stories has always brought her the deepest happiness.

Our principal concern is not, however, with the life and opinions of this gentle writer so joyful in her craft, but rather with her fiction.

Chapter Two

The Mysteries of Eudora Welty

To write discursively and analytically of Eudora Welty's stories can seem daunting for many reasons, not the least of which is the mild distrust she has expressed of some of the methods and ends of literary criticism. "Since analysis has to travel backward," she has stated, "the path it goes is an ever-narrowing one, whose goal is the vanishing point, beyond which only 'influences' lie." The story writer, "bound in the opposite direction, works into the open," confronting and making choices, impelled not by schemes, but by feelings, which come "with an arrow inside them." She has also stressed the danger of looking for patterns in any writer's fiction, since the uniqueness and integrity of each story, its "own full-bodied right and . . . needs of fulfillment," may be overlooked.[1]

Meaning, however, is neither embodied nor perceived with the directness of an arrow finding its target, for the truth of life is ambiguous and often slow to come upon. And the strange habit of the best writers, she has stated, is that they seem to be "obstructionists," as if "they held back their own best interests. . . ." This is because "beauty is not a blatant or promiscuous or obvious quality; indeed, it is associated with reticence, with stubbornness, of a number of kinds."[2]

Eudora Welty *knows* she is mysterious and "obstructionist," but she is so because there is no other way for her to communicate what she must. She asks for a reader of "willing imagination" who will not insist on "a perfect Christmas tree of symmetry, branch, and ornament, with a star at the top for neatness," but will find "the branchings not what he's expecting, . . . not at all to the letter of the promise—rather to a degree—(and to a degree of pleasure) mysterious."[3] In explaining one of her own stories, she says, "Above all, I had no wish to sound mystical, but I did expect to sound mysterious now and then, if I could: this was a circumstantial, realistic story, in which the reality *was* mystery."[4]

Eudora Welty's stories are largely concerned with mysteries of the inner life. She explains that to her the interior world is "endlessly new, mysterious, and alluring"; and "relationship *is* a pervading and changing mystery; it is not words that make it so in life, but words have to make it so in a story. Brutal or lovely, the mystery waits for people wherever they go, whatever extreme they run to."[5] The term "mystery" has here to do with the enigma of man's being, of life and death—man's relation to the universe; what is secret, concealed, inviolable in any human being, resulting in distance or separation between human beings; the puzzles and difficulties we have about our own feelings, our meaning, and our identity. Eudora Welty's audacity is to probe these mysteries in the imaginative forms of her fiction. The critic's task is to try to follow her bold pursuit discursively, to show what the mysteries are and how she tries to communicate them, to disclose some of the patterns within all the wonderful variety of her work. The critic does this with the joyful knowledge that no amount of analysis can destroy the irreducible meaning and beauty of any real work of art, and (in the faith that understanding enhances delight) that his interpretation won't have "killed" the story for any reader.

We begin with the story called "A Memory," which might be recognized as more or less autobiographical even if Katherine Anne Porter (in her sympathetic introduction to *A Curtain of Green*) had not suggested it first, because here in seminal form are some of the central mysteries that have occupied Eudora Welty as a mature writer. It is the *nature* of the child lying on the beach that suggests what is to come, her preoccupation and her discoveries. An incipient artist, the child has a passion for form, order, control, and a burning need to identify, categorize, and make judgments on whatever comes within her vision. She does this by making small frames with her fingers, which is her way of imposing or projecting order on a reality that she has already guessed but not admitted to be a terrifying chaos. She is convinced that reality is hidden and that to discover it requires perpetual vigilance, a patient and tireless scrutiny of the elusive gesture which will communicate a secret that may never be completely revealed.

Parallel with this "intensity" is another equal intensity: that of her love for a small blond boy, a schoolmate about whom she knows nothing, to whom she has expressed nothing, but whom she holds fiercely within the protective focus of her love—a protection of him and of herself and her expectations which is enforced by the dreary regularity of school routine. But one day the boy suddenly has a nosebleed, a shock "unforeseen, but at the same time dreaded," and "recognized." It is the moment when she receives her first clear revelation of mortality, when she perceives the chaos that threatens all her carefully ordered universe, and the vulnerability of her loved one; she recognizes the sudden violence, the horror of reality, against which she is helpless. This event makes her even more fiercely anxious about the boy, for she "felt a mystery deeper than danger which hung about him."

This event is also a foreboding of the experience the girl has on the beach when a family group of vulgar bathers comes crashing into the world of her dream. Here is wildness, chaos, abandonment of every description, a total loss of dignity, privateness, and identity. There is destruction of form in the way the bathers protrude from their costumes, in the "leglike confusion" of their sprawled postures, in their pudgy, flabby figures; there is terrifying violence in their abuse of each other, their pinches and kicks and "idiotic sounds," their hurdling leaps, the "thud and the fat impact of all their ugly bodies upon one another." There is a hint of a final threat to human existence itself when the man begins to pile sand on the woman's legs, which "lay prone one on the other like shadowed bulwarks, uneven and deserted," until there is a "teasing threat of oblivion." The girl finally feels "a peak of horror" when the woman turns out her bathing suit "so that the lumps of mashed and folded sand came emptying out . . . as though her breasts themselves had turned to sand, as though they were of no importance at all and she did not care." The girl has a premonition that without form—the kind she has been imposing on reality by her device of framing things like a picture—human beings have no dignity nor identity, that beyond the chaos of matter lies oblivion, total meaninglessness. This is the vision of reality that must be squared to the dream; and so the girl must now watch the boy, still vulnerable, "solitary and unprotected," with the hour on the beach accompanying her recovered dream and added to her love.

This is one of the sorrowful or "brutal" mysteries that Eudora Welty presents in her stories. The "joyful" mystery is, of course, the careful, tender, ravishing love, the exquisite joy, and the dream. Chaotic reality does not displace the dream; though reality proves to be as terrifying as the child might have guessed, the dream cannot be totally destroyed.

The same mystery is explored in "A Curtain of Green," for the brooding, fearful, scarcely conscious anticipation of the girl in "A Memory" is the anguished knowledge of the bereaved young widow, Mrs. Larkin. In this story we have a similar careful, protective, absolute love, to which comes the violent affront of the most freakish and arbitrary kind of accident: a chinaberry tree simply falls on and kills Mrs. Larkin's husband. When she sees the accident, she assumes instinctively that the power of her love can save him: she orders softly, "You can't be hurt," as though, like God, she can bring order out of chaos. "She had waited there on the porch for a time afterward, not moving at all—in a sort of recollection—as if to reach under and bring out from obliteration her protective words and to try them once again . . . so as to change the whole happening. It was accident that was incredible, when her love for her husband was keeping him safe." Human love is finally powerless against chaos.

Now the young widow must penetrate deeply the meaning of this reality, which is simply to ask the question raised by any devastating accident: why did it happen? She plunges herself into the wild greenness out of which death fell: nature unpruned, uncultivated, formless in its fecundity. In the process of plunging she hopes to discover the essential meaning of nature; the knowledge itself will give her a kind of power over it, even though paradoxically she must abandon herself to it, become a part of it, lose her identity in it, as she does with her hair streaming and tangled, her uncertain wanderings, her submersion in the "thick, irregular, sloping beds of plants." She must look to see what is concealed behind that curtain of green.

Into the focus of her attention comes Jamey, the young black gardener, and once again she tries to seize control of destiny and effect her will, to give some meaning to the confusion and disorder of reality. If her love cannot preserve life, at least her fury and vengeance can bring death. Jamey's mindless serenity, his elusive self-possession, his quiet, inaccessible apartness (suggesting his calm acceptance of life) goad her into wonder and fury. For a moment she experiences a terrible lust for destruction. "Such a head she could strike off, intentionally, so deeply did she know, from the effect of a man's danger and death, its cause in oblivion; and so helpless was she, too helpless to defy the working of accident, of life and death, of unaccountability. . . . Life and death, she thought, gripping the heavy hoe, life and death, which now meant nothing to her but which she was compelled continually to wield with both her hands, ceaselessly asking, "Was it not possible to compensate? to punish? to protest?" Out of oblivion—without malice or motive—she can cause a death, as her husband's death has come, motiveless, out of oblivion; yet her destructive action would also be meaningless because it is *not* compensation for her husband's death: it is even too pointless to be a protest; what would the protest be against? Life and death are arbitrarily given and taken, pointlessly interchangeable—how then can her action, or any human action, have meaning? And yet, how can a human being *not* protest?

No rational answer comes to Mrs. Larkin. There is only release, touched off by the sudden fall of a retarded rain: thus it is a chance of nature that saves her from committing a meaningless murder, just as it is a chance of nature that kills her husband. The rain seems to bring out the quiet and lovely essences, the inner shapes of things in all the profusion of that green place, for "everything appeared to gleam unreflecting from within itself in its quiet arcade of identity." Mrs. Larkin feels the rush of love ("tenderness tore and spun through her sagging body"); she thinks senselessly, "It has come" (the rain and the release). She drops the hoe and sinks down among the plants in a half-sleep, half-faint, which is resignation; a blissful surrender to the mystery of nature, to the inevitable, because "against that which is inexhaustible, there was no defense." But her sleep has the look of death: there is the suggestion that only by sinking herself into final oblivion will she ever be released from her burning compulsion to wrest meanings from nature, to impose order on chaos, to recover her loved one.

These dark mysteries are further explored in a story called "Flowers for Marjorie." The story takes place during the Depression, and Howard and Marjorie, a poor young Mississippi couple, have gone to New York City to find work. Marjorie is pregnant, and Howard has been engaged in a humiliating and fruitless search for a job. He has now reached a point of despair in which he imagines that nothing can ever happen to break the inevitability of the pattern of being without work, without food, without hope. In his view there is no slight possibility of change or chance, a stroke of good luck; time, like their cheap alarm clock, ticks on with a bland, maddening pointlessness, because for Howard time has stopped.

But Marjorie, a warm feminine girl with soft cut hair, quietly and literally embodies an assumption of the significance of time, change, and progression. She has the matter-of-fact, yet deeply mystical knowledge that her rounding body holds a new life. She looks forward to a birth, and to Howard she seems in a "world of sureness and fruitfulness and comfort, grown forever apart, safe and hopeful in pregnancy"—the one flagrant exception to the fixed pattern of hopeless and pointless repetition. As if to tease Howard with the knowledge of her enviable exemption from despair, she has by chance found a bright yellow pansy which she places in the buttonhole of her old sky-blue coat and looks at proudly—"as though she had displayed some power of the spirit." In her human hope and submission, her gentle and loving reproaches against Howard's anxiety, she seems to him almost "faithless and strange, allied to the other forces." He finally shouts at her, out of his deep love turned into terrible despair, "Just because you can't go around forever with a baby inside your belly, and it will really happen that the baby is born—that doesn't mean everything else is going to happen and change! . . . You may not know it, but you're the only thing left in the world that hasn't stopped!"

Then in a moment of wild objection to the affront of time and change in her whole being, of her content, security, and easiness, he seizes a butcher knife and stabs her quickly and without violence—so quickly that the girl stays poised in a perfect balance in her seat at the window, one arm propped on the sill and hair blowing forward in the wind; the relative stillness and composure of her life now become the absolute, ironic stillness of death. Howard watches her lap like a bowl filling with blood. Then he hears the clock ticking loudly and throws it out the window. By his attack on time and change, he has corrected the only apparent flaw in his desperate logic of futility.

The events that follow can only be described as monstrous. Howard, half-numb and hysterical, flings himself on the town, only to be confronted with a series of crazily ironic pieces of good luck. It is as though chance had seized him by the throat and said, "You suppose nothing can happen to change the pattern, and *you* try to seize control. Oh, the universe is full of surprises—only *see* what can happen!"—and then throttled him and taken a gleeful revenge by playing a series of ingenious tricks on him. What a surprise when the slot machine at the bar responds to his last nickel by disgorging itself so profusely that one of the men says, "Fella, you ought not to let all hell loose that way" (for the crazy logic of hell *has* been let loose since

Howard has committed the murder)! And what a finally horrifying surprise when he walks through a turnstile to an arcade and becomes "the ten millionth person to enter Radio City," covered with all of the honor and glory of arbitrarily conferred distinction. ("What is your occupation?" "Are you married?"—as photo-lights flash) and given a huge key to the city and an armful of bright red roses!

He flees in terror back to the flat. There in the little fourth-story room, full of the deep waves of fragrance from the roses, he "knew for a fact that everything had stopped. It was just as he had feared, just as he had dreamed. He had had a dream to come true." Here he is with his gift of flowers for his lovely flower-loving wife (whose round and fruitful lap should be filled with roses instead of a pool of blood)—his good luck, his "break,"his "dream come true." And here he is also with his nightmare come true. He now faces the impossibility of any personally significant kind of chance or change or hope, the absolute and unalterable fact of death.

If love and happiness seem to be permanently insured (as in Mrs. Larkin's case), chance may annihilate them at a stroke; if misery and destruction seem unalterable, so that from despair people act in accordance with what they suppose to be their tragic inevitability (as in Howard's case), chance may surprise them, belatedly and irrelevantly, with a shower of gifts. A change of weather may affect a destiny: a rain shower saves Mrs. Larkin from committing a murder; in "The Whistle" a late spring frost ruins the spring crop of a poor farm couple, driving them to the desperate act of burning all their meager furniture for a moment's warmth. Human beings cannot predict, they cannot control, they cannot protest against, they cannot even begin to understand the inscrutable workings of the universe.

These are the darkest mysteries that Eudora Welty explores until she reaches *The Optimist's Daughter,* for she does not often confront her characters with all the terrors of chance and oblivion. However inarticulate, plaintive, lonely, or frustrating she shows love becoming in the experience of a human being, she rarely again reveals it in its final and stark impotence against the implacable inhumanity of the universe. The stories tell us something about her philosophical and religious vision, which is pessimistic and agnostic.

Through the experience of these characters she seems to be saying that there is no final meaning to life beyond the human meanings; there is no divine "surround," no final shape to total reality, no love

within or beyond the universe (for all its ravishing beauties), however
much of it there may be burning in individual, isolated human
hearts. Through an inevitable act of mind and heart (which is like a
blessed reflex, because love comes willy-nilly, or a compulsion, because the mind must impose its order), the individual makes whatever meaning is to come out of chaotic reality. There are only
fragments of shape and meaning, here, there, and everywhere: those
created by all the world's lovers and artists (the terms often become
interchangeable in her vocabulary). And in Eudora Welty's catholic
and charitable vision, the lovers and artists would probably include
most people at least some of the time. Thus her deepest faith is
couched securely in her deepest skepticism.

One other story in which she plunges into metaphysical questions
is "A Still Moment." In this story three men try to wrest final meanings out of human life from three different points of view. Each of
these men—Lorenzo Dow, the evangelist; Murrell, the outlaw; and
Audubon, the naturalist—is consumed with a desire to know, or do,
or communicate something of burning urgency; and each is essentially
frustrated in his mission. Lorenzo, consumed by divine love, has the
passion to save souls, but his efforts are mocked not only by lack of
response—his inability to light up all the souls on earth—but by far
more threatening internal struggles. These come from his awareness
that nature mocks him in its simplicity, peace, and unconscious effectiveness; that he is more susceptible to nature than to divine beauty;
and that in his frequent encounters with death he manages to survive
less because of his sense of divine guidance and protection than because some strange savage strength and cunning overtake him in the
moment of danger. He is saved by an instinct that he identifies as the
word of the devil, not an angel, because "God would have protected
him in His own way, less hurried, more divine." Because of his precarious and costly faith and the doubts and frustrations and waste
places of his own heart, he flies across the wilderness floor from one
camp meeting to the next, filled with the terrible urgency of his message: "Inhabitants of time! The wilderness is your souls on earth. . . .
These wild places and these trails of awesome loneliness lie nowhere,
nowhere but in your heart."

Murrell, the outlaw killer, who believes himself to be possessed of
the devil, falls in beside Lorenzo and settles on him for his next victim. His method is strangely ceremonial, for he rides beside the victim telling long tales, in which a "silent man would have done a

piece of evil . . . in a place of long ago, and it was all made for the revelation in the end that the silent man was Murrell himself, and the long story had happened yesterday, and the place *here.*" Lorenzo's passion is to save the inhabitants of time before Eternity; Murrell's is to "Destroy the present! . . . the living moment and the man that lives in it must die before you can go on." In the moment of hideous confrontation with the victim just before the murder, Murrell tries to lay hold on the mystery of being. He murders for the same reason that Mrs. Larkin almost murders Jamey: "It was as if other men, all but himself, would lighten their hold on the secret, upon assault, and let it fly free at death. In his violence he was only treating of enigma." Approaching the point of climax which is to be the still moment, he and Lorenzo are like brothers seeking light; for Lorenzo's divine passion is darkened by his sense of the tempter within him, and Murrell is less guilty than his crimes would make him appear because he has no other motive for killing than pure quest for the elusive mystery of being. Evangelist and murderer, soul-saver and destroyer, seem to become as one.

Audubon's light step on the wilderness floor, his serene and loving gaze at the earth, and the birds and animals around him, suggest at first a sharp contrast with the desperate urgency of the two men. He is a man who seems in harmony with nature, "very sure and tender, as if the touch of all the earth rubbed upon him"; a man who needs no speech because it is useless in communciating with birds and animals. But Audubon is presently seen to have his own urgency. Love of nature gives him a compulsive and insatiable need to remember, to record in his journal, and to convey all the varieties of life about him. His vigilant probing of nature is a quest for origins and ends; he does not know whether the radiance he sees is only "closed into an interval between two darks," or whether it can illuminate the two darks that a human being cannot penetrate, and "discover at last, though it cannot be spoken, what was thought hidden and lost." His endless examination of the outside world may disclose to him the mystery of his own identity. "When a man at last brought himself to face some mirror surface he still saw the world looking back at him, and if he continued to look, to look closer and closer, what then? The gaze that looks outward must be trained without rest, to be indomitable."

Here gathered in the wilderness, then, are three fiery souls, each absolute in its consuming desire, for "what each of them had wanted was simply *all*. To save all souls, to destroy all men, to see and to record all life that filled this world—all, all. . . ."

Into the still moment comes the beautiful, slow, spiral flight of the snowy heron; with its unconscious freedom, it lays quiet over them, unburdens them, says to them, "Take my flight." To each comes a revelation, and these revelations are inevitably disparate and subjective. With swift joy Lorenzo sees the bird as a visible manifestation of God's love. Murrell has a sudden mounting desire for confession, and a response of pity; he wishes for a keen look from the bird that could fill and gratify his heart: as though the bird had some divine power, and its sign of recognition could accuse and forgive simultaneously. Audubon gazes at the bird intensely as if to memorize it; and then, because he knows he cannot paint accurately enough from memory, he raises his gun to shoot it. As he does so, he sees in Lorenzo's eyes horror so clear and final as to make him think he has never seen horror before.

Audubon shoots the bird and puts it in his bag. The three men disperse; and for each of them it is as though his destiny has been sealed, the basic issue of his life clarified. Murrell lies in wait for the next victim: "his faith was in innocence and his knowledge was of ruin; and had these things been shaken? Now, what could possibly be outside his grasp?" He is filled with his glorious satanic dreams of conquest and darkness.

Audubon knows that he will paint a likeness of the bird that will sometimes seem to him beautifully faithful to its original; but this knowledge comes with the tragic awareness that even though he alone as artist has really *seen* the bird, he cannot possess or even reproduce the vision because his painting will be a dead thing, "never the essence, only a sum of parts." The moment of beauty can never be communicated, "never be one with the beauty in any other man's head in the world. As he had seen the bird most purely at its moment of death, in some fatal way, in his care for looking outward, he saw his long labor most revealingly at the point where it met its limit." The final frustration of the artist is that he can never capture the final mystery of life, nor convey it to others; no matter how faithfully and sensitively reproduced, nature remains inviolable and unknown.

Riding slowly away, Lorenzo has a terrifying vision, for it suddenly seems to him that "God Himself, just now, thought of the Idea of Separateness." He sees no apparent order or scheme in the divine management of things because God is outside Time, and He does not appear to know or care how much human beings who live inside Time need order and coherence which alone can bring the lover to a final union with the loved object. God created the yearnings, but He did not provide a way of meeting the need. He seems to Lorenzo finally indifferent:

He could understand God's giving Separateness first and then giving Love to follow and heal in its wonder; but God had reversed this, and given Love first and then Separateness, as though it did not matter to Him which came first. Perhaps it was that God never counted the moments of Time; Lorenzo did that, among his tasks of love. Time did not occur to God. Therefore— did He even know of it? How to explain Time and Separateness back to God, Who had never thought of them, Who could let the whole world come to grief in a scattering moment?

In terms of the incident Lorenzo is asking: "Why did you let me see the bird, which was inevitably to love it, and see in it your love become visible, and share that love with the other watchers, only to let it be suddenly and pointlessly destroyed, so that I am now separated both from the beloved object, and from all who saw it or who might have seen and loved it?" Which is like saying, "Why do you allow death to happen?"—the question that also tortures the young wife in "A Curtain of Green."

Yet the "beautiful little vision" of the feeding bird stays with Lorenzo, a beauty "greater than he could account for," which makes him shout "Tempter!" as he whirls forward with the sweat of rapture pouring down his face. He has again felt in his heart how overwhelmingly sensitive he is to the beauty of nature, and also how pointless and baffling is any attempt to relate it to divine love or meaning or plan or purpose; how pointless, then, is his mission to save souls. But he rushes on through the gathering darkness to deliver his message on the text "in that day when all hearts shall be disclosed." His final desperate gesture of faith is that when Time is over, meanings will be revealed; then the breach between Love and Separateness, the source of human tragedy, will be eternally closed. It is a faith that Eudora Welty herself nowhere affirms: she only shows us, in the richly varied characters and situations of her stories, the intensity of the Love, and the tragic fact of the Separateness in the only life we know, which is our present life in Time. She is asking metaphysical questions, but she is attempting no answers. The only solution to a mystery is yet another mystery; cosmic reality is a nest of Chinese boxes.

With a sensitivity as detached as it is tender, so that we may not even notice the sympathy because of the sure, cool objectivity of her art (like Audubon, she is a careful and relentless observer), Eudora Welty brings to life a number of characters each engaged in the private quest for the identity of the self, and the self in relation to the other. She is concerned about what she calls "the mystery of relationship" in all stages of awareness. The questions asked are "Who am I and who are you?" These are related to the questions "How can I get my love out into the world, into reality"—communicated and understood—and "How can I see and know what is going on in *your* heart," which is sometimes to say, "How can I see my love returned and shared, but in such a way as to remain free within myself?"

In "The Hitch-Hikers" and "Death of a Traveling Salesman" two salesmen have a flash of insight into their own identity, which is pathetically and paradoxically that they *have* no identity because they have no place and no focus of love to define them. Tom Harris, the thirty-year-old salesman of "The Hitch-Hikers," appears to have been born with a premonition of his coming isolation, for as a child he had often had the sense of "standing still, with nothing to touch him, feeling tall and having the world come all at once into its round shape underfoot and rush and turn through space and make his stand very precarious and lonely." He lives in a world of hitchhikers, and the title suggests that Harris himself is one of the transients despite the relative economic security provided by his job.

Tom Harris is a wise, tolerant, generous sort; people naturally confide in him and women are attracted to him, but he will not be held back by anyone. He is beyond surprise or shock because of his wide experience. With a peculiarly detached kind of suspense he views the events surrounding a murder committed in his car by one of the hitchhikers, since any strong emotion or violence in his life has always been something encountered, personally removed. There had been "other fights, not quite so pointless, but fights in his car; fights, unheralded confessions, sudden love-making—none of any of this his, not his to keep, but belonging to the people of these towns as he passed through, coming out of their rooted pasts and their mock rambles, coming out of their time. He himself had no time. He was free; helpless."

Immobilized by his fear of attachment, he refuses the chance to tie his present to his past, and both with a future. A young girl, Carol, emerges from that past with her memory of him as a man who talked about himself fascinatingly and played the piano—an entertainer of sorts, like the carefree tramp whose shining guitar had caused Harris to pick up the hitchhikers. In refusing Carol's sweetly frank offer of love, he extinguishes his potential for joyful life as surely as the sullen tramp, Sobby, had extinguished the life of happy-go-lucky Sanford with his mountain music. Without an ounce of exhilaration in the knowledge of his freedom, and embracing with apparent resignation his knowledge of helplessness, he is found in the last scene poised for yet another flight, a puzzling, touching American phenomenon, exceptional only in the degree of his self-awareness.

The salesman of "Death of a Traveling Salesman," R. J. Bowman, comes to this awareness belatedly, by perceiving with the acute eye of a stranger the essence of the simple, rooted life of the couple whose crude hospitality he briefly enjoys. The painful contrast with his own loveless, rootless ways kills him as much as does the protest of his troublesome heart. By the end of the story he is beautifully ready for love, but he cannot live to enjoy it. The two salesmen's tragedy is lack of a "place," a home, a steadying point and focus for their feeling. Eudora Welty shows how being "on the move" can cost a man his life: literally in Bowman's case, though Tom Harris "toughs it out" by a slow process of anesthetizing his heart. Only carefree, amoral, guitar-playing Sanford, the happy hobo in "The Hitch-Hikers," seems able to resist the inner emptiness and lovelessness of life on the road.

The salesmen barely got started in their quest for love and identity; but Clytie, in the story by that name, though less self-aware, has made some small progress. She is ready to emerge, to reach out toward others: she is full of the wonder and mystery of humanity, and there is a kind of breathless, religious awe in the way she scans the faces of the townspeople, seeing the absolute and inscrutable uniqueness of each one. "The most profound, the most moving sight in the whole world must be a face. Was it possible to comprehend the eyes and the mouths of other people, which concealed she knew not what, and secretly asked for still another unknown thing? . . . It was purely for a resemblance to a vision that she examined the secret, mysterious, unrepeated faces she met in the street of Farr's Gin." To the people

of Farr's Gin, Clytie is ready to give that most generous of all gifts—
contemplation: the desire to know without using, the respect for
"otherness," the awe of what is inviolable. But she is suffocated and
nauseated, living in a house of disease and death with her vampirelike
sister, her alcoholic brother, her apoplectic father, and the dead
brother with a bullet hole in his head. These faces come pushing between her and the face she is looking for, a face that had long ago
looked back at her once when she was young, in a sort of arbor:
"hadn't she laughed, leaned forward . . . and that vision of a face—
which was a little like all the other faces . . . and yet different . . .
this face had been very close to hers, almost familiar, almost acces-
sible."

After a horrible experience in which, with "breath-taking gentleness," she touches the face of a barber who comes to shave her father,
only to find it hideously scratchy, with "dense, popping green eyes,"
she dashes out to the old rain barrel, which seems to her now like a
friend, and full of a wonderful dark fragrance. As she looks in, she
sees a face—the face she has been looking for—but horribly changed,
ugly, contracted, full of the signs of waiting and suffering. There is
a moment of sick recognition, "as though the poor, half-remembered
vision had finally betrayed her." That knowledge compels her to do
the only thing she can think of to do: she bends her head down over
and into the barrel, under the water, "through its glittering surface
into the kind, featureless depth and [holds] it there."

What does her action mean? Possibly she has seen the ghastly disparity between what she once was and ought to have been (the loving,
laughing creature of her youth) and what she has become (ugly,
warped, inverted). Also perhaps she realizes that the only love in that
house, if not in that town, was the love *she* made: there was no one
then to embrace, no nature to plunge into but her own, no love possible but narcissistic love, no reality but her own reality, no knowledge
possible but the knowledge of death, which is the immersion into
oblivion. It is another pointless joke in a pointless universe. The final
image of her as fallen forward into the barrel, "with her poor ladylike
black-stockinged legs up-ended and hung apart like a pair of tongs,"
is one of the most grim jokes Eudora Welty has ever perpetrated: it
is only our memory of the wild misfiring of Clytie's love that makes
us see the pathos in her grotesque ending.

The situations in all these stories seem fundamentally tragic or pathetic. It is when the loving heart is awakened in finding an object

that joy speaks out in the stories, almost inaudibly in "First Love," somewhat more clearly in "At the Landing," and loudly and triumphantly in "A Worn Path." Joel Mayes, the solitary little deaf-mute of "First Love," is dazzled into love by a single gesture of Aaron Burr's, a gesture which brings a revelation:

One of the two men lifted his right arm—a tense, yet gentle and easy motion—and made the dark wet cloak fall back. To Joel it was like the first movement he had ever seen, as if the world had been up to that night inanimate. It was like a signal to open some heavy gate or paddock, and it did open to his complete astonishment upon a panorama in his own head, about which he knew first of all that he would never be able to speak—it was nothing but brightness. . . .

A single beautiful movement of human strength and careless grace has crystalized a love that must be as inarticulate as it is sweetly wondering and intense. Quietly, night after night, the little boy sits watching his beloved, adoring his nobility, his mystery, his urgency. The boy's presence is accepted by the conspirators, but ignored. Joel has no way of expressing his love, except by trotting like a little dog around his master, sniffing out the dangers that lie in his path, for Joel constantly senses the imminence of disaster and the dread of coming separation. "Why would the heart break so at absence? Joel knew it was because nothing had been told." And yet even if the moment of revelation *did* come, when love might speak out, he knows there are no words for what it might say. Gazing deeply into the face of the sleeping Burr, he has a terrible wish to speak out loud; "but he would have to find names for the places of the heart and the times for its shadowy and tragic events, and they seemed of great magnitude, heroic and terrible and splendid, like the legends of the mind. But for lack of a way to tell how much was known, the boundaries would lie between him and the others, all the others, until he died." The most he can do for Burr is to quiet his nightfears by gently taking his hand, stopping his nightmare ravings from the ears of potential eavesdroppers. When Burr leaves town, Joel feels he will "never know now the true course, or the outcome of any dream." His love never gets *in the world,* but it is less pathetic than Clytie's because at least it has found an object, it has flowered.

"In the world" is a key phrase in the story of Jenny Lockhart called "At the Landing." It is the hearts of her family that are locked: she is caught in the house of pride, tradition, "culture," and death, folded in the womb of that house by her grandfather. Through the painful birth process of discovery and experience she comes to the landing, the taking-off place, and so out into the world. The world, the forces of life, are symbolized by the river and the flood, which inundate Jenny's house and the graveyard where her relatives are buried. Billy Floyd, a wild creature of mysterious origins who fishes on the river, rides along on the flood and is master of it, is the one who brings her into the world: not only by his sexual violation of her, but more quietly and surely through her adoring response to his wild beauty, through the revelations that come to her about herself and him, and about love, that are the chief concerns of the story.

Jenny learns almost as much above love, about its mysteries and changes, and the mystery of human identity, as it is possible to learn. These revelations come to her by seeing, feeling, and guessing—by intuitive perception. She learns how love "would have a different story in the world if it could lose the moral knowledge of a mystery that is in the other heart": the knowledge forbids an emotional violation, or possession of another's self, which might be worse than the physical assault of rape. Watching Billy ride the red horse becomes for her a kind of anticipation of the sexual act, through which she learns that "the vaunting and prostration of love told her nothing." Sexual experience in itself cannot disclose the mystery of human identity nor bring people together.

But when she sees Billy Floyd in the village store, he seems changed: there is "something close, gathering-close, and used and worldly about him, . . . strong as an odor, the odor of the old playing cards that the old men of The Landing shuffled every day over their table in the street." If she presses him now, corners him in that small place, she will discover his identity, and that will be something small, mean, and faintly dirty—for he is thought by the literal-minded to be "really the bastard of one of the old checker-players, that had been let grow up away in the woods till he got big enough to come back and make trouble." But he conquers her with his defiant look, and she wisely lets him escape, knowing that this is *not* his true and final definition: his origins are more wild and wonderful (is the Natchez Indian in his blood?—is he one of the people of the lost Atlantis?); his nature cannot be defined by the context of the village store and the odors of old playing cards.

She learns too the value of her love and how enormously precious is her whole nature, which must be learned slowly, patiently, tenderly, and guesses that she never *will* be so learned by anyone. She knows also that "what she would reveal in the end was not herself, but the way of the traveler": she has no final revelations to give to any lover; she is only herself, like every other human being, on a perplexing journey through life, engaged in the perpetual and difficult process of finding herself, her meaning, her destination. The most she might do with Billy Floyd is travel with him for a while; he has his own search. Such amazing discoveries Jenny makes in her birth process, and each discovery is the revelation of yet another human mystery. At the end of the story she is only starting her wait for Billy Floyd. She is "at the landing," almost killed by the river men's brutal raping, but still holding fast to her dream of love, "the original smile" on her face.

Jenny's love barely manages to get articulated; its actions in the world are fumbling and largely ineffectual; and at the end of the story she is left, like Joel, separated from her loved one. But the love of Old Phoenix in "A Worn Path" is most triumphantly realized "in the world." It has a clear object—her grandson; it is actualized, put out into reality, not only by her care of him, but in the periodic ceremonial act of her trip along the worn path into town to fetch the "soothing medicine." There are no significant barriers to the expressive love of old Phoenix, and this is reflected also in her sense of familiarity with nature—the ease with which she talks to the birds and animals—and in her ability to live as readily, interchangeably, and effectively in the realm of the fanciful and supernatural as she does in the realm of practicalities. She is, like Dilsey in *The Sound and the Fury,* a completely and beautifully harmonious person—something one does not often find in the fiction of either Eudora Welty or Faulkner.

What happens when love finds fulfillment in the most natural and happy way possible, physically and emotionally, when it is both communicated and returned and is solidly "in the world" through marriage? Is there then an end to the mysteries of the self and the other? In several of her stories Eudora Welty shows there is not; she indicates, in fact, that the one thing any married person cannot do is to assume knowledge of the other, or try to force it in any way, or make a predictable pattern of a relationship, or block the independence, or impede the search of the other. A relationship of love can be kept joyful, active, free, only if each partner steps back now and then to see the other with a fresh sense of his inviolable otherness, his mystery, his absolutely sacred and always changing identity. Out of some deep need to establish the new perspective, to insist on freedom and apartness, one partner may simply run away from the other, withdraw, or go into temporary "retreat." This is a basic situation in "A Piece of News," "The Key," "The Wide Net," *The Robber Bridegroom, Delta Wedding,* "Music from Spain," "The Whole World Knows," and "The Bride of the Innisfallen." The quarrels and separations presented in these stories are not the ordinary, distressing marital quarrels that spring from hate, aggression, and conventional domestic discord, for none of these lovers has ceased to love or want the other. Each of them is simply demanding in his or her own way: "See me *new.* Understand the changes in me, and see how I am apart from you, unknowable and not to be possessed: only then can you possess me fully again."

The theme is given a semicomic treatment in "A Piece of News." Ruby Fisher, a primitive, isolated, and apparently unfaithful young backwoods wife, chances on a newspaper story in which a girl with the same name is shot in the leg by her husband. Though Ruby knows such an action on her husband Clyde's part to be quite improbable—even though he knows of her infidelities—she is immediately struck with the imaginative possibilities of such a situation, and is marvelously impressed and flattered. Images of herself dying beautifully in a brand-new nightgown, with a remorseful Clyde hovering over her, play delightfully in her mind. The romantic view of herself extends to her whole body; and while preparing dinner after Clyde returns, she moves in a "mysteriously sweet . . . delicate and vulnerable manner, as though her breasts gave her pain." When she discloses to Clyde the secret of the newspaper story, there is a moment, before common sense triumphs, when the two of them face each other "as though with a double shame and a double pleasure." The deed *might* have been done: "Rare and wavering, some possibility stood timidly like a stranger between them and made them hang their heads." For an instant they have had a vision of each other in alien fantasy roles—an experience that is pleasing, exciting, and rather frightening.

The theme is again treated with tender humor in "The Key." Ellie and Albert Morgan are dramatically shut off from the outside world by being deaf-mutes. The action takes place in a railroad station where the couple miss their train for Niagara Falls because they cannot hear. The strange little irony of their relationship is that Ellie "talks" too much—with her fingers by sign language. But that volubility of signals shows how she broods over all their discussions, misunderstandings, agreements, "even about the secret and proper separation that lies between a man and a woman, . . . their secret life, their memory of the past, their childhood, their dreams."

An interesting feature of the story is the use of a double narrator-observer: the omniscient narrator provides, as a "receptor" of the couple's problem, a marvelously fiery, compassionate young man with a lovingly humorous detachment who bears kinship to Tom Harris of "The Hitch-Hikers" and to George Fairchild of *Delta Wedding*. He tries, concretely though anonymously, to help the couple, but knows "the uselessness of the thing he had done." He may have godlike prescience and compassion, but he hasn't the power to *change* things. This character is agent rather than focus of the narrator's own sympathy: she has infinite faith in him, but leaves him baffled and thwarted in his large capacities for giving. Nonetheless, the story itself is a gift, which lies in the writer's perceptions and performance—a human vision "charged with sympathy as well as shock." In this as in so many other stories she once again fulfills her wish, described at the conclusion of her introduction to *One Time, One Place,* "to part a curtain, that invisible shadow that falls between people, the veil of indifference to each other's presence, each other's wonder, each other's human plight." The image of the parted curtain, implying disclosure, involves the paradox of human relationships: the closer two people are (and who more than lovers and mates?) the more essential it is to keep the veils in place.

A version of this theme that bears some resemblance to the Cupid and Psyche myth appears in Eudora Welty's romping fantasy, *The Robber Bridegroom.* Rosamond, the lovely heroine, has been kidnapped by a bold bandit of the forest; but she finds the arrangement much to her liking. The one prohibition —the forbidden fruit in her Eden—is any attempt to discover her bridegroom's identity, which is disguised by wild berry stain. Rosamond's idyllic state continues until the satanic stepmother tempts her to break the prohibition and provides her with a recipe for a brew to remove the berry stain. In the night when her bandit lover is sleeping, Rosamond wipes the stains off his face. He awakens, and she is distressed to find that he is only Jamie Lockhart, the well-scrubbed, dull, respectable young man who had come at the request of her father, Clement, to search for and capture the robber bridegroom. Jamie, in turn, now recognizes Rosamond as

"Clement Musgrove's silly daughter," and both of them are thoroughly disenchanted with each other. The truth, as old Clement has seen even with his upside-down version of his daughter's predicament, is that "all things are double, and this should keep us from taking liberties with the outside world, and acting too quickly to finish things off." Once human mystery and complexity are ignored or dissipated by a pressing for simple definitions, the residue is bound to be disappointing.

A "lovers' quarrel" is the cause of the falling out between William Wallace and his newly pregnant, young wife Hazel in "The Wide Net." Hazel is filled with her great experience of coming motherhood: she is elated, solemn, fearful, mysterious, "touchy." William Wallace hasn't taken sufficient account of this: in fact, to make matters worse, he has been out on a drinking spree with one of the boys. Hazel retaliates by writing a letter in which she threatens to drown herself. And so her husband must now go in quest of her, and find, swimming in the depths of the Pearl River, what is the "old trouble":

So far down and all alone, had he found Hazel? Had he suspected down there, like some secret, the real, the true trouble that Hazel had fallen into, about which words in a letter could not speak . . . how (who knew?) she had been filled to the brim with that elation that they all remembered, like their own secret, the elation that comes of great hopes and changes, sometimes simply of the harvest time, that comes with a little course of its own like a tune to run in the head, and there was nothing she could do about it—they knew—and so it had turned into this? It could be nothing but the old trouble that William Wallace was finding out, reaching and turning in the gloom of such depths.

Though "The Bride of the Innisfallen" is an elusive story, its subject is related to that of "The Wide Net." The point of view of most of "The Bride of the Innisfallen" is that of an observing narrator who obviously enjoys the human comedy in the train compartment full of richly varied "types" heading for Ireland, but it is a perspective subtly shared with that of one character singled out for special attention: a young American wife who is running away from her husband. Only at the end of the story does the narrator concentrate explicitly on the mind and experience of the young wife, but then we realize how what she has seen on the trip, and on her perambulations through glorious, fresh, wildly funny, dazzlingly lovely Cork (so it registers for her), *explain* both to us and to her what her "trouble" has been with her husband.

The "trouble" is her excess of hope, joy, and wonder at the mystery and glory of human life, all of which is symbolized to her in the lovely young bride who appears mysteriously on board the *Innisfallen* just as it prepares to land at Cork. This joy the American girl's husband apparently cannot see or share (as William Wallace cannot at first perceive Hazel's strange elation). "You hope for too much," her husband has said to her: that was "always her trouble." How can she preserve this quality which is so much and simply her definition that without it she loses her identity? The question answers itself because joy and hope constantly bound up in her. "Love with the joy being drawn out of it like anything else that aches—that was loneliness; not this. *I* was nearly destroyed, she thought, and again was threatened with a light head, a rush of laughter. . . ." Her real problem is not how to preserve her joy, but how to communicate it to her husband, or to anybody:

If she could never tell her husband her secret, perhaps she would never tell it at all. You must never betray pure joy—the kind you were born and began with—either by hiding it or by parading it in front of people's eyes; they didn't want to be shown it. And still you must tell it. Is there no way? she thought—for here I am, this far. . . . Out of the joy I hide for fear it is promiscuous, I may walk forever at the fall of evening by the river, and find this river street by the red rock, this first, last house, . . . and look up to that window—that upper window, from which the mystery will never go.

There is no "reconciliation scene" in this story as there is in "The Wide Net." The girl leaves the story wandering off happily into a bar. From it she hears a cry flung out "fresh . . . like the signal for a song," and she walks into "the lovely room full of strangers"—people in whom she can delight without fear of exposure ("So strangeness gently steels us," Eudora Welty has quoted a poem of Richard Wilbur). We do not know whether her husband will see her "new" when she returns to him, though we rather hope he may; for how can she possibly be resisted, this heavy-hearted little saint spinning so giddily toward heaven?

In a story called "Circe" (also from the volume titled *The Bride of the Innisfallen*), Eudora Welty celebrates the human mystery by adopting the perspective of a superhuman being. The effort is a tour de force because in her attempts to fathom the nature of Odysseus after she seduces him, Circe begins to look very much like one of the author's human lovers, more than one of whom gaze at the beloved when he is asleep, hoping at that unguarded moment to catch the elusive mystery of his identity. But as a sorceress and magician, though preserved from human frailty and tragedy, and all the uncertainties of time and circumstance (because she can predict the future), Circe envies the human condition. She first contrasts the way of her father with that of the earthly hero. Nature, here personified and deified, is seen to be enviably constant and serene, sure and effective, exempt from human pain, "suffering . . . no heroic fear of corruption through his constant shedding of light, needing no story, no retinue to vouch for where he has been." But in Circe's vision human beings have an equal, though different, glory. She thinks enviously,

I know they keep something from me, asleep and awake. There exists a mortal mystery, that, if I knew where it was, I could crush like an island grape. Only frailty, it seems, can divine it—and I was not endowed with that property. They live by frailty! By the moment! I tell myself that it is only a mystery, and mystery is only uncertainty. (There is no mystery in magic! Men are swine: let it be said, and no sooner said than done.) Yet mortals alone can divine where it lies in each other, can find it and prick it in all its peril, with an instrument made of air. I swear that only to possess that one, trifling secret, I would willingly turn myself into a harmless dove for the rest of eternity!

For what is the "instrument of air" a metaphor? Possibly imagination, intuition, sensitivity, contemplation, wonder, love (whatever, one might guess, is the opposite of cold, rational, loveless, destructive analysis—the metaphor for which would be a blunt mechanical instrument). These delicate "instruments" are the means by which human beings can probe the human mystery, the means by which any lover may meet or be united with any object in the world.

In Eudora Welty's exploration of the mysteries of the inner life, hard and fast lines are not always drawn between the worlds of fact and fantasy; there are half-states, mixtures of dream and reality, or rapid shifts between the two worlds. The facts may lie around somewhere to be pieced together by the diligent, but they may not be insisted on or even particularly interesting or relevant to the meaning of the story. The reader who recognizes this blurring of the lines as *in itself* a demonstrable and intensely personal fact of human experience, welcomes this tendency in human beings because of the release and enrichment fantasy brings into a reality that may be drab or cruel. He perceives its power to crystallize an insight or convey a truth not available to the literal mind in the rational world; he approves of this special form of "realism" and of the techniques that project it.

Robert Penn Warren has perceived a basic difference between the stories in *A Curtain of Green* and *The Wide Net*. He suggests that from the first sentence of the second volume ("Whatever happened, it happened in extraordinary times, in a season of dreams. . . .") we have entered a "special world," in which the author purports not to be completely sure of what happens, in which "the logic of things . . . is not quite the logic by which we live, or think we live, in our ordinary daylight lives."[6] While it is true, as Warren observes, that *A Curtain of Green* displays greater variety in subject matter and mood than does *A Wide Net,* the tendency to fantasy and the depiction of dream life in Eudora Welty's fiction is apparent from the outset. In the earlier stories, however, fantasy is most likely to be presented as a habit of mind of one of the characters; it tends to be a subjective phenomenon that does not distort for the reader the external reality presented. Thus in "A Memory" the child lives in a dream world that is coexistent with the real world, as does the heroine of "Clytie"; the former is made to square the two worlds to her moral and emotional growth; the latter, to her complete destruction. Again in "A Worn Path" Old Phoenix is seen to have her little dreams and abstractions, to slip over into the fantasy world and exist there briefly in a mode as simple and natural as in the real world: she reaches out her hand for a slice of marble-cake offered by a little boy who disappears as suddenly as he appears; she takes the scarecrow for a ghost and so addresses him; she seems to herself to be walking in the sleep of the strings of silver trees and cabins boarded shut, "all like old women under a spell sitting there."

But already in "Powerhouse" and "Old Mr. Marblehall," both from *A Curtain of Green,* the two worlds of dream and actuality are becoming less clearly distinguishable. Powerhouse not only has his fantasy life, but wields it masterfully; he prods and shapes it and then makes music out of it. He has his own brilliant completeness, which in itself is fantastic, and he has a resounding effectiveness "in the world." Through a remarkable and devastating series of descriptive images, the narrator manages to convey what he is: a person who has, all intuitively, encompassed an unbelievably wide range of knowledge and experience—much of it savage, terrorizing, much of it tender, most of it closed to white people, except insofar as he conveys it through his music.

With enormous delight and prodigality the narrator presses for definitions of the nature of Powerhouse, who himself perpetrates a mystery on the crowd, out of which he makes a musical conversation with his quartet. The piece is "Pagan Love Song," the theme is "My wife is dead," and elaborate variations are played upon it as he debates with Little Brother, Valentine, and Scoot, who respond with appropriate horror, sympathy, skepticism (appropriate, that is, to both their temperaments and their instruments). In the black café to which the band repairs for refreshment during the intermission, the theme is again taken up, and more variations—this time spoken—are played upon it. Powerhouse luridly describes how his wife Gypsy, in a fit of loneliness, jumps from a window in her nightgown, "bust her brain all over the world," and is found by Uranus Knockwood, "that no-good pussyfooted crooning creeper, that creeper that follow around after me, coming up like weeds behind me, following around after me everything I do and messing around on the trail I leave."

The waitress, gloriously impressed, breathes, "It must be the real truth." Powerhouse puts his hand to his pocket teasingly, as though to pull out the fatal telegram; but he never produces it. "No, babe, it ain't the truth," he says. "Truth is something worse, I ain't said what, yet. It's something hasn't come to me, but I ain't saying it won't. And when it does, then want me to tell you?" Then he turns up his eyes, smiles dreamily, and the waitress screams in terror and delight.

In this story the line between fact and fantasy has begun to blur. We may reach the safe conclusion that the conventional "gory details" and all the hocus-pocus about the jinxing Uranus (originally a star—Titan of the sky) Knockwood (knock-on-wood) indicate that Powerhouse has only made fantasy of his general and specific fears in order to relieve himself and to entertain his audience; but no provision is made for an unequivocal assertion that Gypsy either has or has not on account of loneliness been unfaithful to Powerhouse or killed herself. For "fact" we should trust Powerhouse's mysterious denials no more than his mysterious assertions, but the point is that we aren't expected to be interested in trusting either literally. We are meant only to perceive and enjoy Powerhouse as everything that his name implies: a tremendous human dynamo that is capable of taking in any raw fact of nature—even sudden death by violence—and, with the energy he generates in the "Powerhouse" of his blood and his imagination, of pouring out the wild order of his music. Fantasy is his product, an important mode of his being, the necessary ingredient of what he is; "the facts of the case" have simply ceased to be relevant. The narrator, assuming the implicitly collective point of view of "civilized" but fascinated white people toward the black jazz musician, abandons herself to the fantasy observed and created, and we are swept along in that abandonment, as we would have been swept into the jazz itself had we actually heard it. Thus both the mode of narration and the subject of the narrative participate in, or project, the fantasy.

"Old Mr. Marblehall," which exhibits an even more marked ambiguity in the relation of fact to fantasy, is the story of an old man's battle against public unconcern and the private sense of boredom and insignificance. Through delicate and complex maneuvers in point of view, involving the reader confidentially in a detached set of disclosures, the narrator shows us both the public attitude of Natchez, the "little party-giving town" he lives in, and Mr. Marblehall's rebellious reaction to this attitude. To the town Mr. Marblehall is nothing ("Nobody gives a hoot about any old Mr. Marblehall"). He is just a little old man from an ancestral house who goes out walking or is driven in his carriage, who is supposed to travel for his health, and who remains insultingly alive and well preserved year after year when he might as well be dead. Mr. Marblehall is determined, however, to be noticed; so he takes a wife and produces a son in his old age, and then looks about furtively for reactions. But nobody gets excited, nobody pays any attention, and nobody is likely to discover that Mr. Marblehall is really leading a double life.

For down in the poorer section of town Mr. Marblehall has another house, another wife, another son: an identical arrangement, but with curious contrasts. The second wife, short and solid and "combustible," is always complaining; the first, tall and disquieted, hovers nervously. The second little boy has the shrewd monkey look, the tantrum-throwing obstinacy of the first son, but he is even more cunning than the first. Mr. Marblehall's name here is Mr. Bird, and his wife tells the neighbors about the horrible and fantastic tales Mr. Bird reads in bed late at night under a naked light bulb—*Terror Tales* and *Astonishing Stories*.

One day, Mr. Marblehall imagines, his secret will be discovered. One of the shrewd little boys will trail him across town, or perhaps he himself will make a public confession—then what astonishment there will be! He consoles himself by thinking how electrified his two wives and sons will be, "to say nothing of most men over sixty-six." He has "caught on, he thinks, to what people are supposed to do. This is it: they endure something inwardly—for a time secretly; they establish a past, a memory; thus they store up life." Having done this, he now waits for "some glorious finish, a great explosion of revelations . . . the future."

But people may never find out, the climax may never come, and nobody cares anyway about being deceived by old Mr. Marblehall. "He may have years ahead yet in which to wake up bolt upright in the bed under the naked bulb, his heart thumping, his old eyes watering and wild, imagining that if people knew about his double life, they'd die."

Though nobody in Natchez cares about him, the reader shares the narrator's obvious fascination with old Mr. Marblehall because of the enormity of his fantasy life, its richness in detail, and contradictory poverty in substance. His second name, Mr. Bird, suggests flight and escape from the ancestral "marble halls" (in which ordinary people dream they dwell, according to the sentimental love song) to something disreputable, despite the presence of house, wife, and child. The furnishings of his fantasy life are tawdry: even mingled with the seemingly enviable lower classes this Mr. Bird is bored, kills time under a naked lightbulb with *Terror Tales*, waits breathlessly to be found out. No wonder he dreams he is a great blazing butterfly stitching up a net, which "doesn't make any sense"—but only to the logical mind. The old man yearns to be gorgeously free and colorful, an actor like his ancestor, a great lover envied for his prowess at an advanced age, a master of women, a spawner of fiendishly clever sons. But instead he has, through the conventions of his carefully circumscribed life and cheaply exotic fantasies, been stitching a net that will in the end catch him—if it has not now. He doesn't know that for Natchez he is already pinned to the wall, a dead specimen of a moribund aristocracy. Yet the story catches him still very much alive, both blazing and bored, as caught *up* he is caught *in* the world of fantasy.

If Eudora Welty's predilection for fantasy was apparent in *A Curtain of Green* (1941), it is loud and clear in *The Robber Bridegroom* (1942). Here the break with strict realism comes from the mixture of characters and events from fairy tales with those of the legendary past, which for the Natchez Trace and River Country of frontier days (the early 1900s) was indeed extraordinary. "Whatever happened, it happened in extraordinary times, in a season of dreams"—the opening line of "First Love" (*The Wide Net,* 1943) to which Robert Penn Warren referred, points first of all to those legendary days when our national history was favorable to dreams of ambition and conquest, glorious heroic or demonic schemes. The historian cannot be sure what happened at the time of Burr's conspiracy, nor what motivated that fabulous rebel; nor what drove the historical characters of "A Still Moment," Murrell, Lorenzo Dow, and Audubon. In projecting these legendary dreams, Eudora Welty is assuming fiction's right to deal with the elusive mysteries of motivation, while admitting its unwillingness to define with factual exactitude.

In its literal sense, "the season of dreams" suggests, further, that the particular weather or atmosphere that a season brings is conducive to all sorts of dream states. In "First Love" the season is winter: the screaming north wind is followed by a preternatural calm in which there is "a strange drugged fall of snow"; the Mississippi "shudder[s] and lift[s] from its bed, reaching like a somnambulist driven to go in new places," and in the "fastness" of Natchez it seems that "the whole world, like itself, must be in a transfiguration." This cold, trancelike atmosphere is appropriate to the story of the deaf-mute whose early journeys to the frontier had affected him as "a kind of childhood wandering in oblivion," and whose "first love" will be breathless, lonely, unspoken, existing only in the dream-country of his heart.

In "Livvie" and "At the Landing" springtime becomes the "season of dreams": the stir of spring excites Livvie, and is "as present in the house as a young man would be"; Jenny's violent initiation to sexual experience takes place when spring floods are ravaging the land, and her sweet, wistful dreams of Billy Floyd are spun out in a sunny springtime pasture. The sleepy noon of a golden day in hot summer is the season for the sensuous, timidly erotic dreams of the three old maids of "Asphodel." In "The Wide Net" Hazel's dreams and hopes of coming motherhood take place when the fully ripened summer edges on autumn. And in "The Winds" little Josie's dreams of childhood and futurity, her instinctive groping on the restless brink of adolescence, are part of the violent equinoctial storm that seizes and shakes her home and shatters the sky with "strangely flowing lightning." These examples show that every season can be "a season of dreams" in *The Wide Net,* that Eudora Welty adjusts the dreams of her characters to their times and seasons, and that the clear focus of her verbal lens upon these worlds of the dreamers often produces a ravishing effect to those readers of "willing imagination" whom she covets. For within these dim and lovely flowering places of the human mind, the mysteries may be seen walking about freely.

The Wide Net contains one story in which "mystery" takes on its most popular denotation—a story which comes close to pure Gothic supernaturalism, despite its realistic frame setting of a New Orleans bar. "The Purple Hat" is the sort of "terror tale" or ghost story Mr. Marblehall might have read under his naked light bulb, though without recognition of the author's superior literary powers. A story of thralldom and addiction, with such fascinating trappings as a shabby old lady's use of a fabulous purple hat decorated with "a little glass vial with a plunger" as agent of seduction in a gambling casino called "The Palace of Pleasure," it is a treat only, perhaps, for the Welty addict, as a parody of the genre. More to be regretted, given the importance of children's fiction in the author's life, is that her single effort at fantasy in that genre, *The Shoe Bird* (1964), failed to be loved by many children. Hers is a fiction for the eternal child in adults— that which keeps them perpetually filled with wonder in a world where secrets grow up to become mysteries and life turns into death, separation, heartbreaking enigma.

If it is only with "instruments of air" that human beings can probe the human mystery and lovers may meet or be united with any person or object in the world, so it is with these delicate "instruments" that Eudora Welty approaches the persons, places, and themes of her fiction; it is what makes for the distinctively lyrical quality of her style. "Relationship is a pervading and changing mystery," she has said; "it is not words that make it so in life, but words have to make it so in a story."[7] Her problem as an artist has been to find the words to convey the mysteries, the elusive and subtle inner states of mind and feeling for which most people (and certainly the people of her fiction) have no words at all: she must be articulate about what cannot be articulated. She is out on a fringe, lonely place—as lonely as the wilderness in "A Still Moment"; there, like Lorenzo, Murrell, and Audubon, she must press for definitions: the meanings, the names of some of the most complex, elusive, and important of all human experiences. And it is inevitable that she should have her failures as well as her successes. Her language is not always adequate to the difficulty of what must be conveyed, which is perhaps the reason why she has been accused of being coy, arch, perversely subtle, too nuanceful or precious.

The wonder is, after all, the large measure of her success. The reason for this we may trace as far back as to the habit of the child in "A Memory," the habit of close observation, of recording, identifying, "placing," both literally and figuratively. For, as she defines it, place is not only the region or setting of a story; it stands for everything in a story that fixes it to the known, recognizable, present, and "real" world of everyday human experience. It is like the solid flesh that both encloses (pins down) and discloses (reveals) the more elusive human thoughts and feelings. "In real life," she says, "we have to express the things plainest and closest to our minds by the clumsy word and the half-finished gesture. . . . It is our describable outside that defines us, willy-nilly, to others, that may save us, or destroy us, in the world; it may be our shield against chaos, our mask against exposure; but whatever it is, the move we make in the place we live has to signify our intent and meaning."[8] In fiction this illusion of reality is created if the author has seen to "believability": "The world of experience must be at every step, through every moment, within reach as the world of appearance." The inner world and the outer surface of life must be interrelated and fused; the imaginative vision must glow through the carefully, objectively painted exterior world.

In her best stories Eudora Welty has seen to "believability" by her use of the familiar local Mississippi settings; her close descriptions of the appearance, manner, gestures of her characters; her infallible ear for their speech rhythms and idioms; her use of plausible and logical plot structures; her concern with physical texture and psychological validity; her use of proper names that are always solidly realistic, local, devastatingly accurate, and at the same time, often richly allusive in their symbolism; her subtle interfusion of the figurative, the historical, the mythical.

Eudora Welty's first published story, "Death of a Traveling Salesman," offers the best illustration of her concern with "believability." Its generating force, as was earlier mentioned, was a neighbor's account of a remark he had heard about a farmer's having to go "borry some fire." It was authentic to the lives of poor Mississippi country people of Depression years. The name of the husband, Sonny, is equally authentic as a boy's, and later adult's, name in Mississippi, making it possible for Bowman, the salesman, initially to mistake the

husband and wife for mother and son. Finally, the name suggests that
ancient fire-bringer, Prometheus, whose presence is evoked by the inciting phrase, "borry some fire." A place name in the story is also
suggestive, Bowman's destination, a town called Beulah. There *is*
such a place in Boliver County, northwest Mississippi: but the higher
validity of its use is that the salesman is on his way to the "Beulah
Land" of Southern gospel hymns.

Her concern with "believability" may be shown again in the way
"A Still Moment"—as formally patterned a story and as close to allegory as any she has written—is most solidly wedded to history in
place and time. For the wilderness is not only the isolated, mythical
desert setting appropriate to mystical revelations, but it is the old familiar Natchez Trace in 1798; the characters are not simply abstract
or apocryphal types of missionary prophet (the good man), criminal
(the evil man), and naturalist (the artistic, detached, contemplative
man), but they are three historical persons who lived and could have
met at that time and place, characters about whom Eudora Welty undoubtedly did her piece of "research."

Most of all, the style itself is the best illustration of her concern
with "believability." The fusion of the elusive, insubstantial, mysterious, with what is solidly "real," can be seen in almost any passage
selected at random from her fiction. The one chosen is a short and
relatively simple description from "Death of a Traveling Salesman."
In this episode Sonny, the husband, has returned from a neighbor's
with a burning stick in tongs; Bowman, the salesman, watches the
wife lighting the fire and beginning preparations for supper:

> "We'll make a fire now," the woman said, taking the brand.
> When that was done she lit the lamp. It showed its dark and light. The
> whole room turned golden-yellow like some sort of flower, and the walls
> smelled of it and seemed to tremble with the quiet rush of the fire and the
> waving of the burning lampwick in its funnel of light.
> The woman moved among the iron pots. With the tongs she dropped hot
> coals on top of the iron lids. They made a set of soft vibrations, like the
> sound of a bell far away.
> She looked up and over at Bowman, but he could not answer. He was
> trembling. . . .

In this passage the simple actions, sights, and sounds, are conveyed
to us sharply and precisely and yet mysteriously and evocatively,
through the mind of a man who experiences an unconscious heighten-

ing of awareness, a clarity of vision, because in these closing hours of his life he is approaching his moment of revelation. He is feeling more deeply than ever before, and hence everything he sees he also feels intensely. We know that throughout the story he is in a semi-delirious state, and thus in realistic terms, we are prepared for all the adumbrations and overtones, the exaggerations, blurs, and distortions of his perception. But strange and elusive meanings are coming to him through all he sees: each act and gesture becomes almost ceremonial; each sight and sound richly allusive, portentous, beautiful, and deeply disturbing. The lamplight registers to him as both dark and light, suggesting the states of dream and reality, his feeling of the warmth, welcome, and shelter of this home and his fear of being left out, as well as the chills and fever of his illness. His sense impressions are blended as the golden light seems to him like a flower with an odor that pervades the walls; the trembling, rushing, and waving of the light are also extended to include the walls, suggesting the instability and delirium of his impressions. The woman does not simply "walk" or "step"; she "moves among" the iron pots, like some priestess engaged in a mysterious ritual, moving among the sacred objects; the sound of the hot coals dropped on the iron lids is muted, softly vibrating; the comparison to the sound of a bell again suggests the ceremonial resonance these simple actions have for the salesman. It is no wonder that at the end of the passage we find him trembling and speechless. Through the evocation of the language we have felt into his complex emotional state of wonder, fear, longing, sickness, pain, love: we have seen it all through his eyes and experience. This is characteristically the way Eudora Welty blends the inner world and outer surfaces of life—the way she sees to "believability."

In observing and recording the mysteries she creates a response of wonder, terror, pity, or delight. Her stories teach us nothing directly except, through *her* vision, how to observe, and wonder, and love, and see the mysteries; for brutal or lovely, they wait for us wherever we go.

Chapter Three
The Weather of the Mind

Anyone fortunate enough to have viewed a sizeable collection of Monet paintings, the privilege of those who visited the Monet exhibit at the Museum of Modern Art in New York in the spring of 1960, and at the Metropolitan Museum in 1978, will have been impressed by that painter's fascination with the effect of changing light, atmosphere, and season on a single motif.

Monet's custom was to set up many canvases before a favorite motif—haystacks, poplars, the Rouen cathedral, his famous water garden—and then paint it several times at different times of day and in varying seasons and kinds of weather, so that an object appearing on one canvas to the eye and imagination as dark and looming in grays, deep purples, and olives, may on a fourth or fifth canvas of the series appear gloriously transfigured in yellows, pinks, and pale blues. As one of his critics has summarized: "It is as if, within Monet's psyche, there were a scale analogous to that of the weather, grading from chromatic luminosity, vibrant with light and joy, through an infinite range of tinted and toned grays implying as many median emotional nuances, and finally down to blackness; nullity; immobility; nonbeing."[1]

If we were to abstract a set of "motifs" from Eudora Welty's fiction and think of them as the objects of her artistic vision, we could draw a useful analogy between the work of the two artists. In one kind of philosophical "weather" and according to one kind of light, the bright objects, the positive values, could be grouped to suggest order, form, control, rationality, discipline, knowledge, predictability: all these would provide the larger context favorable to meaning and purpose in life, to security and protection, to the flourishing of the prime value of love. Opposed to these values would be chance, confusion, disorder, chaos, catastrophe, oblivion: all these would make for exposure and vulnerability; they would be hostile to meaning and purpose in life; they would tend to discourage if not destroy love; and they would eventually be associated with death itself.

Human beings are immersed in this struggle, striving to make order out of chaos, but helpless in the face of the catastrophe that may spring out of nature; trying to live securely in love, but frustrated by the cosmic disorder of a time sequence that brings first the love and then the separateness, or the unpredictable and uncontrollable circumstance that brings separation. Furthermore, these opposing principles are not to be located merely in nature, cosmic reality, the outside world: the vulgar woman who rudely exposes her breasts in "A Memory" is an active though unconscious embodiment of the destructive principle of chaos, as the child is the embodiment of the principle of order. Mrs. Larkin in her submersion in the garden and wielding of the hoe and Howard in his murdering, become more self-conscious embodiments of the paradoxes, conducting their terrible and fatal experiments in meaning. The opposing principles form a continuum in man and the universe of which he is a part.

Now as if the light and weather had shifted over Eudora Welty's shoulder, we find her engaged, in another set of stories, in painting similar motifs, but with a totally different "atmospheric" or value scheme. In these stories we find the bright tones of discipline, order, control, and rationality transmuted to the darker tones of repression, rigidity, or dullness; and the disordered, which in the process of metamorphosis goes through a stage of the ambiguously valued disorderly, at last pops up delightfully as the spontaneous, unconfined, wild, pagan, irreverent, irrepressible. By this changed light, chance and the unpredictable become surprise; abandon loses its former connotations of desolation and decay and shines in the bright rays of carelessness and freedom; exposure and vulnerability dissolve with fear, and are displaced by challenge, mischievousness, and good-humored insolence. Welcome of the unknown supplants fear of it; gloom is routed by joy; and all the tragic limitations of life and love, the conditions that threatened their destruction, have become opportunities favorable to their flourishing.

When one thinks of this second set of values in Eudora Welty's stories, certain images come to mind. Perhaps one pictures Cash standing in Solomon's dignified front room, glorious and dazzling in his new Easter clothes, "all of him young" (the words sing to the delight in Livvie's heart), with a little guinea pig peeping out of his pocket. Or perhaps one pictures King MacLain in irreverent attendance at the funeral of Miss Katie Rainey, cracking chicken bones with his teeth and putting out his bright pink tongue to cool from the hot coffee while the company sings "Nearer, My God, to Thee";

or maybe one sees little Jinny MacLain leaning curiously and boldly over the coffin with tiny green lizards hanging from her ears like earrings; or that funny, wicked old goat, "Papa" from "Going to Naples," who blasts every solemn, tender moment with a long "Tweet" from his weapon of impropriety—the raucous whistle. The mood, the atmosphere, is one of surging, irrestible, pagan joy—"the pure wish to live"—and it is an important atmosphere in Eudora Welty's fiction.

The first clear statement of this view of the oppositions is to be found in "Asphodel" in *The Wide Net*. The story is a somewhat uneasy though fascinating blend of realism, mythology, allegory, and fantasy. Three old maids are on a picnic: they come in a buggy and sit on a hill at high noon in their fluffy, white dimity frocks; they have their baskets and spread cloth, and they eat their chicken, ham, cake, and fruit. Their setting is the golden ruin of the house "Asphodel"— six Doric columns with unbroken entablature on two—and they tell their story of Miss Sabina and Mr. Don McInnis, former owner of "Asphodel," in the manner of a Greek chorus: "their voices serene and alike," now one speaking, now another, and then all together.

The strong-willed, aristocratic Miss Sabina has been forced by her father to marry Mr. Don McInnis, "a great, profane man" with pointed yellow eyebrows, who is dangerous, uproarious, full of hope and laughter, and who stands "astride" everything at the wedding: the room, guests, flowers, tapers, even the bride and her father. He is "like a torch carried into a house." Miss Sabina, who represents the strictest order and control—the antithesis of everything wild, unruly, and sensual—tries to impose her will upon him, but is necessarily defeated: he is not to be tamed and domesticated, and is flagrantly unfaithful. In a fury, Miss Sabina chases him, permanently unsubdued, out of "Asphodel," burns the place, and forbids further mention of his name or that of "Asphodel." She then concentrates on ruling the town, becoming, in fact, its presiding deity—its fate. She runs all its affairs, endows its monuments, names its children, predicts and prophesies each event, and holds everyone in awe of her power. When she passes by at the May Festival, the Maypoles become "hopelessly tangled, one by one"—showing that she has a way of spoiling anything pagan, such as an old fertility rite.

But the one place in town outside her domain is the post office, for there, say the old maids, "we might still be apart in a dream." The post office serves as a medium to the outside world, and the letters the townspeople clutch there are like "all far-away or ephemeral things," suggesting their "secret hope or joy and . . . despair too"— all that is privately sympathetic to the rebellious, pagan instincts Miss Sabina is trying to annihilate with her massive will. Hence her final assault is on the post office, "as if the place of the smallest and longest-permitted indulgence, the little common green, were to be invaded when the time came for the tyrant to die." In she goes, thrashing her lion-headed cane, crying "your lovers!" as she seizes the old maids' letters; she tears to bits with her bare hands every scrap of paper in sight, dancing and raging like one possessed, until she falls dead.

As if to show how ineffectual Miss Sabina's hold on the town has been, the old maids are found on the day after her funeral picnicking at the forbidden spot, "laughing freely all at once," talking and dreaming in the bright sun when their tale is finished. Then suddenly an apparition appears in the form of a bearded man. "He stood motionless as one of the columns, his eyes bearing without a break upon the three women. He was as rude and golden as a lion. He did nothing, and he said nothing while the birds sang on. But he was naked."

The three old maids cry out and scatter off rather unconvincingly, looking back; Miss Cora identifies the apparition as Mr. Don McInnis, "buck-naked . . . as naked as an old goat." Then a number of goats come scampering through the columns of "Asphodel" and leap gaily over the fence toward the three old maids. The ladies scramble into their open buggy and appease the goats by throwing them a little baked hen to eat. As they ride home, Irene expresses satisfaction that Miss Sabina "did not live to see us then" and Cora observes decorously that Mr. Don "ought not to be left at liberty." But Phoebe, who has been all along the most susceptible of the three, laughs softly. She seems to be "still in a tender dream and an unconscious celebration—as though the picnic were not already set rudely in the past, but were the enduring and intoxicating present, . . . the golden day." The "golden age" of classical mythology has become Phoebe's golden day; Pan and his satyrs have been evoked in the appearance of Mr. Don and the chasing goats; order and control, the "civilized" virtues represented by the stiff-frocked, puritanical Miss Sabina, have been amusingly routed in that last but not so strong stronghold of Southern maidenhood.

In "Asphodel" the narrative method is rather puzzling, eclectic, and bizarre, but the theme of the story has a comic simplicity. Mr. Don McInnis, disorder, and the pagan values enjoy an unambiguous triumph. In the story "Livvie," however, we find the reverse: a narrative method disarmingly simple and clear, but a thematic structure far more complex and subtly adjusted to the ambiguities of human experience. The beautiful balance of the opposing values, their easy, natural embodiment in character and situation, the purity of the language, and the sympathy and detachment of the vision, give this story a deservedly high place among Eudora Welty's works.

Livvie's return to life (the original title of the story was "Livvie Is Back") through the death of her old husband, Solomon, and her surrender to Cash, the field hand who comes to claim her, is an obvious but not a complete and clear gain; for there is a corresponding loss and destruction of certain positive values.

As his name implies, Solomon stands for order, control, wisdom, security. His house is "nice"—neat and orderly. Patterns are delightfully worked out in groups of twos, threes, and fours. On each side of the porch, in perfect balance, is an easy chair with overhanging fern and a dishpan of seedlings growing at its foot; a plow-wheel hanging on one side of the door is balanced by a square mirror on the other side. In the house are three rooms; in the living room is a three-legged table with a pink marble top, and on it is a lamp with three gold feet; on the kitchen table are three objects: two jelly glasses holding spoons, knives, and forks, with a cut-glass vinegar bottle between them; even the tiny blood-red roses that bloom on the bushes outside grow in threes on either side of the steps. And there are four baited mouse-traps in the kitchen, one in every corner. Each pictured detail of the house, inside and out, speaks of the balance and symmetry that characterize a dignified, well-disciplined, quiet and peaceful mode of existence.

Safety and security are suggested by the two safedoors that are always kept shut and by the bottled branches of the crape-myrtle trees, a precaution taken, as Livvie knows, to keep "evil spirits from coming into the house—by luring them inside the colored bottles, where they cannot get out again." Solomon's life is moral and pious—he seems to Livvie "such a strict man"; he has his Bible on the bedside table (and uses it); he keeps track of time like a clock, sleeping with his silver watch in his palm "and even holding it to his cheek like a child that loves a plaything."

As mistress of Solomon's golden palace, Livvie passes her days in serenity and comfort; in a sense she shares in Solomon's kingly opulence, though she serves her now-ancient, fragile master by waiting on him in his illness. But since the "nice house" has also been her gilded cage for nine years, she is vaguely restless and discontent, unconsciously oppressed by the wintry atmosphere, by her barren and lonely existence. Once she had ventured forth through the dead leaves in the deep Trace, and there, over a bank in a graveyard, she had had a vision both of her bondage and her possible release. She had seen "in the sun, trees shining like burning flames through the great caterpillar nets which enclosed them," even though "scarey thistles stood looking like the prophets in the Bible in Solomon's house." And she had thought, "Oh for a stirring of the leaves, and a breaking of the nets!"

Her release comes on the first day of spring, which brings a "little puffy wind," and on it the sounds of the distant shouts of men and girls plowing in the red fields and of the small piping cries of children playing. The harbinger of Livvie's release is Miss Baby-Marie, an amusingly vulgar, red-haired woman who travels around selling cosmetics to "white and colored" and is herself covered with "intense white and red" makeup. Livvie is tempted to apply some lipstick, and when she looks in the mirror, her face "dance[s] before her like a flame." The outside world has impinged on her secure, withdrawn world in a form crassly commercial, but its effect is romantically exciting. Pulsating with her new self-consciousness, Livvie is stirred to a further insight which she shares, unspoken, with Miss Baby-Marie as the two of them look at Solomon sleeping: he is about to die. Livvie rushes out for air.

Then Cash comes in his fine Easter clothes, and Livvie is purely dazzled. Cash is, as Robert Penn Warren has suggested, a black buck, a kind of field god;[2] but that identification overlooks the fact that his gaudy clothes have been purchased with money stolen from Solomon, the fact that his luminous baby-pink shirt is the color of Miss Baby-Marie's lipstick. He is a commercially transformed field god, dressed in "the city way"; and if he destroys the nets that are binding Livvie, he is also destroying a certain decency and reserve, even a certain moral order. As she walks beside him, Livvie senses this threat in "the way he move[s] along kicking the flowers as if he could break through everything in the way and destroy anything in the world." Her eyes grow bright at that; she sees "hope in its insolence looking back"; but a little chill goes through her when he lifts his spread

hand and laughingly brings it down, "as if Cash was bringing that
strong hand down to beat a drum or to rain blows upon a man, such
an abandon and menace were in his laugh." Soon afterwards when
Cash sends a stone sailing through the bottle trees, the sounds of broken glass clatter "like cries of outrage"—the outrage perpetrated
against Solomon's prevention and protection. Surely, by implication,
a few more evil spirits have been released to wander freely and work
their mischief in the world.

When Livvie rushes in to Solomon's bedside, she hears his watch
ticking and sees him withdrawn in sleep, his old face looking "small,
relentless, and devout, as if he were walking somewhere where she
could imagine the snow falling." She feels the strength of his austerity, his pure dedication; and that is why the sight of Cash's bright,
pitiless black face is "sweet" to her: she would have to be cruel to
break with Solomon. Now as Solomon sleeps under the eyes of Cash
and Livvie, his face tells them "like a mythical story that all his life
he had built, little scrap by little scrap, respect." The images used to
describe his purpose and method—that of an ant or beetle collecting,
or an Egyptian builder-slave industriously working on the pyramid,
so absorbed in his pursuit that he forgets the origins and meaning of
his work—imply a curious blend of sympathy and criticism. Respect-
ability, as Robert Penn Warren states, is "the dream, the idea, which
has withered";[3] but nonetheless a simple wisdom and nobility characterize the process of this old man's life, the achievement of which is
not entirely vitiated by the dubious value of its goal.

When Solomon wakes up, Cash raises his arm to strike; but the
arm is fixed in mid-air as if held. A mysterious illumination flickers
across Solomon's face: It was that very mystery that Cash with his
quick arm would have to strike, and that Livvie could not weep for."
Though Cash is an impatiently pawing buck, he is momentarily
stayed—if not by the sense of Solomon's mystery, at least because he
feels "a pang of shame that the vigor of a man would come to such
an end that he could not be struck without warning." Cash is sufficiently human to realize human vulnerability, if not dignity: he could
not, without ceasing to be human, do violence to Solomon—push
him over the trembling edge of life—in this moment of the old man's
greatest strength and helplessness. Solomon must be permitted to
surrender his ghost, and he does so with beautiful candor and dignity. Gently he reviews his own purpose for Livvie; without rebellion
he faces the disagreeable fact of his failure (since there was "no pre-

vention"), and the irony of its being Cash who has come to claim Livvie: "somebody I know all the time, and been knowing since he was born in a cotton patch, . . . Cash McCord, growed to size, growed up to come in my house in the end." With humility he confesses his fault: "God forgive Solomon for carrying away too young girl for wife and keeping her away from . . . all the young people would clamor for her back." Finally he offers to Livvie his most valued possession, the symbol of his very life, his dignified, orderly existence; and the moment she receives the silver watch from his hand, Solomon dies.

The denouement is swift and joyful. Back in the front room, Cash seizes Livvie and drags her round him and out toward the door in a whirling embrace. As a final fleeting gesture of loyalty, Livvie keeps stiff and still the arm and hand holding Solomon's watch; then her fingers relax, the watch falls somewhere on the floor, all at once "the full song of a bird" is heard, and outside "the sun was in all the bottles on the prisoned trees, and the young peach was shining in the middle of them with the bursting light of spring."

The triumph of life, youth, passion would appear to be complete. But Eudora Welty has shown us that just as Solomon's death is a necessary prelude to Livvie's new life with Cash, so all of Solomon's values and achievements must suffer a death. The new freedom and joy are not the uncomplicated pagan sort embodied in Don McInnis; they are, in part, a "cash" purchase, and their characteristic hue is a gaudy pink.

The juxtaposition and equal weighting of opposing sets of values to be found in "Livvie" is characteristic of Eudora Welty's work as a whole. To return to the analogy from painting, a single canvas may contain dark, shaded areas and bright splashes of sunshine; it may contain more than a single kind of "weather." "At the Landing," for instance, shows the destructive violence that seems to be a necessary part of coming into life. As the flood ravages land and property, as the body is seized and raped, the human psyche, the mind and heart and soul, will be shaken to the very core of its being, undergo suffering and even death. But only as a result of this destruction can there be a birth of the knowledge, joy, and fulfillment that come from love, adult experience, and wisdom. In "The Winds" Josie re-creates all the glorious diversions, rituals, superstitions, supreme ecstasies of childhood: all these must, in a sense, be destroyed if she is to become a "big girl" like that wistfully adored queen of her heart, Cornella of the golden hair. But Josie is luckier than Cornella, who is lost in the equinoctial storm (the change from childhood to adulthood), because Cornella lacks the stability of home, the comforting presence of mother and father, through whose love and order and control Josie may be gently guided into the hazards of maturity.

What a variety of resonances even the word *home* has in Eudora Welty's fiction: a womb, even a tomb, to Jenny; a stronghold of love and security to Josie; a gilded cage to Livvie; an enviable resting place to the traveling salesman; now a place to fight, to escape from, now a place to return to in *Delta Wedding* and *Losing Battles;* now a narrow, stifling prison; now a focus of stability for the wanderers in *The Golden Apples;* a dear place lost with the loss of beloved parents and violated by an alien intruder in *The Optimist's Daughter.* As the lights and shadows play on that single concept, so variously embodied in Eudora Welty's fiction, we see it as we have always experienced it: as a focal point of the most intense of human loves and hatreds.

To the two extremes of what has been called the philosophical atmosphere or weather of Eudora Welty's fiction, the traditional literary terms of "tragic" and "comic" might well be applied. The weather of her comedy has its own peculiar fluctuations, ranging from humor and merriment to satire and irony. Some of the "seasons and moments" of this comedy are the next subject for our attention.

Chapter Four

Shades of Comedy: "Outside" Stories

In a review of Faulkner's *Intruder in the Dust* Eudora Welty states:

> Faulkner's veracity and accuracy about the world around keeps the comic thread from ever being lost or fouled, but that's a simple part of the matter. The complicated and intricate thing is that his stories aren't decked out in humor, but the humor is born in them, as much their blood and bones as the passion and poetry. Put one of his stories into a single factual statement and it's pure outrage—so would life be—too terrifying, too probable and too symbolic too, too funny to bear. There has to be the story, to bear it— wherein that statement, conjured up and implied and demonstrated, not said or the sky would fall on our heads, is yet the living source of his comedy— and a good part of that comedy's adjoining terror, of course.[1]

As always, Eudora Welty's critical comments about the fiction of other writers is revelatory about her own: most notably, here, the *inherent* nature of the humor, "born in" the stories, and its proximity to terror. And again there is the implicit warning to respect "the complicated and intricate thing": one can't analyze the humor out of a story, distill or reduce it to definable types, and hope to keep it alive and funny.

One of the few generalizations that can safely be made about Eudora Welty's comedy is that it is usually written from what she would call the "outside" point of view. The fictional method is either entirely dramatic, as in the monologues ("Why I Live at the P.O.," "Shower of Gold," *The Ponder Heart*), or largely dramatic: dialogue together with authorial comments providing atmosphere, setting, plot development, the visual characterization of time, place, persons ("Lily Daw and the Three Ladies," "Petrified Man," *Losing Battles*). The speech of the characters is the beginning of comic interest; the humor is "born in" them because the speech is so accurately *theirs,* yet so colorfully and typically *Southern* folk speech. They are the "born storytellers": born into the families that make the stories by their living and dying; inheriting and developing the gift to turn the common and uncommon event into a tale almost as soon as it happens; bearing the gift back and forth to and from each other as rapidly as it is born, entertaining and pleasing by talk and response.

Delightful as it is to hear Eudora Welty's comic stories read aloud, especially by the author herself, it is not necessary; one hears these stories in the inner ear of the imagination. She has seen to that by her "magician's act" of transforming actual speech through selection, concentration, exaggeration, the placement of the indelible word or phrase, the capturing of intonation and accent, more often through idiom and rhythm than through spelling and punctuation. But she "helps herself" to any device that will make speech come alive.

The dramatic monologues seem the right place to begin with a closer look at some of the varieties of the comic element in Eudora Welty's work, since these stories are understandably popular. "Why I Live at the P.O." had its inciting moment in her glimpse through a train window of a woman ironing in the back of a tiny post office: it is this sort of absurdity "born in" life that gives rise to comic fiction. The postmistress of China Grove is Eudora Welty's creation, hilariously though unintentionally funny despite the motive that impels her action—vindictive jealousy of her sister. Her fanatic conviction that Stella-Rondo is setting the family against her forces her into a pattern of alienation and finally isolation from the world about her (the "world" being, in China Grove, mostly her own family). Though acting and thinking with the logic of the paranoid, she is not felt to be so because of the marvelous energy, self-possession, and resourcefulness with which she carries out her revenge (so that our pity is not aroused), and because of the inescapable comedy in her situation, the members of her family and their behavior, and her mode of telling her story.

Stella-Rondo, she thinks, has repeatedly aggrieved and insulted her: by being a younger, favored sister; by stealing and running off with her boyfriend, Mr. Whitaker, the northern photographer; by reappearing not long afterwards with a two-year-old "adopted" child; and finally, as she supposes, by setting the rest of the family against her, one by one. Her story is built on the logic of that steady progress of alienations: what Stella-Rondo did to bring them about, how she herself reacted to the mounting persecution—now with admirable forbearance, now with pacifying explanations, now with righteous indignation—and all the time with the assumed burden of running the family on that hot, hectic Fourth of July.

When the process of Stella-Rondo's evil machinations is complete and everyone is set against her, she saves her pride by moving out to the P.O. Again she works with inexorable logic, disrupting the family as she systematically removes from the house everything that belongs to her: electric fan, needlepoint pillow, radio, sewing-machine motor, calendar, thermometer, canned goods, wall vases, and even a fern growing outside the house that she feels is rightfully hers because she watered it. Finally she is left alone at the P.O., secure in her knowledge of who in the town is for her and who against her; protesting loudly her independence and happiness, she works her revenge by shutting her family off from the outside world.

Her monologue is comic not only because of the apparent illogic of her logic, but because of her manner of speaking. One can see the fierce indignant gleam in her eye as the stream of natural Southern idiom flows out of her: at once elliptical and baroque, full of irrelevancies, redolent of a way of life, a set of expressions, of prejudices, interests, problems, and human reactions that swiftly convey to the reader a comic and satiric portrait of this Mississippi family. The effect of "Why I Live at the P.O." depends not simply on the vividness of evoked scenes and sounds, but also on the implications of vulgarity that counter the comedy of the monologue in an ironic way. Marriage and family life are given their direction by the cheapest advertising, movies, and radio. Allusions to the "gorgeous Add-a-Pearl necklace," to the flesh-colored kimono "all cut on the bias" which was part of Stella-Rondo's trousseau, to the "Kress tweezers" she uses to pluck her eyebrows, and to Shirley-T., her tap dancing, and her head-splitting rendition of "OE'em Pop-OE the Sailor-r-r-r Ma-a-an!" suggest the satiric effects of "Petrified Man."

In "Shower of Gold" (from *The Golden Apples*) and *The Ponder Heart*, Eudora Welty again makes use of the comic monologue. In each case the narrator (Katie Rainey and Edna Earle) is a participant-observer, a garrulous woman with a position of some importance in the community. Each is alert to the most delicate social distinctions, a fountain of local expressions and opinions, stories, and legends; each is also a person of some tolerance and humanity, but possessing "a mind of her own." The auditor is someone who chances by, a stranger to the town who must be informed about persons and situations familiar to its inhabitants. Katie Rainey tells her story to a passerby while she does her churning; Edna Earle tells hers to the first guest who arrives at the Beulah Hotel after the trial and acquittal of her uncle. The story each has to tell is that of a local "hero"; and in the tell-

ing each emerges as a comic type involved in a series of comic situations that develop from the collision of the ordinary world with his
own particular, crazy "humour." King MacLain's "humour" is to take
people (especially women) by surprise; willfully and outrageously he
appears and disappears, according to his whim and appetite. He
brings surprise gifts, he leaves behind surprising signs of his visits.
On one of his surprise visits home, however, a comic reversal occurs.
His own little boys, who do not recognize him, innocently pull a
trick on him. They thoroughly confuse and frighten him with their
Hallowe'en masks and pranks; King gets "up and out like the Devil
was after him—or in him—finally." King here resembles the practical
joker who eventually becomes victim of his own joke.

Uncle Daniel of *The Ponder Heart* has a Dickensian sort of eccentric-
ity. His particular "humour" is his over-generosity: the compulsion
to give away that springs from his enormous, "ponder"ous heart. But
the incongruity of his nature is that this outsized heart has no balancing counterpart of rational and moral intelligence. Lacking the wisdom of the serpent, Uncle Daniel is as foolish as a dove; lacking a
trace of "common sense," he borders on insanity. Out of the clash
between the foolishness of his "wisdom" and the "foolishness" of the
ordinary world of selfishness and calculation, zany relationships and
muddles develop: the absurd marriage between Bonnie Dee Peacock
and Uncle Daniel; the "murder" by tickling ("creep-mousie," Edna
Earle calls it); the riotous disruption of a trial by the hero's explosive
"give-away."

Again the comedy is inherent in the speaker's tone and manner of
speech as much as in characters and situation, and again the comedy
is mixed with irony. The "tragedy" develops because Bonnie Dee's
heart isn't strong enough to match the strength of the Ponder Heart.
"It may be," says Edna Earle, "anybody's heart would quail, trying
to keep up with Uncle Daniel's."

Satire appears in the end as the townsfolk are finally alienated from
their most generous and entertaining citizen because of their greed in
keeping the money he gives away in the courtroom. But the story
does not seem meant to be taken very seriously. The spirit of this
"murder mystery" is buoyant, riding high on the garrulous speech of
the indefatigable Edna Earle, loser in love but a complete winner as
a storyteller.

Humorous characters in Eudora Welty's fiction—as is the case with
most of their famous predecessors in Shakespeare, Fielding, Jane Aus-

ten, and Dickens—are "flat" in E. M. Forster's sense of the word: single-faceted, undeveloping. These characters are tagged by a particular set of actions or expressions, the recurrence of which we expect and meet with increasing delight. Among the passengers in "The Bride of the Innisfallen" and "Going to Naples" we find a rich array of these comic types: the man from Connemara who is always astonished, constantly exploding with "*Oh* my God!"; the fat, hovering little Mama Serto, enthusiastically sponsoring her daughter's romance on the boat going to Naples; and Gabriella herself, perpetually screaming in protest or mere delicious excitement.

In some of its manifestations, Eudora Welty's comedy lightly evokes the mood and spirit of the most ancient rites of comedy: the Dionysiac feasts, the fertility rites of primitive cultures, the folk ceremonies that marked the changes in season or the celebration of birth and marriage. "The Wide Net" is an example of this kind of comedy. The clan's ritual of dragging the river takes place at the turn of a season, shortly before a birth, at a time of change in the life of the young hero who is about to become a father. The ritual is presided over by the leader of the clan (Old Doc), who lives on top of a hill and rules from his porch rocker, who rides the boat during the dragging, and makes philosophical comments on the change of season, the general proceedings, and the "trials" of the hero. For the hero, the ritual involves a testing of strength and fitness, an elemental struggle with potential alien forces or evil powers, and a discovery or revelation of the mysteries of life.

William Wallace's "testing" first comes through his repeated dives into the depths of the river, particularly one long dive into the "dark clear world of deepness" where he has a revelation as to the secret of Hazel's trouble. He finally emerges from this deep plunge "in an agony from submersion, . . . staring and glaring around in astonishment, as if a long time ha[s] gone by," and holding in his hand a small emblem of new life, a little green ribbon of plant, complete with its root. This episode is followed by a bacchanalian feast on the fish of the Pearl River, a brief sleep of satiety, and then the triumphal dance of the suddenly roused hero, who hooks a big catfish in his belt and leaps crazily about until everyone is laughing boisterously.

Immediately after this incident the hero is put to his next test. A strange apparition rises out of the water in undulating loops. It is at once recognized by all as "The King of Snakes!" (the name is thrice intoned, mysteriously). First its old hoary head is seen, then hump after hump of the long black body appears briefly above the surface. It looks meaningfully at the hero, who stares back stoutly, then it disappears. The hero has faced up to the threatening evil powers in life, has stared down the King of Snakes, and this fantastic confrontation is part of his initation to his new role as defender and protector of the family.

After the small company has endured a heavy thunderstorm and witnessed the hazards of nature in the fiery fall of a great tree struck by lightning, it descends in triumphal procession to the town of Dover. Only two more "trials" remain for the hero. First, on the way home, he must prove to his officious friend, Virgil Thomas, that he, William Wallace, is the hero of the affair; beating Virgil in a fight, he makes his friend swear that it was *his* wife, *his* river-dragging, *his* net. Finally he must recapture his wife. This is easily accomplished by a scolding on either side and an affectionate paddling by William Wallace. When Hazel lies smiling in the crook of his arm, it is "the same as any other chase in the end." But it is finally Hazel's victory, since she has initiated and invisibly guided the hero in his quest and trials. She leads him by the hand into the house, "smiling as if she were smiling down on him." The change in the relationship has been as definite and mysterious as the change in her body and in the ripening season.

Although the story moves along naturally and credibly within its own realistic terms of setting, event, and character (except for the somewhat mythical proportions of the King of Snakes), it contains many delicate allusions to archaic fertility ceremonies with their celebration of the rebirth of the hero or king who survives his agon or conflict. Hence "The Wide Net" may be enjoyed as a modern evocation of comedy in its most ancient ritualistic forms.

In the appearance of the mask of Silenus—in any revival of the unruly, irrepressible Dionysian self in Eudora Welty's fiction—we are again in touch with the ancient sources of comedy. In "Asphodel" we find him personified in the rude and golden Mr. Don McInnis, with his satyr's beard, whose career and appearances totally disrupt the Apollonian rule of Miss Sabina. In *The Golden Apples* the mask appears on the face of the merry and lascivious King MacLain, with his hard little horns butting against the walls of life. In this aspect of humanity the powerful life force is revealed; the resource and insolence of growing things; sexuality, fertility, birth and rebirth, pleasure, fulfillment; the triumph and progress of the race over the defeating forces of tragedy and death.

Eudora Welty often takes ritual action very seriously—especially the most simple and primitive rituals of the home, or the private rituals that come from a repeated performance of an action of love (Old Phoenix's trips down the worn path). But in the larger ceremonials that take place at community and family gatherings, she is likely to have an eye alert for the comic and satiric possibilities inherent in the manners and morals, social life and entertainment of a highly organized and subtly stratified folk community. She perceives that whatever the purpose or occasion for bringing people together—a wedding (*Delta Wedding*), a funeral ("The Wanderers," *The Optimist's Daughter*), a courtroom trial (*The Ponder Heart*), a picture-taking ("Kin"), a family reunion (*Losing Battles*)—the product is pleasurable excitement for participants. For spectators, the occasion provides a rich and amusing display of the small actions, customs, modes of dress and speech, behavior and attitude, that go to make up the life of a Southern town or family. With infectious zest and a genial humanity she crowds these group canvases like Brueghel paintings, exposing the small vanities, follies, delights, blunders, incongruities of the clans. Yet the most characteristic tone of this group comedy is tolerant, sympathetic, even affectionate: she enjoys the oddities and whimsicalities that become more obvious because concerted, in these shared acitivites and rituals.

Readers of her stories will have their own private collection of such comic pictures, which, although they may be ever so incidental to the essential meaning of a story, hang delightfully in odd corners of the mind. Among these may be the picture (from *Delta Wedding*) of an unbelievably enormous tubbed fern, fluttering and vibrating as though in a gale, and moving forward, apparently under its own power, through a dismayed group of Fairchilds (though it is actually borne on a broomstick by four small staggering black boys). The loan of this fern is a certain Miss Bonnie Hitchcock's idea of how to honor the Fairchilds on the occasion of Dabney's wedding: a double ineptitude and comic blunder, not only because of the unwieldy, virtually unplaceable size of the plant, but because of its having been sent only a few months earlier for the funeral of the bride's aunt. Or the following courtroom scene from *The Ponder Heart,* in which the intimate quizzing of Miss Teacake Magee, Uncle Daniel's first wife, is broken off by an immensely practical question:

"Why were you divorced, may I ask?" says Old Gladney, cheerful-like.
"I just had to let him go," whispers Miss Teacake. That's just what she always says.
"Would you care to describe any features of your wedded life?" asks old Gladney, and squints like he's taking Miss Teacake's picture there with her mouth open.
"Just a minute," says the Judge. "Miss Edna Earl's girl is standing in the door to find out how many for dinner. I'll ask for a show of hands," and puts up his the first.
It was a table full, I can tell you. Everybody but the Peacocks, it appeared to me. I made a little sign to Ada's sister she'd better kill a few more hens.

From start to finish the trial is deliciously "hick," local and personal. The austerity and lofty justice of the law collapse utterly in the face of the intimacy and perversity of the Southern small-town friends and neighbors.

Losing Battles is one long feast of such scenes, largely those of the clan together in celebration, renewal, defiance. They aim to enjoy themselves and do, and they serve up, with all the talk, food, and drink, and mostly unconsciously, huge portions of comedy. In these scenes the narrator often uses a "wide-angle lens," encompassing a variety of activity, alert to what "funny business" may be transpiring in any quarter, allowing everyone space for pleasure or outrage, while the reader participates in the antic life of the Vaughn-Beecham clan and their friendly enemies.

Remarkable in Eudora Welty's comedy is the artful pacing and mixing or sequence of contradictory moods, most evident, perhaps, in scenes partially or wholly farcical. A slowly paced scene in *Losing Battles,* deliciously protracted over twenty pages, is that of the bedlam on Banner Top in the attempted rescue of Judge Moody's Buick—an operation involving a human chain headed by Jack, an old truck, a large cedar gradually uprooted, a stunningly inventive series of farcical events and actions, and a stream of exclamations and comments, each hilarious and each tailored to fit the character who utters the words. Swift pacing is even more common in Eudora Welty's short fiction, being more suited to the concentrated form of the short story. In "Moon Lake," for example, a group scene, mostly of young girls at camp with a few adults, is occasioned by a resuscitation. An orphan, Easter, is thought to be dead by drowning, but the Boy Scout Loch, who works to revive her on a camp table, has not given up, and finally, it seems miraculously, she comes back to life. Her body arches and falls, her feet kick the Boy Scout, who tumbles backward off the table onto an officious, disapproving camp mother, Miss Lizzie, who herself plops down in half and sits ridiculously on the ground with her big lap spread out. The scene is a triumph of mixed moods, passing rapidly from the sublime to the ridiculous. For virtuosity of comic writing Eudora Welty has few peers: among American writers one can find them only in two other southerners, Twain and Faulkner.

The Robber Bridegroom (1941) represents a unique form of comedy among Eudora Welty's works. It includes the "epic boast" of the southwestern tall tale, folk clowns and their antics, farcical situations, and the classical "happy ending"—but with a difference. Just as the terror adjoins the comedy in this work, so does the historical adjoin the fantasy.

In 1975 she explained the process of the novella in some detail to the Mississippi Historical Society, in an address titled "Fairy Tale of the Natchez Trace."[2] She stated that she had not attempted to create "a *historical* historical novel," for all its having been a story laid in and near Rodney about 1798, but rather a blend of the facts and legends of that time and place with Grimm's *Fairy Tales*. From such well-remembered stories as "The Robber Bridegroom," "The Fisherman and His Wife," "Jack the Giant Killer," "The Little Goose Girl," "Rumpelstiltskin," and "Snow White and the Seven Dwarfs," she drew several familiar character types, themes, and situations: the beautiful golden-haired heroine, the wicked ugly stepmother, the bandit bridegroom, the forest hideout, the warning raven, the locket talisman, the talking head in a trunk, the counting out of gold in the robber's lair. From Mississippi history and legend are drawn such folk heroes and types as Mike Fink, champion keelboatman; the Harpe brothers, bandits noted for their barbarous cruelty ("Harpe's Head" being to this day the name of a place where the decapitated head of one of these bandits was placed as a warning to other outlaws); Clement Musgrove, the innocent and successful planter; and Indians, outlaw bands, mail riders, and rich New Orleans merchants.

Each character in the story either is, or becomes, more than one of the types. The heroine Rosamond is a romantic girl who has "every fairy-tale property," but she is also a "straightforward little pioneer" who chooses to preserve her life over her virtue.[3] In comparing Grimm's "Robber Bridegroom" with her own version of that tale, Eudora Welty shows the original story as far more horrible than her own: for its heroine's beautiful body is dismembered and salted, whereas Rosamond suffers no such fate. But Mississippi history holds worse things than any fairy tale with its well-authenticated accounts of babies being brained and thrown into oil, scalpings, eviscerations, corpse stuffings, and massacres. Other less lurid social realities included the deceit, sly bargains, and exploitation of other people's misfortunes that make of Goat and his family comic characters, not only "folk clowns," but "collateral forerunners of the family Snopes."[4]

Jamie Lockhart's double identity as bandit and New Orleans dandy, outlaw, and hero is only one of several aspects of duality shown in the story—such unbounded energy there was in those early days of the Natchez country, the author explains, that "leading one life hardly provided scope enough for it all."[5] Thus all the characters in their several roles are legitimately fathered by the driving spirit of their time and "the wild and romantic beauty of their place." Her explanation reminds the thoughtful reader not only of the degree of historicity in this fantasy of the Southwest frontier, but of the perennial truths of the old fairy tales, with their comic and comforting accommodation to the eternal child in us all of the coexistence of death and life, terror and felicity, evil and good.

Tolerance and affection have been a constant element in much of Eudora Welty's comedy: we find it in the first story of *A Curtain of Green,* "Lily Daw and the Three Ladies" (1937), as well as in "Going to Naples" (1954), the last story of *The Bride of the Innisfallen.* But a more caustic type of laughter can be found only in her first volume, and that chiefly in "Petrified Man" (1939), a story that has no close parallel among her other stories. Justly popular, it captures the comically vulgar gossip of women in a beauty parlor, whose preoccupations and attitudes cause the story to take on a darker shading. Behind its "dramatic" narrative method is a chilled, appalled recognition of abysmal vulgarity and the scathing, annihilating laughter of satire.

The theme of "Petrified Man" is woman's inhumanity to man. As the title suggests, the men have been "petrified"—both terrorized and turned to stone (in effect, rendered impotent)—by the women. Ironically it is in the ritual process of being feminized, made "beautiful," that the women become physically horrible. For them the beauty parlor is a "den of curling fluid and henna packs" in which they are "hidden" and "gratified."

But a peculiar sort of gratification it is. The apparatus, which suggests torture rather than indulgence, includes such things as wave pinchers, dryers, henna packs, cold wet towels, permanent machines, pungent fluids. The techniques are equally unpleasant, even brutal: strong red-nailed fingers press into a scalp; cold fluids trickle down the neck or into the eyes; a customer is "yanked up by the back locks and sat . . . up"; one complains, "You cooked me fourteen minutes"; another is complained about by an operator, "She always yelled bloody murder . . . when I give her a perm'nent." The place has not even the advantage of being clean. A little boy makes tents with aluminum wave pinchers on the floor; an operator flicks her cigarette ashes into a basket of dirty towels; an ashtray full of bobby pins spills on the messy floor. After as well as during the treatment, the women are made to look horribly ugly, big-headed, like a collection of Medusas—and the serpents' tongues are in their mouths. Their hair either stands out in a hideous electric frizz, or falls out, or both ("hennaed hair floated out of the lavender teeth like a small storm-cloud"). An operator gazes at herself in the mirror and observes, "I declare, I forgot my hair finally got combed and thought it was a stranger behind me"—indicating how far it stands out.

The three main characters in the story—a beauty operator, Leota; her customer, Mrs. Fletcher; and Leota's friend, Mrs. Pike (also a beautician before her marriage)—are the women whose petrifying domination of their respective husbands is exposed. Through a variety of physical, psychological, and cultural irregularities or perversities, the traditional roles of male and female are ironically reversed. Leota is physically larger than her husband, Fred, and financially supports him. Mr. Pike, as well as Fred, is without work, and both men are loudly condemned by their wives for stupidity and indolence. Through a debasing intimacy and collusion with one another, and the divining powers of their fortune-teller "gods," these wives predict the future and manage the affairs of their husbands. They nag, accuse, thwart, force the men—who have reached the "bad age" of forty-two—into such male retreats as fishing trips. The women's favorite forms of entertainment seem to be gossiping, reading romance and terror fiction, having beauty treatments, and viewing male freaks at traveling shows—pickled Siamese twins, forty-two-year-old pygmies, and a "petrified man" whose joints have been turning to stone since the age of nine.

Mrs. Fletcher, though belligerently asserting her own superiority to the other women in a hundred minutiae, is clearly another dominating female who prides herself upon her skillful management of her husband ("Mr. Fletcher can't do a thing with me"). She gets him to comply with her will by pretending to sick headaches, forcing him to do bending exercises to prevent him from becoming "petrified," and cleverly consulting his advice on "something important, like is it time for a permanent, not that I've told him about the baby" (she is pregnant).

The preoccupations of these women are all sexual and maternal, but in curiously perverted ways. Having destroyed what might be natural in marital relations, their taste runs to the sensational and freakish. The petrified man is an object of pleasantly horrified speculation: "How'd you like to be married to a guy like that?" Pregnancy is shameful; to be accused of it is an insult; the condition is considered deplorable and concealed as long as possible; the husband is held vaguely culpable for this cruel assault on his wife's beauty. "Beauty," to these women, is more important than motherhood. Leota memtions the case of a certain Mrs. Montjoy who insisted, against the will of her helpless, frightened husband, on coming to the beauty parlor for her weekly shampoo and set on the way to the hospital after the onset of her labor pains. The children do not appear to be wanted or cared for: the one child we see in the story, Mrs. Pike's "Billy Boy," is rather nasty, prematurely "smart." Shunted around from hat shop to beauty parlor, he plays with such toys as wave pinchers and is made to feel disagreeably underfoot—as indeed he is.

It is, of course, the shrewd Mrs. Pike (as her name suggests, she is sharp-nosed and "cold as a fish") who, from a picture in one of Leota's magazines, identifies the petrified man of the freak show as a former neighbor, a Mr. Petrie, wanted for a series of rapes ("four women in California all in the month of August"). The various reactions to this disclosure enforce the point of the story. Mrs. Pike is interested only in collecting her $500 reward, but Mr. Pike at first resists informing on a neighbor, remembering the kindness of the "ole bird" who was "real nice to 'em, lent 'em money or somethin'." Mr. Pike is simply told "to go to hell"; Mrs. Pike turns Mr. Petrie in and collects her reward. Leota is irrationally furious with Mrs. Pike for using her magazine to make the identification and for robbing her of the reward. Mrs. Fletcher, hearing about the dreadful Mr. Petrie, enjoys a pleasant revulsion and is somehow vindicated in her hatred of the woman who has divined the fact of her pregnancy.

The reader's reactions are complicated: probably, in a feminist era, one should not guess what a "common" reaction might be. The grotesque turn of events *is* somewhat amusing. At least one man—Mr. Petrie—has turned violently, if only briefly, against the collective monstrosity of female sexual action with a comparable male monstrosity of action. But then, in becoming the petrified man of a freak show, he settles into the mode of impotence, helpless in his guilty yet victimized state. Whether this is because women are reacting to centuries of male domination in a hopeless seesaw of competition for dominance is not implied. The story, through comic speech and action, presents only what may be taken as symptoms, without exploring causes, or taking any sort of moral position. Yet it is difficult not to see the man who becomes a "petrified" freak as the symbol of a society in which relations between the sexes have become monstrous. This meaning is enforced by the title, which indicates not a particular person, but a general appalling state of morals and manners—the traditional concern of satire. The brilliance of this story derives from the combination of its matter-of-fact, smile-producing fidelity to some of the most familiar types, attitudes, modes of behavior and speech of one level of modern American society, and its horror-producing vision of the modern Medusa turning to stone the man who gazes on her, the two of them frozen in hideous postures like some piece of ancient grotesque statuary. We can say of this story what a critic has said of the comic spirt of Jonathan Swift: it "frightens us out of laughter into dismay."[6]

"A Visit of Charity," an "inside" story, is also ironic and satiric, but its tone is less caustic than that of "Petrified Man." Marion, a fourteen-year-old Camp Fire Girl, is obliged to make a visit to an Old Ladies' Home in order to collect points. Her mood is anything but charitable: she approaches the undertaking with a legalistic sense of duty. Once inside, she is awed, frightened, disgusted. She is closeted in a dark, wet-smelling room with two rather terrifying old women. One reaches quickly with clawlike hands to snatch Marion's cap and the flowers from her hands; the other, lying in bed, bleats like a sheep and has its red eyes.

An initial comic contrast is made between the two women: the first is unconvincingly saccharine, flattering and ingratiating to the young visitor, calling the flowers "pretty—pretty"; the other, who is brutally frank, hostile to this and all other Camp Fire Girl visitors, announces sharply that the flowers are "stinkweeds." The comic and grotesque quickly shift to pathos, however, when we hear the reason for the candid one's misanthropy. Bleatingly she voices terrible accusations and desperate complaints against the violation of her privacy by the hated roommate and against the emptiness and indignity of their lives. "Your head is empty, your heart and hands and your old black purse are all empty. . . . And yet you talk, talk, talk, talk, talk all the time until I think I'm losing my mind. . . . Is it possible that they have actually done a thing like this to anyone—sent them in a stranger to talk, and rock, and tell away her whole long rigmarole?"

Then Marion suddenly looks at the bitter old woman intently, and for the first time she wonders deeply: it is apparently her first moment of genuine penetration of another. She breathes a soft inquiry—"How old are you?"—as she bends over the old woman, whose anger dissolves in the face of this unfamiliar attention and turns into a pathetic whimpering. Marion quickly flees from the room and escapes the final pleas of the first woman for a nickel or a penny "for a poor old woman that's not got anything of her own." It is about as large a dose of ugly reality as Marion can take. With the reflexive, cruel self-protection of youth against all the threats to its joy that human misery may present, she flies out to reclaim a hidden apple, boards a bus, and begins to eat.

The irony of the story—the discrepancy between the expected and the actual—is implied in the title. The Old Ladies' Home is supposed to be a charitable institution, but it is instead a final container and breeding-place of human misery, a hell for the living dead. The child's visit has none of the overtones of moral sweetness and light usually expected of visits of charity: the experience is one of terror, to be escaped, blotted out, as quickly as possible. It is as though the brutal fact of this place and its inmates, and the contrast between resilient youth and defeated old age, have been stumbled on and then recorded. No accusing finger is pointed, no one is particularly to blame. But in her biting into the apple there is a subtle hint that this little Eve has had her initiation to the knowledge of evil.

We have, in fact, left the realm of comedy altogether in those stories in which Eudora Welty seems to be walking down a dark corridor opening doors on scenes and situations in which the characters are discovered in various painfully grotesque postures and actions induced by the brutal ironies of life. "The Whistle," "Clytie," and "Keela, the Outcast Indian Maiden" are examples of these stories and the last two doubtless contributed to the notion of some early reviewers of *A Curtain of Green* that Eudora Welty was "preoccupied with the demented, the deformed, the queer, the highly spiced."[7] While it is true that she often depicts the abnormal, especially in her early work, it is scarcely with an eye to the sensational or melodramatic. The focus is never on the grotesque for its own sake, for the twinge of horror it evokes.

In "Keela, the Outcast Indian Maiden," however, we seem to be confronted with an external fact as grotesque and brutal as we could imagine. Significantly enough, it was not imagined at all; it was literally stumbled upon in the real world: On assignment at a fair, she heard about a little black man in a carnival who was made to eat live chickens. The focus of the story is not, however, upon the central horrible fact but upon the reactions of the three principal characters both to the fact and to each other.

Steve, the young man who served as barker for Keela's "act" in the carnival, is driven around restlessly, cruelly burdened with a sense of guilt for a crime against humanity that he committed in relative innocence—relative because it had apparently never occurred to him that a savage "outcast Indian maiden" might also be an object for pity rather than commercial exploitation. But Steve had never viewed that frightening, alien creature as human, and moral enlightenment had come to him only when he had witnessed the effect of compassion working through the kindly stranger who identified Keela as a human being, familiar and near, a club-footed little black man sharing in the common human feelings. This is why Steve's imagination now broods compulsively on every detail that heightens the pathos of Keela's predicament, the outrage to humanity, the irony of his own guilty ignorance—the fact that the little deformed man was whipped up off a fence "like a cyclone happens," that "back in Miss'ippi it had it a little bitty pair of crutches an' could just go runnin' on 'em!," that "you could see where they'd whup it."

But no one can fathom the nature of Steve's anxiety: not the witness or "confessor," and still less the victim. The café proprietor, Max, is placid, even kindly; but his sensibility is closed to the deeper levels and nuances of human suffering, and he wants no trouble. Max sees his function simply as that of helping Steve find the man he wants, and he helps only because of his simple interpretation of Steve's anguished talk and behavior: to Max the man is "nuts." Steve needs a shared response of horror at his guilty action, a knowing, appalled sympathy, a moral judgment; but all he gets from Max is a bit of mild bafflement, bored patience and tolerance, tired little ironies, and irrelevant generosity. Because Steve isn't taken seriously, the fatal sense of responsibility settles on him more heavily than ever. He is even denied the satisfaction of making reparation, since he has no money to give Little Lee Roy.

But the final irony of Steve's moral predicament is that the victimized man himself has no comprehension of what his experience has meant. Steve quickly perceives this, and so scarcely addresses the little man, whose present attitude makes him irrelevant to Steve's whole problem. As Steve tells his story, Little Lee Roy sits quietly and happily, now and then emitting small murmurs and squeals of delighted recognition. He is flattered by the visit; pleased at the revival of this uniquely colorful episode in his life; tickled at the account of the debasing fraud, as though he had been party to some ingenious cleverness. The stranger who befriended him he has forgotten; Steve he "remembas" with obvious approval. Some anesthesia seems to have numbed his memories of misery and an indignity that he may, in fact, never have felt. The smiling little man, his simplicity closely associated with that of the chickens perching on either side of him on the stairs and the sparrow alighting on his "child's shoe," has no more than a child's moral intelligence, and even less than the child's capacity to remember pain. At supper that night he reports the day's interesting diversion to his children: "two white mens come heah to de house . . . talks to me about de ole times when I use to be wid de circus—"; but the children cut him off shortly with a "Hush up, Pappy." Perhaps they have heard the story often enough.

Thus the reader's vision is shifted from the loud, shocking central fact of the story to a wondering contemplation of the strangely contrasting positions of the main characters in relation to it. As in "A Still Moment," the triangle of relationships is occasionally pointed up almost diagramatically when the narrator steps back to take a picture of the scene—for a fleeting moment freezes the relationships into a silently revealing shape. "The little man at the head of the steps where the chickens sat, one on each step, and the two men facing each other below made a pyramid." The dialogue is between the two men below; Lee Roy, the little King (*le roi*), with his chickens sitting like little mindless, instinctive vassals on either side of his perch, is "above" the other two, impervious; all three are, for different reasons, detached from each other, each occupying his own corner of the pyramid, not really communicating with the other two. It is another vision of "love and separateness": the love shown through Steve's pity and sense of responsibility, Max's imperturbable kindliness, and Little Lee Roy's childish delight in his visitors; the separateness, through their total failure to comprehend each other in and through the central fact of Lee Roy's terrible experience.

The grotesque and ironic are allied with pathos and tragedy rather than comedy in this story, as also in "Clytie," "Flowers for Marjorie," and "The Burning." These stories are included in a chapter about Eudora Welty's comedy because much of her work seems to reveal the modern perspective on comedy, which is often dark, aware of its close relation to pathos and tragedy. In a discussion of "Our New Sense of the Comic" Wylie Sypher speaks of how "the direst calamities that befall man seem to prove that human life at its depths is inherently absurd. The comic and tragic views of life no longer exclude each other. . . . The comic and the tragic touch one another at the absolute point of infinity—at the extremes of human experience. . . . We have, in short, been forced to admit that the absurd is more than ever inherent in human existence: that is, the irrational, the inexplicable, the surprising, the nonsensical—in other words, the comic.[8] And is it not the absurd that confronts us through the experience of Howard ("Flowers for Marjorie"), who experiments "rationally" in an apparently irrational universe; or in the dilemma of Steve; or in the monstrosity of the women in "Petrified Man"; or in the alienation of the town of Clay from Uncle Daniel Ponder because of the affront of his generosity? In Eudora Welty's fiction the absurd may evoke laughter or terror, pity or fear—more often in combination than singly. All of these feelings lie close together; all are part of the various and rapidly shifting "weather of the mind" which responds with clarity and immediacy to complex human experience.

The terror adjoining the comedy—Eudora Welty herself has shown us this, along with such disparate writers as Chekhov, Kafka, Faulkner, and Samuel Beckett. However, the fact that among her stories we may find such diverse manifestations of the spirit of comedy as those of ancient ritual and mythology, of the "humorous" character of nineteenth-century fiction, and of Southern folk humor—as well as the satiric, ironic, and "absurd"—is evidence of the remarkable range and catholicity of her comic version.

Chapter Five
Delta Wedding: "A Comedy of Love"

The bride of *Delta Wedding,* Dabney Fairchild, receives from her two maiden aunts the wedding gift of a tiny porcelain lamp with a delicately painted cylinder chimney on top of which rests a perfect small teapot. On this cylinder is a picture of a little town with trees, towers, people, windowed houses, a bridge, and a sky full of clouds, sun, stars, and moon. But when the candle inside the cylinder is lit, there appears a glowing redness from within and the little town amazingly takes fire, since the heat of the candle produces the illusion of the motion of flames. This beautiful little lamp resembles a kind of china night-light familiar in her childhood to Eudora Welty, which she describes in her essay on "Place in Fiction," and then uses as a metaphor of what happens in fiction. "The lamp alight is the combination of internal and external, glowing at the imagination as one; and so is the good novel." In real life these inner and outer surfaces lie close together, are "implicit in each other"; and to render that reality, the novel must be "steadily alight, revealing."[1]

The metaphor is applicable to much of Eudora Welty's own work, and especially to *Delta Wedding.* In this novel the surface shapes, the pictures, the external life presented are so extraordinarily plentiful, however, that our attention may be devoured by this inexhaustible richness. To begin with, we have the Fairchild clan—Battle and Ellen Fairchild and their eight children (the second of whom is to be married to the plantation overseer Troy), and a dozen or more of aunts, uncles, and cousins, all of whom live in nearby family homes or have collected for the wedding; in addition, there is an array of black servants attached to the family. "Shellmound" is a burgeoning home, as thoroughly lived in as any house in fiction or out, with its large collection of high, shabby old rooms, floral rugs and matting, rocking chairs, and "little knickkacks and playthings and treasures all shaken up in them together" as the family steadily swells in size: a house "where, in some room at least, the human voice was never still." The ceaseless variety of chatter and activity works up to a pitch unusual even for "Shellmound" as the wedding day approaches and trains are met, relatives visit back and forth, embrace and kiss, dances are attended, cakes baked, children's games played, and enormous meals consumed. (A typical Fairchild menu consists of "chicken and ham and dressing and gravy, and good, black snap beans, greens, butter beans, okra, corn on the cob, all kinds of relish, and watermelon-rind preserves, and that good bread," and, since the family is having "just a pieced dessert, without George to fix something special for—some of Primrose's put-up peaches and the crumbs of the coconut cake.") A bright rainbow of color is provided by clothing and flowers; and the fecundity of earth, the soft ripeness of plantation cotton, the profuse natural growth in the warmth of the Delta September season, enforce the pervasive sense of plenitude. But all this busyness is still only surface, the external painting on the cylinder chimney; inside the flame is glowing, with all the beauty, excitement, and danger that fire connotes: and that fire—the inner life of the central characters— is the essential life of the novel, lighting up the rich surface texture.

The focus is generally on the nature of the Fairchild family: on what distinguishes the men from the women, the insiders from the outsiders (that is, those who have "married in"), the perplexities of their relationship to each other, and the solitary, unique, joyous, or painful growth of each private sensibility, both as it reflects the others and as it begins to discover itself. Despite all their family warmth and shared activity, the Fairchilds are intensely private identities. Their significant thoughts and feelings seldom break into words, their perceptions are intuitive, their "analysis" is internal. Sitting around together in the "closest intimacy," they yet bask in the "greatest anonymity"; at times they seem "more different and farther apart than the stars"; and even the bride and her mother have "gone into shells of mutual contemplation—like two shy young girls meeting in a country of a strange language." When the music of Mary Lamar Mackey's nocturne comes from another room, the house becomes "like a nameless forest, wherein many little lives live privately each to its lyric pursuit and its shy protection." Though the baffling, frustrating, lonely side of "separateness" is shown in the novel, its attractive rather than its tragic aspect is stressed. "Separateness" protects the vulnerable and provides a shell against exposure, so that within each shell the tender life may silently evolve with trembling or joy, enduring its burdens of pleasure or of pain.

The specific event that points up several problems of identity and relationship in the novel takes place two weeks before the opening events. Most of the family have been picnicking, and on the way home, tired and singing, they walk on the railroad track. One of the cousins, a simple-minded child named Maureen ("funny in her head"), catches her foot in the trestle; and as Uncle George kneels down to try to release the foot, a local train, the "Yellow Dog," comes bearing down. The others jump, but George does not: he wrestles with the caught foot while Maureen senselessly spreads her arms out across the path of the engine. The train comes to a stop; there is a "tumbling denouement"; and then Robbie Reid, George's young wife, who has been viewing the impending tragedy with terror, cries out in violent protest, "George Fairchild, you didn't do this for *me!*"

The complex implications of this incident reverberate through the story, for right after it Troy and Dabney go up the railroad track and get engaged; Robbie bursts into open rebellion; Shelley shames herself by revealing a symptomatic cowardice. Thinking of it later, Ellen feels that "perhaps that near-calamity on the trestle was nearer than she had realized to the heart of much that had happened in her family lately—as the sheet lightning of summer plays in the whole heaven but presently you observe that each time it concentrates in one place, throbbing like a nerve in the sky."

The "hero" of both the trestle incident and the novel is George Fairchild. His action defines his nature, which is scrutinized and contemplated endlessly, patiently and impatiently, with awe and vexation, with detachment and devouring. He is seen always from the outside, and it is exactly because of the thoroughness with which he is seen through the minds and hearts of his wife, sisters, and nieces that we realize the depth and breadth both of love's knowledge by intuitive penetration, and its helpless ignorance. Eudora Welty has walked her readers around George several times over—the relative length of the novel form gives her an opportunity for leisure, amplitude, and variety of circumspection—so that we seem to know everything about him. But in the end she is, by implication, throwing up her hands and saying, "See how much *can't* be known—who and what *is* he, or anybody?"

George is the family idol and the inheritor and living exponent of the legend about Denis (brilliant, free, intense, squandering of his love), the brother who had been killed in World War I: the two of them had been "born sweet." Dabney perceives that Uncle George, "the very heart of the family," is different from the rest of them; and once, thinking about him, she recalls a couple of incidents that seem to clarify his rare and precious nature:

> She saw Uncle George lying on his arm on a picnic, smiling to hear what someone was telling, with a butterfly going across his gaze, a way to make her imagine all at once that in that moment he erected an entire, complicated house for the butterfly inside his sleepy body. It was very strange, but she had felt it. She had then known something he knew all along, it seemed then—that when you felt, touched, heard, looked at things in the world, and found their fragrances, they themselves made a sort of house within you, which filled with life to hold them, filled with knowledge all by itself, and all else, the other ways to know, seemed calculation and tyranny.

She remembers too an incident from childhood in which she had unexpectedly come upon George in the woods, naked, fresh out of the bayou, catching a knife flung by one of two little black boys, stopping their violent and dangerous wrestling, and then "disgracefully" taking them both against his side. Dabney had protested against that—"all the Fairchild in her had screamed at his interfering—at his taking part—*caring* about anything in the world but them." She is awed at the kind of sweetness that could be "the visible surface of profound depths—the surface of all the darkness that might frighten her. . . . George loved the *world,* something told her suddenly. Not them! Not them in particular." Her fear springs from her awareness that deep, universal love can never be made to focus singly, simply, protectingly, on any one family or person: the Fairchilds can never possess him, he can and will not exist solely for them. It springs too from her unfaced sense that this kind of love is an end product of an active, courageous participation in all human life, of suffering sustained, of terrors met and subdued. George the beloved, the peacemaker, is apart from the family that mothers him indulgently and yet relies upon him as its conscience and protector.

There are others in the family who perceive this special quality in George. Shelley records in her diary: "I think Uncle George takes us one by one. That is love, I think." Laura, the little motherless cousin who comes to "Shellmound" for the wedding, thinks how "it was right for him to stand apart" because his kindness, unlike that of the other Fairchilds, was "more than an acting in kindness, it was a waiting, a withholding, as if he could see a fire or light, when he saw a human being—regardless of who it was, kin or not, . . . and had never done the first thing in his life to dim it." She wants to protect him from the crowding in of the Fairchilds. If "Shellmound" would only burn down, she wildly dreams, she could rescue him and then "give him room"—let him be "mean and horrible—horrible to the horrible world." Laura too is experiencing the desire individually to protect and be protected by this strangely detached, universal love.

George has, of course, already broken loose from the family bonds (if they ever held him) in taking as his wife little Robbie Reid, a local store clerk. The marriage is considered shockingly "beneath" a Fairchild, and Dabney too is breaking the social code by marrying Troy, an overseer. Robbie loves George deeply and knows his "real and forgetful and exacting body," "the heat of his heavy arm, the drag of his night beard over her"; she responds to his pure, helpless need of her. But she is greatly troubled by the continual and insistent demands of the Fairchild women, who seem to ask "small sacrifice by small sacrifice, the little pieces of the whole body!" It seems to Robbie that in his action on the trestle George is making an instinctive if not a conscious choice between the Fairchilds and herself; it is as if all the Fairchilds, and George himself, assumed that the final sacrifice of love and loyalty had to be made unhesitatingly to the idiot child of the legendary Denis rather than to his own wife.

To Robbie her husband's rescue of Maureen seems related to all the intangible, aristocratic loyalties that she cannot feel or understand and therefore deeply resents. George "evidently felt," she thinks, "that old stories, family stories, Mississippi stories, were the same as very holy or very passionate. . . . He looked out at the world, at her, sometimes, with the essence of the remote, proud, over-innocent Fairchild look that she suspected, as if an old story had taken hold of him—entered his flesh. And she did not know the story." Ever since her marriage Robbie has felt terribly "out of it," and now her resentment springs into open rebellion when it seems that the Fairchilds may demand even his life, which would, in fact, be her own life, since she loves him enough to want to "turn into him."

After the trestle incident, she runs away from George in a fury, leaving him in solitary, noncommittal hurt and puzzlement on the eve of Dabney's wedding. During the process of her long spiritual journey back to him, the agony of which is symbolized by her long walk on the killingly hot, dusty road from the store to "Shellmound," she tortures into fully recognized existence the reasons for her fear and hatred. The Fairchilds' family love of George is too fiercely possessive and binding; it is threatening, unworthy of him.

George needs a love of "pure gold, a love that could be simply beside him—her love. Only she could hold him against that grasp, that separating thrust of Fairchild love that would go on and on persuading him, comparing him, begging him, crowing over him, slighting him, proving to him, sparing him, comforting him, deceiving him, confessing and yielding to him, tormenting him, . . . those smiling and not really mysterious ways of the Fairchilds."

But if she supposes she must save him from the Fairchilds, from dedicating his life to the family myth, she knows, to her humiliation and pain, that it cannot be by more of her own pleading and demanding. With shame she recalls her own weakness, when she had, by her look of terror, called out to George "to come back from his danger as a favor to her," and had seen him thrust away "the *working* of the Fairchild mask," the mask of pleading for more and more of his giving. "Unless," she thinks, "pleading must go on forever in life, and was no mask, but real, for longer than other things, for longer than winning and having."

Robbie has seen the family demands on George's potential sacrifice and indulgence, and she has observed too his rejection of whatever is selfish in those demands. She even has the wisdom of recognizing herself, briefly, as neither better nor worse than the other Fairchilds in her pleading for and to George. She must resign herself to the fact of the inexhaustible human need for love and to the final elusiveness of the beloved in the face of love that is greedy or pleading. George may appear to be granting special favors to this one and that, but he is not—even to his most passionately loving wife. There is both dramatic and moral propriety in Robbie's having to come back to *him*; for if a heroic action ever appears wrong, it is wrong only to the person whose identity has been so completely emptied into that of the hero that the two lives seem risked instead of one. The awe-filling poise, the seemingly inhuman detachment of a universal love, is a source of frustration or even of terror to any human being who loves in the "normal"—that is, the personal, "attached"—way. Dabney and Laura touch this mystery only lightly because of their relational distance from George; Robbie, as his wife, is plunged into it fully.

And yet Robbie knows that the very quality that makes George's love independent will also make him take nothing for granted in their relationship. He will woo her all over again when she comes back to him, "as if she were shy"; he will need to come back to her "as a little spring where he had somehow cherished only the hope for the refreshment that all the time flowed boundlessly enough." The traveler, the proud, independent adventurer, the detached lover, is the supplicant too. She knows that he needs her, wants her, loves her in a simple lover's way—she has that to fling at the Fairchilds and to protect her pride.

As a favored center of consciousness in the novel, Ellen is the most balanced of the major characters, the most mature and objectively "reliable." She stands in the midst of the family as mother, wife, sister; but she is not a Fairchild, not by nature a plantation mistress; she is only, "in her original heart, . . . a town-loving, book-loving young lady of Mitchem Corners" (Virginia). Out of her frantically busy life, she watches with tender concern the growth of her children and all the developing relationships around her; and she sees everything: Dabney's wild hope and expectation of life; Laura's pathetically eager desire to be drawn into the family and stay on at "Shellmound"; Shelley's emotional tightness, her inward fear and outrage at her younger sister's marriage; Battle's and his sisters' disapproval of Dabney's marriage to an overseer; Robbie's grievances against the Fairchilds; George's apartness ("she felt that he was, in reality, not intimate with this household at all"). Through love's observation she knows everybody from the inside, hopes for everybody, and with exquisitely gentle tact and grace, works for harmony in patient ways that are rather like those of Mrs. Ramsey in Virginia Woolf's *To the Lighthouse*.

The climax of the novel occurs in the scene following Robbie's return to "Shellmound." As luck would have it, George is out visiting the two maiden aunts, and the rest of the Fairchilds are finishing dinner. Half sick, dirty and tired, Robbie must suffer the humiliation of joining them at the table and hearing one of George's older sisters, Tempe, voice the family accusation: *"Why* have you treated George Fairchild the way you have? . . . Except for Denis Fairchild, the sweetest man ever born in the Delta?" Robbie's immediate response is a stout inward rebellion against what she considers their insufferable vanity, their inability to feel deeply, their injustice in demanding from her a penitent attitude, and their intolerance and refusal to love outside the family.

Just then a little crisis occurs. One of the black servants rushes in crying, "Miss Rob' come in lettin' bird in de house!"; another cries, "Bird in de house mean death!" The family jump up from their chairs, and a chase ensues during which are heard cries of excitement, distress, challenge—"Get it out! Get it out!" Ellen is left to confront Robbie alone in a meeting supremely taxing to Ellen's honesty, tact, courage, and love. For a potentially destructive force has indeed come with Robbie's entrance into the family and the outcome of her relationship with George is somehow both harbinger and omen of the coming relationship of Dabney with Troy. To the sound of beating wings, and with a muffled sense of excitement and danger, Ellen "has it out" with Robbie, hears the reason for all her hurt and protest, and admits: "There is a fight and it's come between us, Robbie." But she insists that the fight is not over George, who would be hurt and shamed to know of the quarrel and who should not be "pulled to pieces, and over something he . . . very honorably did." The real fight, she says, is *"in* us, already, . . . *in* people on this earth, not between us, and there is a fight in Georgie too. It's part of being alive. . . . The fight in you's over things, not over people. . . . Things like the truth, and what you owe people." Ellen sees that the internal fight is a condition of life itself, and so necessarily George struggles as he tries to live honorably and independently as well as lovingly, as he tries to reconcile his various loyalties and to resist what is merely possessive in the Fairchilds or his wife.

As she speaks, Ellen has subconsciously blended the throbbing, beating sound of the bird wings with a memory of the sound of fire bells ringing; the cries of pursuit and the general sense of danger and climax with another time of panic when the gin had caught fire several years back and she had fainted and miscarried a child. Now George suddenly appears at the door, shirt torn back, shoulders bare, "looking joyous." Ellen cries "Is it out? Is the fire out?"; then to George, "Don't let them forgive you, for anything, good or bad. Georgie, you've made this child suffer." Finally relief sweeps over Ellen; she has said what needed saying, a series of catastrophes has been miraculously avoided. "The Yellow Dog had not run down George and Maureen; Robbie had not stayed away too long; Battle had not driven Troy out of the Delta; no one realized Aunt Shannon was out of her mind; even Laura had not cried yet for her mother. For a little while it was a charmed life. . . ." Ellen faints, but is revived after a half hour; the bird is caught; and it turns out, appropriately, to be a brown female thrush.

Ellen's further reflections on the meaning of what has transpired form a major part of the concluding sections of the novel. In odd moments she thinks about George's "resembled indifference—his apparent lack of intense concern over such major events as Dabney's marriage or Robbie's anguish; "but little Ranny, a flower, a horse running, a color, a terrible story listened to in the store in Fairchilds, or a common song, and yes, shock, physical danger, as Robbie had discovered, roused something in him that was immense contemplation, motionless pity, indifference." There is a "wild detachment" in him that she finds akin to her own feeling—"perhaps she had fainted in the way he was driven to detachment."

Ellen's sense of kinship with George has been deepened by their shared experience of separate encounters with a mysterious, incredibly beautiful girl found roaming in the woods. The girl had seemed almost mythical—a dryad of the woods who appeared to "shed beauty." Ellen had taken her by the hand and tried to speak warningly, protectively, "about good and bad, . . . about men, our lives." But the lost girl had been intent and self-sufficient, more challenging than vulnerable in her fresh beauty; she had asked the way to the "big road" and Ellen had waved her toward Memphis, "the old Delta synonym for pleasure, trouble, and shame." George tells Ellen that when he had met the girl, he took her "over to the old Argyle gin and slept with her." Ellen is rocked at this (as is the reader), but she quickly recovers, knowing George to be incapable of any degrading action: he took the girl, Ellen seems to feel, exactly when she was ready and looking for sexual initiation. Despite his "fierce energies" and "heresies," he leaves the world "as pure . . . as he [finds] it; still real, still bad, still fleeting and mysterious and hopelessly alluring to her." Later their secret is darkly extended when they learn that the girl in her wanderings has been accidentally killed on the railroad track, as if to prove that George's challenge of death was no harmless joke because a train on a track could indeed kill.

Watching George at the dance after the wedding, it seems to Ellen as though "any act on his part might be startling, isolated in its very subtlety from the action of all those around him, springing from long, dark, previous abstract thought and direct apprehension, instead of explainable, Fairchild impulse." Given this complexity of mind, it is inevitable that George should act in such careless defiance. "He was capable—taking no more prerogative than a kind of grace, no more than an ordinary responsibility—of meeting a fate whose dealing out to him he would not contest; even when to people he loved his act was 'conceited,' if not absurd, if not just a little story in the family." And so, too, George was "capable of the same kind of love. Indeed, there danced Robbie, the proof of this. To all their eyes shallow, unworthy, she was his love; it was her ordinary face that was looking at him through the lovely and magic veil, little Robbie Reid's from the store."

What George is and what he does seem to constitute an important answer to the problems raised in some of Eudora Welty's earlier stories: problems about how to exist in the face of potential accident or catastrophe, vulnerable to the whims of fate; how to act freely and without fear; how to live through and out of love. Again it is the free act of giving that makes life significant, beautiful, even heroic. Deeply felt through Ellen's perspective is an admiration of this divinely careless attitude; this joyous or courageous embracing of experience; this throwing of the self in the way of every kind of potential danger, "ready for anything all the time," "magnificently disrespectful"; this unflinching confrontation of death in all its myriad forms, physical or emotional: a state that looks simple and spontaneous, but is in fact supremely sophisticated, fully aware, lying beyond infinite complexities of thought and experience. Seeing George's glorious independence, Ellen knows how useless is even her own form of solicitude for him, her tolerance and compassion:

He appeared, as he made his way alone now and smiling through the dancing couples, infinitely simple and infinitely complex, stretching the opposite ways the self stretches; . . . but at the same time he appeared very finite in that he was wholly singular and dear, and not promisingly married, tired of being a lawyer, a smiling, intoxicated, tender, weather-worn, late-tired, beard-showing being.

Eudora Welty's vision of both the enormous possibilities and limitations of love, the theme of "love and separateness," has also been fully explored in this novel, and under optimum conditions: namely, where the characters are fully aware adults; where there is a great deal of love and the possibility of communication to begin with, because of the existence of social and personal contexts and relationships favorable to its flowering; and because the novel form provides space for more extensive analysis of the complex thoughts and feelings involved than would a short story. It is, on the whole, not a tragic vision of love's possibilities; the novel, as John Crowe Ransom named it, is a "comedy of love."[2]

The question remains how all this "inner glow" of *Delta Wedding* is seen through, or fused with, the profuse "outer surface." Since the "plot" is largely a matter of the internal development of the charac-

ters, some readers have found the novel episodic, crowded with minor
events, lacking in structural coherence, and anticlimactic in the way
its central external event—the wedding itself—is reduced to the
plainest sentence: "Mr. Rondo married Dabney and Troy." The structural coherence of the novel is found, however, in the internal de-
velopments already described: in them we find the basic situations,
complications, tension, crisis and resolution that we look for in well-
constructed fiction.

But it must be admitted that the fusion of the outer and inner life
in the novel is not always complete. There is a good deal of skipping
back and forth, which at its worst produces this kind of writing:

As Ellen put in the nutmeg and the grated lemon rind she diligently assumed George's happiness, seeing it in the Fairchild aspects of exuberance
and satiety; if it was unabashed, it was the best part true. But—adding the
milk, the egg whites, the flour, carefully and alternately as Mashula's recipe
said—she could be diligent and still not wholly sure—never wholly. She
loved George too dearly herself to seek her knowledge of him through the
family attitude, keen and subtle as that was. . . .

That intelligent and sensitive housewives engage in such analysis of
their loved ones while baking cakes is undeniable, but the realism of
the narrative method in this instance remains fundamentally awkward. There is nothing in the language of this passage to weld the
two different sets of experience. The fusion, where and when it occurs, comes through the creation of atmosphere and the free use of
metaphor and symbol. Eudora Welty informs and infuses her descriptions of the physical world—woods, river and field, time and texture
of day or night, house interiors, even external events—with the emo-
tions of her characters. The language that projects the inner world is
sympathetic to the language that conveys the outside world. Two examples of this correlation have already been suggested: an atmosphere
of cruel and killing midday heat on a dusty road is related to Robbie's
sense of terrible exposure, hurt, ordeal, as she takes the long hot walk
in the boiling sun; and the atmosphere of panic and excitement
caused by the bird chase provides a counterpart to Ellen's sense of crisis in confronting Robbie on her return.

But the technique may be seen functioning already, and more delicately, in the opening pages of the novel. Laura is riding the train
into the Delta country, which is closely and beautifully painted; but
the description is charged throughout with the intense, compressed

anticipation and excitement of the little traveler—who feels terribly grown up (all of nine years old), yet is a bit frightened and young, as she reviews each delight of landscape: the tones and colors of field and sky which open themselves upon her eye, memory, and imagination. With an almost dizzying joy and solemnity she re-enters the land of enchantment, so that the train seems to be racing with the yellow butterflies outside the window; the slightest, gayest note of panic is sounded when a white foxy farm dog runs beside the train barking sharply; the large clouds seem "larger than horses or houses, larger than boats or churches or gins, larger than anything except the fields the Fairchilds planted"; the land lies flat and level, but it shimmers "like the wing of a lighted dragonfly"; it seems "strummed, as though it were an instrument and something had touched it." In order both to endure and increase the pleasure, Laura sinks her teeth delightedly into a banana; then later she watches the sky color change till "all that had been bright or dark was now one color," a glowing "like a hearth in firelight." At the conclusion of the opening passage we find the explicit statement: "Laura . . . felt what an arriver in a land feels—that slow hard pounding in the breast." But we have felt the little heart beating excitedly all through the description.

The scene of Dabney's early morning ride out to view "Marmion" is another illustration of the creation of picture and atmosphere as a correlative to inner experience. Dabney is as young, fresh, and lovely as the fully described morning. She is much in love with Troy, but more with "sweet life" itself. With the same free, bounding spirit she exhibits in riding her red filly across the plantation, she throws off the burden of the family honor in her thoughts (as she will presently in her action by marrying Troy); for she hates whatever kills or limits life and is determined "to give up nothing" to prove her happiness. But the whirlpool in the Yazoo River, into which she later gazes broodingly for a few moments, remembering stories about its many victims and watching the alien life of twisted cypress roots and water snakes turning and moving there, represents her fears about the dark and threatening aspects of her uncertain future as a married woman and mistress of "Marmion." In this manner Eudora Welty fuses inner and outer event, external atmosphere and internal feeling.

Atmosphere becomes symbol in many of these instances, and so it is with the patterns of light and dark in the novel. Isolated lights surrounded by darkness suggest human isolation or mystery; light from within, shining out from or illuminating a surface, may suggest insight or communication. Out in the night after the wedding Ellen sees the whirling dancers "burning as sparks of fire to her now, more different and apart than stars"; but a moment later she sees George's mind "as if it too were inversely lighted up by the failing paper lanterns—lucid and tortuous." In the closing scene of the novel, after their supper picnic, the family are lying on the grassy blanket beside the Yazoo River, singing "softly, wanderingly, each his way," looking at the stars falling. The insects all over the Delta are noisy, and "a kind of audible twinkling, like a lowly starlight, pervade[s] the night with a gregarious radiance." So the family is "gregarious"; the desultory chatter, teasing, and relaxed speculating about the future provide the "audible twinkling"; but each person is essentially drawn up into quiet reflection and solitude; each is a bright star, a beautiful, separate, mysterious identity in the wide dark sky.

According to another pattern, light may suggest what is familiar and comforting, the security of childhood and innocence, against which darkness suggests what is terrifying or potentially destructive in life—passion, experience, change, the unknown future. The nightlight is used according to this symbolic pattern. As a little family treasure, a delight to children, a gift of the two maiden aunts, who call it "a friendly little thing," it is something cherished by the innocent, a stay against darkness and fear, a thing enjoyed within the light and warmth of the family circle. Riding back beside her sister, India makes a circle with her fingers, imagining she holds the lamp carefully; it seems to her "filled with the mysterious and flowing air of night." When Dabney accidentally drops it while running forward to meet Troy (who appears to India as "a black wedge in the lighted window"), she is symbolically shattering not only her innocence and childhood within the family, but a part of the family unity itself, its "coziness," one of its legends in a concrete object—all that the two aunts would like to preserve intact, along with their own and their nieces' virginity. "It's all right," Dabney says "coolly enough" after the accident (though she weeps later as if feeling it "part of her being married that this cherished little bit of other people's lives should be shattered now"). But it isn't all right to India, who flings herself sobbing against George's knees and has to be consoled and teased about "an old piece of glass that Dabney would never miss." George protects and comforts the women of his family, but he cannot and will not preserve them from the "facts of life"—from experience or the wrongheaded fear of it.

The trestle incident, which undergoes continual metamorphosis from fact to legend and back again to fact, also has symbolic functions related to the theme of innocence and experience. The train is on a track coming from the outside world; George has gone to this outside world; he now comes back as a visitor into the enclosed, protected, self-sufficient world of the Fairchilds—"Shellmound," a mound of shells, an isolated group of essentially private, inwardly sensitive people, who are living more or less on top of each other in a large, white, overcrowded house. The train which comes from the outside is only the familiar "Yellow Dog," but it is a train that *can,* and later *does,* kill. George's act of heroic abandonment on the track is both a protective action and an invitation to experience, or a similar abandonment, to all his young viewers (significantly the adults are not along). He is showing them all clearly that danger *is* involved in living a free, courageous life, but that is the kind of life he himself embodies and unconsciously challenges them to share.

Troy and Dabney respond by immediately taking their own pledge for a leap into experience—they decide to marry. Shelley responds with an initial terrorized retreat from experience, sexual involvement, mature relationships, and accident and death. For a while she closes even more tightly into her own "shelley" self and into her family shell, "communicating" only with her diary, setting her will against her sister's plunge into experience. She is greatly troubled, feeling that "alarm and protest should be the nature of the body," that life is "too easy" and can change too quickly, that it is never "inviolate." But during the course of the novel she begins to mature, becomes reconciled to the closing of her girlhood relationship to her sister, and is earnestly trying to conquer her various fears. In the end as she is driving the car along the trestle, she is struck all at once with the idea that it would be "so fine to drive without pondering a moment into disaster's edge"—so up and over the trestle she goes before the "Yellow Dog." Mr. Doolittle patiently stops a second time, and Shelley is thoroughly humiliated. The minute she gets over the trestle, she despises her action, "as if she had caught herself contriving." She is learning that genuine fearlessness does not need to make its own occasions for abandonment, or play a game of Russian roulette; life provides such occasions without willful invitation. She should meet experience courageously, not force it.

Hence, to those who witness, react to, ponder the trestle incident, there follows a new view of reality and experience: a clear image of

the way to face their threats fearlessly in the life and action of the
beloved uncle, husband, brother; a refined potential for significant
communication and meaningful relationships; a clearing of the air of
illusion, but a deepening of the awareness of mystery.

Because the focus of *Delta Wedding* was taken by some readers to
be the way of life of the traditional South (or at least what Southern
plantation society had become by 1923), it was attacked by such
Northern liberal critics as Isaac Rosenfeld (in the *New Republic,* 29
April 1946) and Diana Trilling (*Nation,* 11 May 1946). They complained that the novel failed to show the relationship between the
world of the Fairchilds and Southern society as a whole, and that the
attitude taken toward the Fairchild mode of life was neither critical
nor morally discriminating. Even John Crowe Ransom (*Sewanee Review,* Summer 1946), though generally admiring of the sensibility
and "high art" of living achieved by the Fairchilds as the end product
of their socially and economically structured society, wondered
whether they were not being "heedless of the moral and material
shortcomings of their establishment." Eudora Welty's readers, he
said, would surmise that she had witnessed such a society in her
youth and had identified herself with the child Laura (as being
roughly Laura's age in 1923); he wondered whether the reader might
not even conclude that "there was no strategic conception behind this
novel other than that Miss Welty was nostalgic for a kind of life that
already had passed beyond recognition"—a time before either the introduction of mechanical cotton-pickers and cultivators or the rise of
racial tension.

These critics were complaining about the apparent lack of social
criticism in the novel, but none of them, I think, had seen clearly
that "the South" as such was not its chief concern. Nor was the
"Southern problem" assumed *not* to exist by reason of exclusion, since
no attempt was made to present the Fairchilds as socially or economically typical of any large or significant sector of Southern society.
"Shellmound" is a separate place, "inside"; "the world" (always, to
be sure, the Southern world) is "outside"; it is Memphis, the city
where George has his law practice and lives with Robbie Reid in a
"nice two-story flat," the city to which the beautiful lost girl is
headed; it is Ellen's original home in Mitchem Corners, Virginia;
Troy's hill country; Jackson, the home of Laura and her father, where
the air is different from "Shellmound's" air of "pleasure and excite-

ment." The author's perspective, in actual life as well as functionally in the novel, is that of an "outsider." Eudora Welty never lived in the Delta country, and she visited it only once (the town of Greenville, overnight), while she was writing *Delta Wedding*. Her story was partly based on stories and legends of the Delta country told by the old people in her community, and it was probably as much a product of imaginative guesswork and "research" as "A Still Moment" or "First Love."

Eudora Welty has made the life at "Shellmound" convincing, but she has not presented it with a total lack of moral discrimination. An implied affection for the Fairchild way of life is balanced by an implied criticism of its tendency to self-protective isolation, its snobbery, the piety surrounding its legends. This criticism is embodied in the stance of George and in the thoughts and actions of the "outsiders" in the family—particularly Ellen and Robbie, and to a lesser extent, Troy. Even Dabney comes to the perspective of an "outsider"; for, reflecting on a chapter in the family history that involved a duel over land, she thinks, "Honor, honor, honor, the aunts drummed it into their ears. . . . To give up your life because you thought that much of your *cotton*—where was the love, even, in that? *Other* people's cotton! Fine glory! Dabney would not have done it." The question perpetually raised in the novel is "where is the love?" in any action or attitude. The central heroic action of George on the trestle is suspect until "the love in it" is disclosed; family loyalty, the basis of family cohesion, is everywhere suspect. The vision that produces the society also provides its testing ground.

Eudora Welty's account of why she set her story in 1923 is instructive.[3] She used that date, after some preliminary research, as the only year in which there had not been, either in the world at large or that region in particular, some external catastrophe such as a war, a depression, or a flood. The novel was published in 1946: it was then presumably written during the last stages of World War II. In apparent defiance of the immediate facts of time and history (such a monstrous fact, for instance, as that of the dropping of atomic bombs), Eudora Welty lifted a particular place and time out of history in order to learn what might be continuing and permanent in human relations.

We might think of the characters in "Shellmound" as forming a kind of "control group" in an experiment designed to isolate and discover what the possibilities of human love are under the best possible circumstances. In this small, closely knit society there are no outside causes for grief or pain: no war or natural catastrophe, no extremes of poverty or wealth, no sense of rootlessness or insecurity which are by-products of competitive urban society, no serious racial or social disharmony. Furthermore, there is no marked tendency to moral ugliness in any character: we find rather less than the usual human selfishness, rather more than the usual affection and tenderness. In short, the "givens" of the novel are wholly congenial to the flourishing of every sort of love—romantic, conjugal, domestic, filial. (This is in contrast to such stories as "Clytie," "A Curtain of Green," and "Flowers for Marjorie," in which an impossible home situation, sudden death by accident, and a major economic depression—all external causes—ruin the possibilities for human happiness.)

But even in the secure world of "Shellmound" catastrophe threatens, and in every heart are the potentials of fear, distrust, selfishness, introversion—all of which produce the "separateness." "The fight is *in* us, *in* people on this earth," says Ellen, telling us, in effect, where the battles are fought in this novel: telling us to look not simply at the pretty paintings on the china lamp, but through the surface to the dangerous and beautiful flame within, "steadily alight, revealing." *Delta Wedding* is a gentle inquiry into the workings of human love, reaching conclusions that are credible and balanced as well as joyful. As such it may be rediscovered by readers who have dismissed the novel as a social document.

Chapter Six
The Search for the Golden Apples

The most complex and encompassing of Eudora Welty's works is a group of stories that she perceived to be "interconnected" as she wrote them, with characters reappearing at different stages in their lives. Separately published over a period of about two years, revised, arranged in a loosely chronological order, and with the addition of one major story, the collection was published in 1949 under the title *The Golden Apples*. It is now widely recognized as one of the finest examples of a genre broad and loose in form, the short story cycle, which includes such American classics as Sherwood Anderson's *Winesburg, Ohio* and Faulkner's *The Unvanquished*.

The term *cycle* is particularly appropriate in reference to *The Golden Apples* for many reasons. The stories begin and end with Katie Rainey, first as narrator and observer of the comings and goings of the wanderers and homebodies of Morgana, Mississippi. The book ends with her death and funeral rites. Forty years and a full generation have passed—like a turn of the sky or a cycle of the stars and planets. The astronomical images, blended with allusions to Greek, Roman, Celtic, and Germanic myths and legends of ancient heroes, are vital to the book. Each star—each individual character—has importance and uniqueness; each is, in the several stages of its career, a kind of heroic constellation, "a Perseus, Orion, Cassiopeia in her chair, or the Big and Little Bear, maybe often upside down, but terribly recognizable." And in combination, in their relationships, these heroes form yet other, larger constellations, rising and setting according to the loftier determinations of the stars and planets, of fate itself. They come together, they meet and cross paths, with or without recognition; they return, after many days or years, to their former place, or to their final resting place. To watch them is indeed to experience a cycle, lofty and awesome as the cycles of the sky.

And yet the world of the stories is richly textured, the real, everyday world of flowers, quilts, the churning of milk, the next meal, the

marital quarrel, small-town gossip. Eudora Welty is concerned with
individual persons and their problems, glories, and failures. Her
achievement is to make us see these small-town southerners from the
perspective of myth, and even beyond that, of nature itself, in its
varying and changing forms, personified and even deified by ancient
peoples. Her triumph is to weld these varied and contradictory
purposes so completely that the characters are never more than utterly
realistic, yet no less than fabulous, heroic, the long shadow of myth
extending far out from each mundane, wandering heel.

The thematic unity of *The Golden Apples* may be approached
through a poem by William Butler Yeats in which the title appears:

> The Song of the Wandering Aengus
>
> I went out to the hazel wood
> Because a fire was in my head,
> And cut and peeled a hazel wand,
> And hooked a berry to a thread;
> And when white moths were on the wing,
> And moth-like stars were flickering out,
> I dropped the berry in a stream
> And caught a little silver trout.
>
> When I had laid it on the floor,
> I went to blow the fire aflame,
> But something rustled on the floor,
> And some one called me by my name:
> It had become a glimmering girl
> With apple blossoms in her hair
> Who called me by my name and ran
> And faded through the brightening air.
>
> Though I am old with wandering
> Through hollow lands and hilly lands,
> I will find out where she has gone,
> And kiss her lips and take her hands;
> And walk among long dappled grass,
> And pluck till time and times are done
> The silver apples of the moon,
> The golden apples of the sun.

The poem concerns the quest of one of Yeats's favorite Celtic hero-
gods, Aengus, associated with youth, beauty, and poetry. The

speaker is "possessed," passionate and restless, and he goes out in the starlit night to fish with a pole both natural and magical, a stripped hazel wand with a red berry (fruit) for bait. With it he catches a silver trout, which undergoes metamorphosis, becoming a "glimmering girl," a beautiful visionary invitation and lure, who calls out his name, then disappears. Now he is forever in quest to find and possess her, to enjoy eternal happiness, to pluck the apples of which the blossoms in her hair gave promise—the apples which are silver by moonlight, golden by sunlight.

Snatches of this poem appear in the story called "June Recital," welling up in the thoughts of Cassie Morrison when memories of the past, set off by the *"Für Elise"* theme, break over her. She knows that both Miss Eckhart and Virgie Rainey (her old piano teacher and her friend) are "human beings terribly at large, roaming on the face of the earth," and she knows that there are others like them, "human beings, roaming, like lost beasts." In the middle of her sleep that night she sits up, says a snatch of the poem (*"Because a fire was in my head"*), then falls back to sleep. The chapter concludes: "She did not see except in dreams that a face looked in; that it was the grave, unappeased, and radiant face, once more and always, the face that was in the poem." The face that looks in on Cassie looks out at us in many guises on every page of the book, for the search of the passionate, tireless, wandering Aengus is the search of all the wanderers in *The Golden Apples:* for the glimmering vision which is love, adventure, art, through the achievement of which the golden apples may be plucked, change experienced, or individual fulfillment realized. And yet, to any Morgana son or daughter, a dream of fulfillment may be only a fata morgana described by Eudora Welty in an interview as "the illusory shape, the mirage that comes over the sea . . . My population might not have known there was such a thing as *Fata Morgana,* but illusions weren't unknown to them, all the same—coming in over the cotton-fields."[1] For the golden apples, as Thomas McHaney has shown, are not single in their meaning, but "multitudinous." They represent "not merely objects of longing and desire or the goals in a quest filled with jeopardy; they are discord, illusion, distraction, and all that is precious and rare. Taken together they are the fruits of life, the golden fruit of existence, not forbidden but sometimes foreboding; not unattainable but always difficult to seize; perpetually worthy and capable of celebration."[2]

King MacLain is the first of the wanderers, celebrated, comically, through the monologue of the wise and garrulous Katie Rainey, busy

at her churning. Her gossipy idiom plunges us at once into the middle of the life and ethos of this small Southern town, and it conveys
exactly the mixed admiration and sense of outrage felt by Morgana
folk as they contemplate King's amorous career. King stands boldly
opposed to what is moral and orderly in their society, mocking both
wives and husbands in their respectively submissive roles, tempting
and triumphantly seducing the wives, flouting and cuckolding
the husbands, appearing and disappearing mysteriously at whim. In
his pagan abandon and sensuality, his open defiance of sobriety and
decorum, he is allied with such characters as Don McInnis of "Asphodel" and Cash McCord of "Livvie" (curiously, all three surnames are
Irish or Scottish Gaelic). Though outrageous like Don McInnis and
still another "outrage," Uncle Daniel of *The Ponder Heart* (to whom
he is related in warmth, generosity, and an apparent lack of rational
and moral intelligence), like both of these men, he is courteous and
courtly in manner, and like them he also appears in a dazzling and
impeccably crisp white suit.

King's mythical counterpart is the Zeus of the roving eye, who involved himself in a series of amours with mortal women. His wife,
Snowdie Hudson, is like Danäe, who though confined by her father,
was visited and impregnated by Zeus in a "shower of gold," a glorious stream of sunlight. Snowdie has been established in a house built
especially for her by her father. An albino, with eyes susceptible to
light, she is a sweet, gentle girl who appears "whiter than your
dreams" in her wedding dress. And when, shortly after one of King's
visits, she comes to inform Mrs. Rainey that she is expecting a child,
Mrs. Rainey says, "It was like a shower of something had struck her,
like she'd been caught out in something bright. . . . There with her
eyes all crinkled up with always fighting the light, yet she was looking out bold as a lion that day under her brim, and gazing into my
bucket and into my stall like a visiting somebody." (It is worth not-
ing that Danäe's son, through her union with Zeus, is Perseus.)

King is widely adored for his mystery, his legend, his exoticism
(like some ancient merchant he travels, selling tea and spices), his
coming by surprise ("Fate Rainey," Mrs. Rainey complains of her
husband, "ain't got a surprise in him, and proud of it"), his bringing
of gifts, his sexual prowess; and above all, perhaps for his ability to
make of every woman a goddess, a queen, a legend to herself. It is
this achievement that King boasts of when he is old and appears at
the funeral of Mrs. Rainey: he tells how he had once given her a

swivel chair to use at her selling post on the roadside. "Oh, then, she could see where Fate Rainey had fallen down, and a lovely man too; never got her the thing she wanted. I set her on a throne!" But he is also considered both a show-off and a scoundrel not only for deserting his faithful and courageous wife but also for irresponsibly populating the countryside: "children of his growing up in the County Orphan's, so say several, and children known and unknown, scattered-like." The clearly "known" children are Snowdie's twins, Randall and Eugene; the "unknown" children will be a matter for further speculation.

On the whole, Eudora Welty treats the career of King MacLain in a comic manner, with little attempt at complexity of characterization. King is more absurdly human than supernaturally heroic. On one of his surprise visits home he arrives on Hallowe'en, and is himself surprised by the twins, who are frighteningly masked for the nonce and chase around him on their roller skates like little possessed demons, scaring him off in a panic. On another visit, described in the story titled "Sir Rabbit," he cleverly outwits the stupid husband of his willing and gleeful victim, Mattie Will Sojourner (Mattie "will," and she *will* wander), in a hunting encounter in some woods near Morgana. The scene of King's assault of Mattie Will evokes the experience of Leda in Yeats's famous "Leda and the Swan" sonnet. Eudora Welty seems to be working simultaneously with what is common and heightened in the action—the quality that makes it at once actual and mythic. The use of Mattie Will's consciousness makes possible both wonder ("when she laid eyes on Mr. MacLain close, she staggered, he had such grandeur") and a reduction to the commonplace ("she was caught by the hair and brought down as suddenly to earth as if whacked by an unseen shillelagh"). When she has "put on her, with the affront of his body, the affront of his sense too," she finds "no pleasure in that": the experience of King's "whole blithe, smiling, superior, frantic existence" is ambiguous. When he has finished with her, she feels she has become "Mr. MacLain's Doom, or Mr. MacLain's Weakness, like the rest and neither Mrs. Junior Holifield nor Mattie Will Sojourner"; she is part of the legend, "something she had always heard of."

But the tone of the story is largely comic; the prepotent male can't be allowed to be Olympian, except for a moment or two to the dazzled girl. Later, after Mattie Will has come upon him snoring against a tree, his once fiery limbs looking to her "no more driven than any man's, now," she thinks of a depreciatingly funny little rhyme:

> In the night time
> At the right time
> So I've understood,
> 'Tis the habit of Sir Rabbit
> To dance in the wood—

In the last story we find, to our surprise, that King has returned home from his wandering voluntarily and permanently at the age of "sixty-odd." Snowdie, having spent all her parents' money unsuccessfully tracing him through the Jupiter Detective Agency of Jackson, is curiously discontent—ashamed of herself for having tried to find him, confessing in private to Virgie Rainey, "I don't know what to do with him." But despite the visible signs of old age and senility in King (a coffee cup trembles in his hand, his mind is a wandering storehouse of anecdotes from the past), he is permanently defiant; his stiffly starched white suit looks "fierce—the lapels alert as ears," recalling the impudent rabbit in this old gentleman. He retains the irresponsibility of amorality; he can never be coerced or wheedled. And when at Mrs. Rainey's funeral he makes a hideous face at her daughter Virgie Rainey, it is to her like "a silent yell at everything"—propriety and decorum, law and order, human misery, the implications of time's passing, fate, tragedy—a yell at death itself, "not leaving it out." It is a simple joyous assertion by an old man with an untamed spirit of "the pure wish to live."

Among the wanderers King seems to have plucked more than his share of the golden apples; but then he is a "flat" character, undeveloping, mythical, existing outside the complex moral world; nor is he offered seriously as a type of the ideally fulfilled man. The stories relating his amorous career are entirely comic in tone.

In the second story, "June Recital," we are introduced to several other Morgana wanderers, chief among whom are the piano teacher, Miss Eckhart; Virgie Rainey, in her rebellious sixteenth year; and Loch Morrison. The point of view in this section is divided between that of Loch Morrison and his sister Cassie. Loch is a restless youngster with "a fire in his head," supposedly confined to his bed with malaria. Through a telescope and later from the branches of the tree into which he scrambles from his window, he curiously views the events that transpire in the large abandoned MacLain house next door. Cassie, who in her own room is busy dyeing a colorful scarf in preparation for a hayride, has a more limited view of the activities in the

MacLain house from her window, but through her consciousness and memory we learn the implications of the mysterious goings-on next door. Throughout, the reader enjoys a richly multiple, almost cinematic perspective, being able to see both the Morrison and MacLain homes; the variety of persons, rooms, and activities in and around both; and the comings and goings on the street. Loch's eyes and boy's imagination record, sometimes inaccurately; Cassie remembers and ponders; the reader is left with the delightful task of constructing, relating the parts, interpreting.

From his window and tree posts Loch observes with proprietary interest two unrelated little dramas taking place on two levels of the MacLain house (a possible third is sheer comic byplay: Old Man Holifield, a night-watchman from the gin mill, sleeps through everything). In one of the bedrooms upstairs Virgie Rainey is gaily romping with a young sailor—making love on a bare mattress, eating pickles from a bag, chasing and being chased. Downstairs an old woman, whom Loch mistakenly takes to be the mother of the sailor, comes in; with quantities of shredded paper, she elaborately and ritualistically "decorates" the room in preparation for burning. On the piano she places a large magnolia and later a ticking metronome. Before lighting the fire she plays, three times over, the opening bars of a piece called *"Für Elise."* Cassie hears the theme, and from a kind of conditioned response she murmurs, "Virgie Rainey, *danke schoen.*" Then, through Cassie's thoughts, we learn how the two little dramas are related: the old lady is really Miss Eckhart; the mysterious and grotesque ceremonial below is a mock celebration, a desperate act of thwarted love, hope, ambition, unconsciously directed against the breezy, abandoned young lady upstairs.

Miss Eckhart has traveled the farthest of all the wanderers, and she has achieved the least obvious fulfillment in her lifetime. "Home" to her must once have been Germany, and how the large, dark-haired, iron-willed, and passionate woman with her alien tongue happened to come with her old mother to this small Southern town, no one ever learns. But she takes a room with Snowdie MacLain and sets up a "studio" in which she gives piano lessons, the annual climax of which is the gala "June Recital." Miss Eckhart's life, one gathers, is largely boring and frustrating since her pupils are without talent, and she has no other occupation save the care of her old mother. She is a stern and exacting teacher: one after another, each little girl sits quivering under her bosom "like a traveler under a cliff," waiting for the sharp smack of the fly swatter on the back of her hand (Miss Eckhart hates flies), yielding to the discipline of the metronome. But Virgie Rainey is in every way exceptional. Unlike the others, she is musically gifted and sensitive, obviously Miss Eckhart's one bright hope among her pupils (hence her refrain after Virgie finishes playing, "Virgie Rainey, *danke schoen*"). Unlike the others, Virgie is also spirited, independent, and fearless; she rejects the use of the obnoxious metronome, displays temper and "bad manners" at her lessons, asserts her will about the playing of certain pieces. She reveals that "Miss Eckhart, for all her being so strict and inexorable, in spite of her walk, with no give whatsoever, had a timid spot in her soul. There was a weak place in her, vulnerable, and Virgie Rainey found it and showed it to people."

The "vulnerable" place had also become apparent in Miss Eckhart's passion for Mr. Hal Sissum, a shoe department clerk who played the cello each evening in the Bijou (the local movie house). Mr. Sissum had discovered Miss Eckhart's surprisingly pretty ankles, and when he had played one sweet soft summer evening at a "speaking-night," plucking the strings above her while Virgie had ceremonially looped her with a clover garland, Miss Eckhart had sat "perfectly still and submissive." But Mr. Sissum had drowned in the Big Black River, and at his grave during the funeral Miss Eckhart had expressed her grief by a strange, hysterical rocking back and forth—as though she had become a living metronome. Once only, during a thunderstorm, had Cassie and Virgie witnessed and heard the release of that passionate nature in Miss Eckhart's wild playing of a Beethoven sonata, a self-exposure that was alarming because "something had burst out, unwanted, exciting, from the wrong person's life. This was some brilliant thing too splendid for Miss Eckhart. . . ."

Virgie becomes Miss Eckhart's last hope for vicarious fulfillment— the child must go out into the world, Miss Eckhart repeats over and over; she has "a gift." "In the world, she must study and practice music for the rest of her life. In repeating all of this, Miss Eckhart suffered." Because she knows the independent nature she is dealing with, she senses, even before it happens, that Virgie will flout her and determine her own way. From studying serious music, Virgie goes straight to playing the piano at the Bijou, and her hand immediately "loses its touch." She matures overnight: "with her customary swiftness and lightness she had managed to skip an interval, some world in-between where Cassie and Missie and Parnell were, all dyeing scarves. Virgie had gone direct into the world of power and emotion. . . ." No awkward, tentative adolescence for Virgie: she plunges herself directly into an affair with a sailor. Poor Miss Eckhart, her ideals, her discipline, her music, are abandoned.

In being so confounded in her career as in love, Miss Eckhart is proving herself once more a natural-born victim, plaything of a hostile fate. This tendency to disaster had revealed itself early in her Morgana career when she had been attacked and beaten one night by a black man. After she recovered, people had expected and hoped she would move out: "perhaps more than anything it was . . . the terrible fate that came on her, that people could not forgive Miss Eckhart." But she stayed on, "as though she considered one thing not so much more terrifying than another"—being beaten or murdered physically was no worse than being emotionally tortured. Not only fate but the town itself seems opposed to her fulfillment, just as the townspeople are indifferent to Virgie's flowering as a pianist; they are hostile, as small towns always are, to artistic impulse, idiosyncracy, "foreignness," ambition, restlessness—to hunger for the golden apples. "Perhaps nobody wanted Virgie Rainey to be anything in Morgana any more than they had wanted Miss Eckhart to be, and they were the two of them still linked together by people's saying that. How much might depend on people's being linked together?" Fate clips wings, sometimes through disaster, but more often slowly and subtly through provincial blindness and narrowness.

When Snowdie sells her home and returns to MacLain, Miss Eckhart is put out of the house. She has no more pupils; and after her mother dies, she is a pathetically lonely creature, eventually winding up a charity case on the County Farm. Returning to the abandoned MacLain house, Miss Eckhart now seems, in her attempt to burn the studio, the old piano, the metronome, the magnolia blossom (Virgie had often come to lessons bearing one of these exotic blossoms), suicidal as well as murderous; she is destroying all that was once precious to herself but is now meaningless and lost. She is lighting, in effect, her own funeral pyre and, in the process, literally lights a fire on her head.

To complete the pattern of the ineffectuality of her life, her attempt at a glorious, retributive finish is thwarted by fate and the town in the form of a timely (or untimely) appearance of King MacLain and a pair of town comics, Old Man Moody, the marshal, and Mr. Fatty Bowles. They put out the fire, and Miss Eckhart, having suffered the indignity of having her hair burned off in a second desperate attempt to revive the fire, is taken away in full view of the town, her head wrapped in "some nameless kitchen rag," her gray housedress "prophetic of an institution." Virgie and the sailor run out of the house; the sailor, still only half dressed, darts toward the river. Virgie clips up the street in a defiantly bright apricot voile dress, swinging a mesh bag on a chain, clicking her heels "as if nothing had happened in the past or behind her, as if she were free, whatever else she might be."

The ladies coming from their "Rook" party look on unsurprised: "people saw things like this as they saw Mr. MacLain come and go. They only hoped to place them, in their hour or their street or the name of their mother's people"—to make something known and fixed out of this event, a story or a legend; to take the sting, the surprise, the comedy or tragedy, out of the glorious, pathetic, baffling humanity around them. "Then Morgana could hold them, and at least they were this and they were that. And when ruin was predicted all along . . . even if they mightn't have missed it if it hadn't appeared, still they were never surprised when it came." The town is giving "the treatment" to Virgie and Miss Eckhart: a "placing" that is tantamount to indifference or dismissal.

Only Cassie and Loch, who have excitedly run out in front in petticoat and nightie, are surprised and shocked, which is the same as "caring." When Cassie sees Virgie clicking along toward Old Man Moody's party, she knows there will be a confrontation of the two principals of the drama:

> "She'll stop for Miss Eckhart," breathed Cassie.
> Virgie went by. There was a meeting of glances between the teacher and her old pupil, that Cassie knew. She could not be sure that Miss Eckhart's eyes closed once in recall—they had looked so wide-open at everything alike. The meeting amounted only to Virgie Rainey's passing by, in plain fact. She clicked by Miss Eckhart and she clicked straight through the middle of the Rook party, without a word or the pause of a moment.

The reader recoils at what seems a shattering snub to the brave, ruined woman who had counted on and hoped so much for the girl. But later in her moonlit bed Cassie, who thinks about the strange meeting, realizes that it is much too late for any sign or communication between the two. They are too far apart: neither can, any more, blame, or thank, or help the other:

What she was certain of was the distance those two had gone, as if all along they had been making a trip (which the sailor was only starting). It had changed them. They were deliberately terrible. They looked at each other and neither wished to speak. They did not even horrify each other. No one could touch them now, either.

Danke schoen. . . . That much was out in the open. Gratitude—like rescue—was simply no more. It was not only past; it was outworn and cast away. Both Miss Eckhart and Virgie Rainey were human beings terribly at large, roaming on the face of the earth.

Virgie's roaming has only begun, but Miss Eckhart's is nearly over. Two more journeys for her: one to a mental hospital in Jackson, and then her last, through the kindness of Miss Snowdie, to her long rest in the MacLain graveyard. It is a painful career to contemplate.

In contrast is the career of the third wanderer to whom we are introduced in "June Recital," Loch Morrison. His adventurous and rebellious spirit does not show itself in explicitly sexual activity, as does King MacLain's, but he is a boy-wonder with a heroic name (Lochinvar), a youthful Perseus.

Loch is staunchly independent and scornful of girls, of the "civilities," of danger; lonely and apart in his activities and imagination, "all eyes like Argus, on guard everywhere," he is restlessly waiting for the glorious, heroic opportunity. His possessive love of the abandoned MacLain house springs from its appealing, romantic wildness and its invitation to adventure. Opportunity blossoms excitingly with Miss Eckhart's attempt at arson, and provides Loch with his first occasion for a heroic rescue mission: he dives headfirst out of the tree branches to capture the "time-bomb" metronome.

This action is a comic foreshadowing of the serious and effectual rescue that he carries out in "Moon Lake" when he dives into the murky lake bottom to bring back the half-dead orphan, Easter, and resuscitates her through the drawn-out ordeal of artificial respiration. The adults who witness this process—the indignant Miss Lizzie Stark who shouts, "What's he *doing* to her? Stop that," and Ran MacLain, who sets the "seasoned gaze" of the twenty-three-year-old on Loch's rhythmical movements over Easter on the table—note the oddness of the act. The incident is a superb example of Eudora Welty's mastery of delicately ambiguous tone and of gently intimated symbolism, since the reader is both amused at the varied human responses to sexual suggestion, and yet moved and sobered by the deeper implications of this strange physical correspondence. The stakes are really life and death, and the young Boy Scout is as fully and passionately, even though as mindlessly and mechanically, engaged in giving life as he would be if involved in the act of love.

Like the Perseus of the picture hanging in Miss Eckhart's studio, one of whose adventures had been the saving of Andromeda from being attacked and drowned by a sea monster, Loch must be allowed his pride and his vaunting. This vaunting is partly witnessed, partly imagined, by two of the young camp girls, Nina and Jinny Love, when they wander toward the Boy Scout's tent on the evening after all the excitement, and see him in silhouette, undressing by candlelight. After he examines his case of sunburn in the Kress mirror, he comes naked to the tent opening where he stands leaning on one raised arm, his weight on one foot, looking out quietly into the night:

Hadn't he, surely, just before they caught him, been pounding his chest with his fists? Bragging on himself? It seemed to them they could still hear in the beating air of night the wild tattoo of pride he must have struck off. His silly, brief, overriding little show they could well imagine there in his tent of separation in the middle of the woods, in the night. Minnowy thing that matched his candle flame, naked as he was with that, he thought he shone forth too. Didn't he?

He is as plausibly human as King, and a youth of undoubtedly heroic parts; but he is beyond no one's gentle laughter, and looks, in the end, self-consciously gawky, "rather at loose ends." Yet his restless heart drives him away from restricting Morgana to New York City, where, as his sister Cassie notes wistfully, he has "a life of his own."

Throughout *The Golden Apples* we find juxtaposed two sets of characters. There are the wanderers who are expressive in action, wild, rebellious, free, overflowing, self-determining; but they are driven by fierce hungers and yearnings. The characters who serve as their foils appear to be re-actors more than actors. They tend to be passive, helpless, outreaching; their characteristic activity is quietly unobtrusive and inward, for they observe and learn, feel and wonder. But they have their own kind of power. As the wanderers suggest such deities as Zeus, Perseus, and Aengus, their foils may be thought of as prophets or seers, with the capacity to see through the surface of events, persons, relationships, to their strange, deep meanings. They achieve insight about life, themselves and others, not through any supernatural revelation, but through sensitivity and the exercise of the moral imagination. Thus their power is private and internal, evident only to the reader, as is the patient work of their soft, giving hearts.

They admire the strong characters; they both sigh for and are frightened by freedom and by the large, bold gestures of their independent loved ones who come and go at will or impulse—the gods among them with their noble, godlike gestures. These characters exist to know and adore; they are the "still points" in humanity, resting places, stable and secure, for all their inward growing and sympathetic roving after the wanderers. Their instincts are cautious and protective: they want to ward off the disaster that inevitably threatens the freely experimental life. They are almost necessarily feminine, or very young. Examples of the type are Jennie Lockhart of "At the Landing," Joel Mayes of "First Love," and Laura and Ellen of *Delta Wedding*. In *The Golden Apples* they are Cassie Morrison and Nina Carmichael, though some of the softness and sensitivity of the type may also be seen in Snowdie and Eugene MacLain.

In her relation to Miss Eckhart, Virgie, and her brother Loch, Cassie—admiring, timorous, sensitive, virginal—is the reflecting "still point." Even as a child Cassie finds in Virgie "her secret love, as well as her secret hate"—she envies the glorious freedom and the careless assurance of Virgie's musical talent. Out of this love springs her power of perception. She knows, for instance, what Miss Eckhart is feeling. "She found it so easy—ever since Virgie showed her—to feel terror and pain in an outsider; in someone you did not know at all well, pain made you wonderfully sorry." At one point she even wonders whether this secret knowledge might not have provided her with an opportunity to help the woman. "Somewhere, even up to the last, there could have been for Miss Eckhart a little opening wedge—a crack in the door. . . . But if I had been the one to see it open, she thought slowly, I might have slammed it tight for ever. I might." She is prophetic even about herself, perceiving that knowledge of another's heart may be a formidable weapon, and choice, rather than outward or inward law, determines whether such knowledge shall be used kindly rather than ruthlessly.

In her relationship with her brother Loch, Cassie is the adoring, passive spectator. The time when he was a child and she had wanted "to shield his innocence" is past, even though she bursts into tears because of worry about his malaria when she sees him out in front in his nightie with a row of big pepper-and-salt colored mosquitoes perched all along his forehead. But Loch is already out on a limb figuratively as well as literally when she watches him cavorting in the tree overhanging the MacLain house. Unlike her brother, she is not a wanderer: "She could never go for herself, never creep out on the shimmering bridge of the tree, or reach the dark magnet there that drew you inside, kept drawing you in. She could not see herself do an unknown thing. She was not Loch, she was not Virgie Rainey; she was not her mother. She was Cassie in her room, seeing the knowledge and torment beyond her reach, standing at her window singing. . . ." Here Cassie almost seems to become the bard, the one who remembers and celebrates in ballads. But her traveling is only in imagination. As we might expect, she remains unmarried and at home in Morgana; she cares for her psychotic father, tenderly regards the careers of the wanderers from a distance, and patiently constructs memorials for the dead. She is one of those characters who, like Snow-die MacLain, might make the word *home* connote security and love, rather than stifling confinement, to any wanderer.

In "Moon Lake" we are introduced to another wanderer, Easter. She is dominant among the orphans and "advanced" for her age both physically ("she had started her breasts") and experientially; she is a wild tomboy who plays mumblety-peg and runs around enviably dirty. Easter is quite possibly an offspring of King MacLain, evidence being, first of all, Katie Rainey's remark that several of King's children are growing up in the County Orphan's. Then there is the "withstanding gold" of Easter's hair, which forms a crest on top of her head and seems to "fly up at the temples, being cropped and wiry" (the golden crest may be associated with King's golden panama hat, and the pompadour cap so fiercely loved by Loch Morrison). Finally, there are Easter's own remarks about her parentage: "I haven't got no father. I never had, he ran away. I've got a mother. When I could walk, then my mother took me by the hand and turned me in, and I remember it."

Like a true daughter of King, Easter is independent and adventurous, wandering away from camp into the woods, smoking a piece of cross-vine, seeking out new forms of excitement with Jinny Love and Nina, running about with her dress stained green behind, dreamily floating out on the lake in an abandoned boat. Her eyes, which are "neither brown nor green nor cat," have "something of metal, flat ancient metal" in them, so that their color could have been found "somewhere . . . away, under lost leaves—strange as the painted color of the ants. Instead of round black holes in the center of her eyes, there might have been women's heads, ancient." This strange, half-mythical child with her ancient eyes also has her secret ambition: she is going to be a singer. With the "ring of pure dirt" around her neck, her bold explorations of the woods and lake, and her early dedication to music, she seems to be a child of nature and art with no visible relationship to Morgana as a social order, still less the confining institutional life of an orphanage—a "visiting somebody."

Nina Carmichael stands in relation to Easter as Cassie does to Virgie in "June Recital." Nina is tremendously impressed, admiring, envious of Easter's "beatific state" of being "not answerable to a soul on earth"; yet she is protective and pitying—or rather wanting to pity—for she is waiting for her heart to be twisted by the knowledge that her delightful new companion is an orphan. Easter serves for Nina as Virgie does for Cassie in being a means to growing moral insight by way of imaginative projection. Lying on her cot in the tent at night, Nina thinks and dreams of the exciting possibilities of "slipping into" the experience of persons quite different from herself; she wants "to try for the fiercest secrets. To slip into them all—to change. . . . To *have been* an orphan."

Nina then has a sense of the night personified and holding a special relation to Easter. The passage that follows is significant both as a foreshadowing of coming events and as a symbolic account of the nature and destiny of the two types of characters juxtaposed in the novel: the wanderers and their static, reflective counterparts:

Nina sat up on the cot and stared passionately before her at the night— the pale dark roaring night with its secret step, the Indian night. She felt the forehead, the beaded stars, look in thoughtfully at her.

The pondering night stood rude at the tent door, the opening fold would let it stoop in—it, him—he had risen up inside. Long-armed, or long-winged, he stood in the center where the pole went up. Nina lay back, drawn quietly from him. But the night knew about Easter. All about her. Geneva had pushed her to the edge of the cot. Easter's hand hung down, opened outward. Come here, night, Easter might say, tender to a giant, to such a dark thing. And the night, obedient and graceful, would kneel to her. Easter's callused hand hung open there to the night that had got wholly into the tent.

Nina let her own arm stretch forward opposite Easter's. Her hand too opened, of itself. She lay there a long time motionless, under the night's gaze, its black cheek, looking immovably at her hand, the only part of her now which was not asleep. Its gesture was like Easter's, but Easter's hand slept and her own hand knew—shrank and knew, yet offered still.

"Instead . . . me instead. . . ."

In the cup of her hand, in her filling skin, in the fingers' weight and still-ness, Nina felt it: compassion and a kind of competing that were all one, a single ecstasy, a single longing. For the night was not impartial. No, the night loved some more than others, served some more than others. Nina's hand lay open there for a long time, as if its fingers would be its eyes. Then it too slept. She dreamed her hand was helpless to the tearing teeth of wild beasts. At reveille she woke up lying on it. She could not move it. She hit it and bit it until like a cluster of bees it stung back and came to life.

The night in this passage may be related to the "dark magnet that kept drawing you in" which Cassie sees as her brother's lure, but not her own. It is the dark or unknown side of life, attractive and beauti-ful, yet dangerous, leading to possible death of the heart or a literal death: the fate that threatens persons who live with the hand and the heart thrown carelessly open, freely, experimentally, courageously. The fact that the night "loves" and "serves" these persons indicates their paradoxical relation to experience and fate: they are partly vic-timized by it, partly inviting, even controlling and subduing it. The figure of night as a giant Indian, summoned by Easter and kneeling at her side, shows that susceptibility to both love and death is a sig-nificant element in the fearless nature. The night comes as a great wild lover to woo the maiden, but he is also reminiscent of *"Der Tod"* in Schubert's famous song, who sings to the maiden, *"Gib deine Hand."* The child is clearly marked either for some special tragedy or some special escape and fulfillment—perhaps for both.

Nina's hand imitates the careless gesture, but it is distinguished from the orphan's hand in being aware, in "knowing," yet "offering still." Nina is filled with "a single ecstasy and longing"; she wants herself to be open to love and experience, to accept the fate of the wanderer. The "fire in her head" is "compassion"; she yearns to suffer tragedy with and for the other. Out of a desire to live fully and freely she "competes" with the other. "Instead . . ." she prays to the dark unknown presence; "me instead. . . ."

When Nina finally goes to sleep, the hand also "sleeps." During the night in a dream the open hand lives its entire life independent of the girl, yet attached to her, making her suffer sympathetically the pain and terror of experience. When she awakens in the morning, the hand is dead; the life in that offered hand seems over. But she brings it back to life by the ruthless action of hitting and biting it. Thus its brief night's history has anticipated Easter's coming ordeal of death and resurrection (by a similarly cruel method); and in addition, it has shown forth the entire life process of such wanderers as Virgie Rainey and Ran and Eugene MacLain, who will experience their own deaths by despair and rebirths by a resurgence of joy and hope.

The nature of Easter's near-tragedy again shows the large part played by chance or accident in Eudora Welty's vision of the universe. The orphan is standing high up on the diving board, watching the swimming lesson, when Exum, a little black boy bent on nothing but sheer mischievous fun, gives Easter's heel "the tenderest, obscurest little brush" with a green willow switch. She drops as though hit in the head by a stone, and apparently the heavy fall of her body causes it to be imbedded deep in the muddy lake bottom. Only after Loch has made several attempts to find her and has surfaced with "long ribbons of green and terrible stuff, shapeless black matter" in his hands is he finally successful. When Easter is brought up she is not only more dead than alive, but hideously disfigured, changed into some terrible lake-bottom growth—tongue rolled backwards, teeth smeared with mud, wet hair lying over her face in "long fern shapes," a dark stream of water rolling from her mouth down her cheek. All the little girls have a long solemn look at the "berated" and "betrayed" figure, "the mask formed and set on the face, one hand displayed, one jealously clawed under the waist"—they have seen, most of them for the first time, the ugliness of death. When Easter is finally revived after hours of work, Nina thinks: "At least what had happened to Easter was out in the world, like the table itself. There it remained—mystery, if only for being hard and cruel and, by something Nina felt inside her body, murderous." Catastrophe has been seen and faced as a *fact*. The change is not in the horror or mystery itself, but in the girl's attitude toward it. Catastrophe or death that is actually visible or recognized is less terrifying than catastrophe that is imagined: the threatening, the "unknown" has been objectified, fully met "in the world"; it can be survived both by victims and spectators.

The careers of Randall and Eugene MacLain, the twin sons of King and Snowdie, are presented in "The Whole World Knows" and "Music from Spain." In the earlier sections of *The Golden Apples* the twins

are almost indistinguishable: they are seen from a distance as rather
mischievous, feebly disciplined little monkeys who always leave their
doors "wide open to the universe" when they go out to play, and let
in the flies so annoying to Miss Eckhart. They are next seen in "Sir
Rabbit" as a pair of fair-banged fifteen-year-olds who come trotting
up like a pair of matched circus ponies to engage Mattie Will Sojourner in a spring-inspired sexual romp—an incident that serves as
a prelude to Mattie's greater adventure with King, and shows the
twins, in actions as well as appearance, to be "the very spit of their
father." But in the stories devoted to each, the two brothers are
clearly differentiated; they are alike only in a common woe: marital
discord, failure in love.

"The Whole World Knows" is an almost unrelieved lamentation,
a singularly distressing account of a sordid scandal into which Randall
is unwillingly swept. It takes the form of a soliloquy that is half confession, half supplication, as though spoken to a priest or even to
God. To his wandering, unhearing father, King, Ran pours out the
tale of his estrangement from his wife and his tragic affair with
Maideen Sumrell. His words are drenched with confusion, grief, loneliness, a sense of guilt, a desire for self-justification, a need for the
paternal understanding and guidance that we know will never be
forthcoming.

Before all the trouble begins, Ran has apparently been on his way
to becoming an established citizen of Morgana. He has married young
Jinny Love Stark (some ten years his junior) and is working as a teller
in the Morgana bank. Then one summer Ran leaves his wife and returns to a hot, dismal room in his old home, the MacLain house, now
run for boarders by a Miss Francine Murphy. Why has he left Jinnny?
The "up-and-down of it, . . . the brunt of it," according to Miss Perdita Mayo—one of the town's leading old maids, gossips, and general
opinion-makers and takers—is that "Jinny was unfaithful to Ran"
with young Woodrow Spights, who works beside Ran in the Morgana
bank. But Miss Perdita, for all her common sense and humanity
("I'm a women that's been clear around the world in my rocking
chair"), cannot see what lies behind the fact of Jinny's infidelity, nor,
apparently, can anybody. Jinny's mother, who has had her own trouble with an alcoholic husband, shows her resentment when she says
to Randall, "You men. You got us beat in the end. . . . We'd know
you through and through except we never know what ails you. . . .
Of course I see what Jinny's doing, the fool, but you ailed first. You
just got her answer to it, Ran." To this Ran thinks in bafflement,

"And what ails me I don't know, Father, unless maybe you know."

The reader is able to divine what is ailing Ran only by watching his reactions to Jinny's character. She is one of those free spirits who cannot be touched by misery, frustration, tragedy; they won't—they can't—take life seriously. When all goes well, they radiate delight into the hearts of their lovers, but often they baffle and enrage, simply because they are so untouchable, unmalleable, closed to all those terrible dark worlds of inward suffering. Their gayety and carelessness are narcissistic and affect others as a stinging, unconscious reproach and mockery.

Jinny's careless, self-centered joy was already established in "Moon Lake." In contrast to the sober, reflective temperament of Nina Carmichael, Jinny was carefree and resilient; she was a child who skipped gaily because even the swamp sounds came to her as "a song of hilarity." It is not surprising to come upon her some ten years later—a young woman who might have been miserable separated from her husband—standing in front of a mirror, smiling frivolously, and carelessly hacking off chunks of her pretty brown hair as she says lightly, "Obey that impulse—." Ran's reaction to her on this first visit back to the Stark house after the separation is inevitable: "That lightness came right back. Just to step on the matting, that billows a little anyway, and with Jinny's hair scattered like feathers on it, I could have floated, risen and floated." Her very presence hints of metamorphosis.

The rage that counterpoints Ran's delight is seen in an incident in which he asks Jinny to sew on a button missing from his sleeve. While she performs this intimate domestic task, the girl is agonizingly close to him; yet she is so untroubled that his thoughts become murderous. With inward violence he imaginatively shoots her full of bullet holes:

I fired pointblank at Jinny—more than once. . . . But Jinny didn't feel it. She made her little face of success. Her thread always went straight to the eye. . . . She far from acknowledged pain—anything but sorrow and pain. When I couldn't give her something she wanted she would hum a little tune. In our room, her voice would go low and soft to complete disparagement. Then I loved her a lot. The little cheat. I waited on, while she darted the needle and pulled at my sleeve, the sleeve to my helpless hand. It was like counting my breaths. I let out my fury and breathed the pure disappointment in: that she was not dead on earth. She bit the thread—magnificently. When she took her mouth away I nearly fell. The cheat.

To Ran, Jinny is a cheat because she refuses to be affected or frustrated; she refuses to feel deeply or to suffer with or for him or anyone else—least of all herself; and that is, perhaps, "cheating" on an important area of human experience.

Ran takes up with an eighteen-year-old country girl named Maideen Sumrall, partly for company, but mostly because Maideen looks like a fresh and "uncontaminated" Jinny, without the mockery in her face and with lovely brown hair shoulder-length rather than butchered by scissors and "ruined." Maideen is simple and good-natured, but Ran makes a literally fatal mistake in supposing that "there was nothing but time between them." Not only does Maideen turn out to be malleable to his will but far worse, she is as disastrously vulnerable as Jinny is invulnerable. After an excursion to Vicksburg, the two collapse half drunk in a roadside cabin, where Ran's suffering and cruelty to Maideen reach their climax. During the night he attempts suicide unsuccessfully with an old pistol of his father's and then takes Maideen in a quick, loveless conjunction. Later he awakens to hear her weeping beside him, "the kind of soft, patient, meditative sobs a child will venture long after punishment." Now in soliloquy to his missing father he wails, "How was I to know she would go and hurt herself? She cheated, she cheated too."

Maideen has "cheated" in taking her experience too seriously, too tragically, in ironic contrast to Jinny's kind of cheating. It is Maideen's breast, rather than Jinny's, that ends filled with "the bright holes where Ran's bullets had gone through." Only in the last story do we learn how irrevocably the girl has "hurt herself": soon afterwards she dies by suicide, found on the floor of the place where she works by Old Man Moody. But the fact of her suicide gives point to Ran's desperately futile plea, "Father! Dear God, wipe it clean. Wipe it clean, wipe it out. Don't let it be."

The final cry of Randall's soliloquy—"And where's Jinny?"—is apparently answered, for the two are seen back together a decade later at Mrs. Rainey's funeral. At one point during the afternoon Virgie is subjected to Jinny's insistence that she marry—everybody ought to marry, Jinny feels, because "only then could she resume as Jinny Love Stark, her true self," careless and independent, not bound by marriage. But as if to suggest that at least an armed truce has been achieved between Ran and Jinny, we find at the funeral their curious and delightful children.

Randall's "wanderings" have been largely confined to Morgana—he knows he belongs there, even though his mother has called him to come back under her roof in the town of MacLain, and though he sets off restlessly for Vicksburg because he has "looked at Morgana too long." Morgana has been the scene of his triumphs as well as his scandals, defeats, and disasters. The son of King has become reigning prince (mayor) of Morgana, a man whose career, like that of his father, is a legend to the community:

> They had voted for him . . . for his glamour and his story, for being a MacLain and the bad twin, for marrying a Stark and then for ruining a girl and the thing she did. . . . They voted for the revelation; it had made their hearts faint, and they would assert it again. Ran knew that every minute, there in the door he stood it.

"The whole world knows" (because Morgana is the whole world to Morgana) about Randall MacLain.

"Father, Eugene! What you went and found, was it better than this?" asks Randall in his soliloquy. If his brother, the twin who grew up gentle like his mother, could have heard that question, he would have had to answer sadly, "No, no better." The reasons for his answer are provided in "Music from Spain," the one story of *The Golden Apples* that is not set in Morgana. Told in the third person, mostly from Eugene's point of view, the story has a natural economy of structure, since Eugene's odyssey takes place on a single day in San Francisco, and the carefully related events lead with a gradual crescendo to the climax and resolution. The central action is initiated by a sudden, impulsive move on the part of Eugene, which expresses and unleashes in him a long-pent-up sense of protest and rebellion. One morning at breakfast when Eugene's wife makes some "innocent" remark to him—"Crumb on your chin" or the like—he leans across the table and slaps her face. Then, without giving her the usual goodbye kiss, he leaves the apartment and steps out on the street to walk and reflect about the meaning of his strange, aggressive action.

Eugene has traveled so far from Morgana only to find himself more effectively trapped in a marriage gone bad than he might ever have been at home. His wife Emma is in every way a curious contrast to Randall's wife Jinny. Older and heavier than Eugene, she is a plump, fussily feminine, busy-tongued, self-indulgent little woman whose traits are in contrast to Jinny's youth, slim boyishness, and mocking abandon. Given to self-crucifixion, Emma naturally crucifies everyone

around her. In sharp contrast to Jinny, she is an indefatigable, nox-
ious, almost professional sufferer.

Not that Emma hasn't some reason for suffering: a year earlier, little Nan, their sunny, lovable child, had died. But that loss has been
Eugene's as well as Emma's, and there has been no relief from her
prolonged, narcissistically bloated grief. Because Emma is so
"touchy," Eugene cannot attack her response to the loss: "if a quarrel
did spring up; she would cry . . . she had a waterfall of tears back
there." As a result, there is no more love between them. Out of his
layman's reading of his unconscious, Eugene decides that *"He struck
her because he wanted another love. The forties. Psychology."* The slap he
feels has been "like kissing the cheek of the dead. . . . How cold to
the living hour grief could make you."

The initial protest made, Eugene follows with another and decides
not to work at Bertsingers' Jewelers that day. Beginning his wanderings, he passes through Market Street and notes with disgust the tawdry, pathetic appeals of this Vanity Fair, for "Market had with the
years become a street of trusses, pads, braces, false bosoms, false
teeth, and glass eyes. And of course jewelry stores." Just beyond Bertsingers' the doorway of a market is crowded with flowers. Eugene
wishes he could have worked there—cracked crabs with a mallet or
grown flowers instead of bending all day like a drudge over "meticu-
lous watches." Viewing the "daily revelation" of the fog lifting from
the city, he has a surge of fresh longing, such as he had felt years ago
in Mississippi, to wander and see distant places, or once again to return to "that careless, patched land of Mississippi winter, trees in
their rusty wrappers, slow-grown trees taking their time, the lost
shambles of old cane, the winter swamp where his twin brother, he
supposed, still hunted." Walking the streets, he experiences a strange
sympathy with the lawless, chaotic life of the big city: "he would
know . . . anything that threatened the moral way, or transformed
it, even, in the city of San Francisco that day: as if he and the city
were watching each other—without accustomed faith. But with interest . . . boldness . . . recklessness, almost."

Just then Eugene spies walking ahead of him in traffic the Spanish
guitarist he and Emma had heard in solo recital the previous evening
at Aeolian Hall. Suddenly the Spaniard is almost hit by an automobile: Eugene springs forward and saves him from a possibly fatal accident. The two men shake hands in relief and delight, but Eugene
suffers a shock of disappointment that the Spaniard cannot speak En-

glish. Since no words of thanks or deprecation can be spoken, the two stroll on together. Eugene notes that the big fellow has remained imperturbable, and he reflects that the Spaniard "had walked out in front of the automobile almost tempting it to try and get him, with all the aplomb of—certainly a bull fighter." Thus the Spaniard is immediately established as one of life's heroic, fearless ones; like that other fabulous musician, Powerhouse, this man is self-possessed, bold, generous of spirit. And again, as with Powerhouse, Eudora Welty joyously turns the lavish power of her descriptive gift on this admirable, inscrutable creature of paradoxes: wild and primitive with his thick black hair, crude table manners, and fierce bull-like nostrils, but dignified and tender with his music, noble in his gestures and bearing.

The Spaniard is a perfect companion for Eugene on this day of pilgrimage to freedom and rebirth. Articulate, the old fellow would probably have been of little use to Eugene: rendered mute by the language barrier, Eugene is pressed to a more primal form of communication, the almost physical blood-knowledge that we usually associate with the vision of D. H. Lawrence.

With Eugene serving as host, the two advance to a restaurant for lunch, where Eugene's mind grows fantastical thinking up possible clues to the stranger's secret life, the exotic, perhaps dangerous acts perpetrated, "and always the one, dark face, though momently fire from his nostrils brimmed over, with that veritable *waste* of life!" From these aroused thoughts spring images from his own past—a favorite piece of music played when he was Miss Eckhart's student; an engraving of "the kneeling Man in the Wilderness . . . in his father's remnant geography book, who hacked once at the Traveler's Tree, opened his mouth, and the water came pouring in"—the Traveler he had once believed to represent his unknown father, and with whom he now identifies himself.

Back on the street the two witness an accident. A little woman trips, sinks in the streetcar's path and is instantly killed. People close around in morbid curiosity; the Spaniard shakes his head, but there is no sign that he has made a connection between his own near-accident and this one. Eudora Welty has only shown, as in *Delta Wedding,* that real accidents occur as well as near-accidents; there is little security for the individual in a universe largely governed by chance.

Eugene takes his guest on a streetcar out toward the edge of the city, and the two walk up and down hill after hill in a steady progress toward the sea. Once they come to a high point where the Spaniard suddenly swings around to survey the world behind them. "He tenderly swept an arm. The whole arena was alight with a fairness and blueness at this hour of afternoon; . . . the laid-out city looked soft, brushed over with some sky-feather. Then he dropped his hand, as though the city might retire; and lifted it again, as though to bring it back for a second time. He was really wonderful with his arm raised." The gesture is heroic, suggesting divine powers of creation and benediction, as if the Spaniard were bringing the city into its beautiful being like a piece of music. The raised arm is related to Perseus's vaunting in Miss Eckhart's picture and to that youthful heroic reflection in Loch; in *The Golden Apples* it is the gesture of men who have gloriously achieved and conquered.

The two men advance to the cliffs of "Land's End" and begin scrambling over brown rocks with the sea exploding wildly beneath and a strong wind turning back the gulls in their flight. While the sun sets, the Spaniard leads a tortuous progress through rough paths and caves. Eugene has begun throwing out remarks like "You assaulted your wife" from the safe position of not being understood. At last on the edge of a cliff, where a touch could topple the Spaniard over the edge, Eugene seizes and clings to him, "almost as if he had waited for him a long time with longing, almost as if he loved him, and had found a lasting refuge." The Spaniard lets out a "bullish roar," followed by a "terrible recital" of words that strike Eugene as fearless and shameless. Eugene nearly falls and has to pull himself back by seizing the man. He then runs to chase the Spaniard's big black hat (caught in the wind), puts it on his own head, runs back to the Spaniard, and this time is himself held with "hard, callused fingers like prongs." He feels disembodied, weightless, lifted up in the strong arms of the Spaniard and swung around "pillowed in great strength." The whirling dizziness affects his body like the coming of passion, and he thinks of Emma advancing to meet him, her arms lifted in the "wide, aroused sleeves," closing around him, "returning him awesome favors in full vigor, with not the ghost of the salt of tears." This is the way it should be:

If he could have spoken! It was out of this relentlessness, not out of the gush of tears, that there would be a child again. . . . If he could have stopped everything, until that pulse, far back, far inside, far within now, could shake like the little hard red fist of the first spring leaf!

He was brought over and held by the knees in the posture of a bird, his body almost upright and his forearms gently spread. In his nostrils and relaxing eyes and around his naked head he could feel the reach of fine spray or the breath of fog. He was up-borne, open-armed. He was only thinking, My dear love comes.

What has happened in this remarkable scene of climax? Some fateful encounter has taken place between the two men: half in play, half in dead earnest, each has momentarily seized the fate of the other, grappled with and closely confronted the other. But the Spaniard is the stronger. First when Eugene puts on the great warm black hat and later when he flies like a bird over the sea out from those strong hands, he undergoes metamorphosis. The stranger's life-force seems to have flown out from the hat and hands into Eugene's blood, so that he briefly participates in the Spaniard's powerful, fearless mode of being. From this change springs passion; and out of that could spring a new life, a new child. The episode is parallel to the climax of "Moon Lake." The hero of each book, through an action suggestive of the sexual act, brings to life one apparently dead: both Eugene and Easter are put literally into the posture of love by the unconscious "lovers" of their lives—those who have life to give from the glorious "waste" of their own lives.

Eugene's story does not end happily. His change, his rebirth, have, after all, not been shared by his wife, nor has Eugene's experience miraculously provided him with words to describe it. He returns home to find Emma exactly the same—petty, unimaginative, smugly opinionated, dominating as usual—far indeed from the passionate woman who had met Eugene in his ecstatic vision on the cliff. He hears Emma and a neighbor reduce his marvelous friend to a scurrilous Latin type who exhibits "bad taste" by laughing out loud with a woman in church. One senses the deep misery and hopelessness inundating him again. His wife's nature has settled firmly into a mold basically hostile to spontaneity, happiness, or fulfillment.

The later history of Eugene is brief and poignant. Returning to Morgana, he dies of tuberculosis apparently soon afterwards. Passing the cemetery where Eugene is buried in the MacLain plot, Virgie Rainey remembers the story of this sadly strange son of King:

Eugene, for a long interval, had lived in another part of the world, learning while he was away that people don't have to be answered just because they want to know. His very wife was never known here, and he did not make it plain whether he had children somewhere now or had been childless. His wife did not even come to the funeral, although a telegram had been sent. A foreigner? "Why, she could even be a Dago and we wouldn't know it." His light, tubercular body seemed to hesitate on the street of Morgana, hold averted, anticipating questions. Sometimes he looked up in the town where he was young and said something strangely spiteful or ambiguous (he was never reconciled to his father, they said, was sarcastic to the old man—all he loved was Miss Snowdie and flowers) but he bothered no one. "He never did bother a soul," they said at his graveside that day, forgetting his childhood.

Eugene is one of those wanderers who, like Miss Eckhart, pluck the golden apples only in a rare, isolated moment or two during an entire lifetime. They remain essentially thwarted, crushed, victimized by the cruel and devious workings of fate.

The final section of *The Golden Apples,* "The Wanderers," has many functions in the structure of the book as a whole. As an epilogue, it provides the denouement of several careers, lends perspective to the meaning and interrelations of these life histories, and gives a sense of mutability. It also provides a fully detailed portrait of the Morgana community by showing it engaged in a major tribal ritual, that of the funeral; furthermore, it recapitulates and makes concluding statements of the major themes of the book. But it is perhaps chiefly the story of Virgie Rainey, who, as a woman now past forty, is the most perceptive and emotionally mature of the wanderers and is getting a belated start (after an early abortive attempt) on her long search for the golden apples. The ending of the book is really, therefore, another beginning, and the sense of an epic cycle is achieved.

The initiating action of "The Wanderers" is the death, by heart attack, of old Mrs. Fate Rainey, narrator of the first section. For decades, from her selling post at the turn of the MacLain Road, Katie Rainey has watched the passing and trafficking and has been a central and familiar community figure who records and represents the change as well as the constancy of Morgana life. To Virgie the old woman has been a bondage both dear and confining. After running away briefly at seventeen with her sailor, Bucky Moffitt, Virgie returns home, living out through the long years of her endless youth (her dark hair never loses its spring) a battle between affectionate loyalty and a sense of oppression. Katie Rainey has caused Virgie to impose on her own life a pattern inimical to her talents and desires: an office job in which her skillful pianist's fingers are rigidly set to typing, or turned to farm and domestic chores—milking the cows, dressing the quail, cooking and sewing.

In never losing her beauty nor her desire or capacity for love, Virgie seems a daughter of Venus in bonds. Early morning of the day of her mother's funeral finds her vigorously cutting down overgrown grass and shrubs in the yard, the choked-out roses scratching her and drawing blood. But while she performs this heavy chore, she is aware of the morning star hanging in the sky. "She could feel dimmed round Venus still, for she must feel some presence, there was always something, someone, and Venus watching her made the imperceptible work almost leisurely, then again fierce." Still beautiful and passionate, Virgie has confined her rebellion against small-town moral codes to an affair or two discreetly conducted with some inferior man (the only kind available); the town knows this, and Mrs. Rainey is exposed to their twittering gossip, but dignity requires that she ignore their lack of "chivalry."

Her love for Virgie and a subliminal memory of her own youthful independence provoke the pity and understanding that prevent her from a terrible confrontation with her daughter; yet stubbornness keeps her always fretting after the girl, demanding that she appear when expected in order to perform the necessary chores according to schedule. Pride, affection, and a costly control have kept this difficult relationship going until it is finally broken by death. When Mrs. Rainey is struck by her final heart attack, Virgie is busy cutting out a dress from some plaid material. "There's nothing Virgie Rainey loves better than struggling against a real hard plaid," the old lady thinks with the first thrust of pain; and her last clear feeling before she staggers to the bed is a desire to be "down and covered up, in, of all things, Virgie's hard-to-match-up plaid." Discipline achieved against odds—this has been the source of Katie Rainey's pride in her daughter ("It's a blessed wonder to see the child mind"); and the obedience and affection that motivate it have been the warming mantle spread over the old woman in her declining years.

Soon after her death the whole community, white and black, descend on the Rainey house, and the funeral rites begin with the "laying out" of the corpse (beautifully performed, all agree, by old Snowdie), with housecleaning and the preparation of great quantities of food and drink, the cutting and arranging of flowers, and the gathering of the clan. Virgie displays none of the anticipated signs of hysteria or grief to the expectant visitors; when she finally weeps briefly, it is out of a generalized sense of loss at the old order's passing, which no one understands. She is busy but detached, watching and waiting until, at the close of the first night, when all but Snowdie (who stays to sit with the corpse) depart, they seem "to drag some mythical gates and barriers away from her view." Then she goes down to the river, takes off her clothes, and slips in. A strong physical sense of union with nature suffuses her, for "all was one warmth, air, water, and her own body . . . one weight, one matter." Swimming, her body is soothed and sensitized, and the sand, pieces of shell, grass, and mud which touch at her skin seem "like suggestions and with-drawals of some bondage that might have been dear, now dismember-ing and losing itself." She experiences an emotional ablution, an emptying, a sensation purely sensuous but strangely disembodied, edging on metamorphosis, "suspended in the Big Black River as she would know how to hang suspended in felicity." Not in the tribal rites and clichés, but only in this personal ritual with its subtle, in-sinuating mode of address to her mind and senses, does Virgie find clues to the unspeakable meaning of the great change in her life.

And so through the funeral services the following afternoon, though she is bereaved, the only experiences meaningful to Virgie are the private or spontaneously shared ones. When an orgy of weeping has been induced by the minister's remarks and a child's singing of a sentimental hymn, Virgie watches King MacLain steal back and forth from a table in the hall to pick at the ham, and she then sees him push out his lip and make his hideous face at her, "like a silent yell." The sound of his cracking a little bone in his teeth refreshes her. Hearing the happy sounds of the MacLain children playing outside, she experiences another moment of alliance—she doesn't know whether with Ran or with King. With or without benefit of friend-ship or intimacy, Virgie knows that these are her people, her kind. They are all rebels—King, his son, his impious, curious grandchil-dren, and Virgie herself—all have the "pure wish to live," to be indi-vidual; they refuse to be crushed by life or by death, or by the stultifying effects of sentimental conformity or piety.

Later in the day, returning home from the cemetery, Virgie has a sense of the "double coming-back." She remembers the time of her return at seventeen when on the way from the train to her home she had looked about her "in a kind of glory." Then, as now, having gone through an experience of despair, she had felt the beauty of the golden earth meet some ineffable impulse of life and hope in herself, and the issue was a rebirth, a resurgence of joy. "Virgie never saw it differently, never doubted that all the opposites on earth were close together, love close to hate, living to dying; but of them all, hope and despair were the closest blood—unrecognizable one from the other sometimes, making moments double upon themselves, and in the doubling double again, amending but never taking back."

The impulse of hope now drives Virgie away from her home and on to some unknown place and condition of the future. She gives away or packs up for storage all her mother's belongings, and sets out in her old car. Seven miles out from Morgana, the town of MacLain is the natural stopping-off place for Virgie to make her final reflections—the last dearly familiar place, drenched with the legends and memories of the wandering MacLain clan, several of whom are already buried in the cemetery (and King himself, surely the next to go). Here, too, Miss Eckhart is buried. On the stile in front of the courthouse Virgie sits quietly as Mr. Mabry, her last lover, passes by unnoticing; she is "bereaved, hatless, unhidden now, in the rain" and finally, all alone. Then she remembers a picture Miss Eckhart had hanging on her wall, showing Perseus with the head of the Medusa. Only now does she begin to comprehend its meaning:

> The vaunting was what she remembered, that lifted arm.
> Cutting off the Medusa's head was the heroic act, perhaps, that made visible a horror in life, that was at once the horror in love, Virgie thought—the separateness. She might have seen heroism prophetically when she was young and afraid of Miss Eckhart. She might be able to see it now prophetically, but she was never a prophet. Because Virgie saw things in their time, like hearing them—and perhaps because she must believe in the Medusa equally with Perseus—she saw the stroke of the sword in three moments, not one. In the three was the damnation—no, only the secret, unhurting because not caring in itself—beyond the beauty and the sword's stroke and the terror lay their existence in time—far out and endless, a constellation which the heart could read over many a night.

What Virgie half-sees, since her vision as an active wanderer-heroine now blends with that of the passive seer-prophet, is both the polarity or alternations of human experience and their fusion beyond time. She remembers that vaunting of Perseus's lifted arm in Miss Eckhart's picture, and with it, the Medusa's severed head; she must "believe in" the victim along with the heroic slayer. The reiteration

of the motif of love and separateness in this passage recalls the crucial
scene from "A Still Moment." Audubon has performed a heroic act
in slaying the white heron: heroic because his will and intelligence as
artist and naturalist have asserted themselves over his natural feeling
for the bird's beautiful life. Since he cannot paint from memory, he
must kill the bird to save its beauty for the eternal world of art. The
bird becomes victim, and to Lorenzo, the witness, the effect is one of
horror.

To be sure, the bird is innocent, unaware, and lovely whereas the
Medusa seems evil and hideous, a death-bringer. But in the legend
the Medusa is victim from the start: originally a beautiful Gorgon,
raped by the lord of the sea in the temple of Athene (Minerva), she
is transformed by the jealous and enraged goddess into a monster.
Medusa's hair, the most glorious attribute of her beauty, is changed
into revolting snakes, the fascination of which turns all gazers into
stone. The victim now possesses a deadly power to victimize, which
Perseus can evade only by viewing her reflection in his protective
shield and slaying her while her snaky head sleeps.

In this use of the myth, and in Eudora Welty's vision generally,
evil is never pure and unambiguous, nor is heroism a simple matter
of the triumph of good over evil. Whoever conquers does so to the
cost of someone or something else, producing in the moment of destruction physical and metaphysical horror. To the merely human eye,
from which the larger, eternal perspective is withheld, such acts of
violence are horrible because they bring the death that is the final
cause or essence of all separateness in life or in love. And so the protest is raised when an act of destruction, however heroic, is witnessed.
The human way is to see actions and relationships "in their time," as
music is heard, in a succession of moments; the human way is to feel
out, or through, the whole painful process of tragedy and heroism.
Just now, for Virgie, there is no "hurt," only the revelation of a "secret" or mystery, since the incident pictured is without immediacy;
the implications of the heroic action have been transmuted and distanced to the world of art, where like a constellation loftily removed
it may be eternally read, studied, contemplated.

If the human burden is tragedy (separateness), the human glory is
the ability to absorb that tragedy, to project it in the forms of art,
and then to give to others this knowledege turned to beauty. All this
Beethoven had done for Miss Eckhart, and Miss Eckhart had done for
Virgie:

Miss Eckhart, whom Virgie had not, after all, hated—had come near to loving, for she had taken Miss Eckhart's hate, and then her love, extracted them, the thorn and then the overflow—had hung the picture on the wall for herself. She had absorbed the hero and the victim and then, stoutly, could sit down to the piano with all Beethoven ahead of her. With her hate, with her love, and with the small gnawing feelings that ate them, she offered Virgie her Beethoven. She offered, offered, offered—and when Virgie was young, in the strange wisdom of youth that is accepting of more than is given, she had accepted *the* Beethoven, as with the dragon's blood. That was the gift she had touched with her fingers that had drifted and left her.

In Virgie's reach of memory a melody softly lifted, lifted of itself. Every time Perseus struck off the Medusa's head, there was the beat of time, and the melody. Endless the Medusa, and Perseus endless.

In time, our present human life, the tragic pain and the triumph, the horror and the beauty, the despair and the joy, the frustration and the fulfillment, the separateness and the love, exist in an endless counterpoint: this is the experience of Virgie Rainey, and of every wanderer in *The Golden Apples*.

Finally emergent in Virgie's knowledge and experience is the transcendence of art, once unknowingly communicated through her in a June recital when, at the age of thirteen, she had played the *Fantasia on Beethoven's Ruins of Athens* and the red of her sash had wet and stained her "as if she had been stabbed in the heart." Though the gift has left her, the tragic, romantic knowledge, with its defeat and triumph, has ripened fully.

Eudora Welty's use of a mythology made thoroughly indigenous in *The Golden Apples* has already been noted. Among classical works, Ovid's *Metamorphoses* seems most often evoked, and not only because of its rich gathering of Greek and Roman myth and legend, tales within tales told by a thousand tellers in a loosely flowing but swiftly paced, sophisticated, and image-laden poetic narrative. Ovid's magnificent work, with its theme of transformation, leaves the reader convinced that man and nature, human and divine, heaven and earth, antiquity and divinity, youth and age, fantasy and reality, all melt and merge into one another—a state of expectancy also induced in the reader who comes to *The Golden Apples* with a "willing imagination."

Together with the theme of metamorphosis we find that of quest: the odyssey of Eugene, the search for a father of Randall, of all the wanderers for fulfillment and joy. Woven through the book we also find patterns of developing images and symbols that serve important structural functions: they relate and unify the individual careers presented in the book, they support and embody its themes, they are the means by which the texture of an event or feeling is conveyed, they invest the prose with the quality of poetry.

One cluster of these images grows out of the title and its use in the Yeats poem. Plucking the golden apples is the prelude to tasting and enjoying the fruit: fruit and things golden are generally associated with pleasure and fruition; frequently, though not always, they are associated with sexual and emotional fulfillment through love. The golden rays of the sun make earth fertile: King visits and impregnates Snowdie in a shower of gold; he leaves Mattie Will Sojourner in light "like golden smoke"; his familiar sign is the golden panama hat. Finally, his offspring are crowned with golden hair: the twins, Easter with her crest of "withstanding gold," and little Fan, King's grandchild, whose hair when she flies out in play is "a band of sunlight soft and level," or when at bedtime it ripples all around her face, is like "a little golden rain hat."

To young ones, for whom experience and fulfillment lie dimly and alluringly in the future, a golden harbinger may intimate the coming mystery in a moment of quiet reflection. Loch hears the distant songs of Cassie and her friends returning from their hayride. He looks out into the dark leaves of the tree, then sees beyond a low cloud lighted, looking like "a single low wing. The mystery he had felt like a golden and aimless bird had waited until now to fly over." In the camp at Moon Lake the sound of Loch's golden horn playing taps is a "fairy sound, . . . a holding apart of the air," evoking the dreams and longings of the young girls in the tents; seeing the boy in the distance, Nina puts him into "his visionary place." To Virgie, however, who at seventeen is already initiated into both love and despair, golden light is a sign of returning joy and hope. When the fields glow in the "ripe afternoon" of her return home after running away, she feels like dancing, "knowing herself not really, in her essence, yet hurt; and thus happy."

References to ripening, or ripe, juicy, sweet fruit ("the golden apples of the sun") are usually associated with sexual anticipation or fulfillment. From his bedroom window Loch views not only the progress of the affair between Virgie Rainey and her sailor but the ripening of figs on the old rusty fig trees nearby. Loch is waiting for the day when the sailor will take the ripe figs. "When they cracked open their pink and golden flesh would show, their inside flowers, and golden bubbles of juice would hang, to touch your tongue to first." To Loch the fig tree is "a magic tree with golden fruit that shone in and among its branches like a cloud of lightning bugs," and he dreams of "the sweet golden juice to come." When Virgie Rainey comes in to Miss Eckhart's for her piano lessons, she is often "peeling a ripe fig with her teeth." To the teeth of Mattie Will Sojourner, set in the small pointed ear of a MacLain twin, the ear has "the fuzz of a peach."

Because the time of fruition is usually brief and precious, ripe fruit may also be associated with the idea of time's fleeting. Once Nina thinks of ripe pears, "beautiful, symmetrical, clean pears with thin skins, with snow-white flesh so juicy and tender that to eat one baptized the whole face, and so delicate that while you urgently ate the first half, the second half was already beginning to turn brown. To all fruits, and especially to those fine pears, something happened—the process was so swift, you were never in time for them. It's not the flowers that are fleeting, Nina thought, it's the fruits—it's the time when things are ready that they don't stay."

Butterflies and humming birds appear with a cluster of associations related to those of the golden apples. Butterflies are again associated with delight, sexual pleasure, or exoticism; they are the sign of the lover, as Psyche, beloved of Cupid, appears with butterfly wings. Miss Eckhart gives to Virgie the gift of a butterfly pin to wear on her shoulder. In "Moon Lake" Nina sees the silhouette of two lovers, each on one end of a canoe floating on the bright water, and looking like "a dark butterfly with wings spread open and still." In San Francisco Eugene spies a butterfly tattooed on the inner side of the wrist of an exotic-looking young man with a black pompadour and taps on his shoes; later he sees a strangely beautiful woman, a mulatto or Polynesian "marked as a butterfly is, over all her visible skin. Curves, scrolls, dark brown areas on light brown, were beautifully placed on her body, as if by design, with pools about the eyes, at the nape of her neck, at the wrist, and about her legs too, like fawn spots, visible through her stockings. She had the look of waiting in leafy shade, . . . of hiding and flaunting together"—a fascinating creature in whom the process of metamorphosis seems to have been arrested. Nature's strange camouflage offers protection; yet these markings are decorative, attracting attention and possibly luring a potential lover into a secret, shady spot. Eugene imagines that the Spaniard has such

a retreat, "a dark and shady place" which he seeks out; "for it was
natural to suppose . . . that the solidest of artists were chameleons."

When "The Wanderers" was first published separately in *Harper's
Bazaar*, it appeared under the title of "The Humming Birds." The
basic analogy is this: as the small aerial wanderers suck sweetness
from flowers, so their human counterparts try to suck sweetness from
life. But in their swift darting, hummingbirds also suggest the mystery and elusiveness of joy; in their peculiar mode of hanging suspended while they suck, they suggest both physical suspension in
space (swimming, floating, or flying) and the suspension in time (the
sense of being outside time) that comes with the moment of ecstasy
(the word means, literally, the state of being outside oneself).

The hummingbird image is first introduced in Cassie's reflections
as she sees one of them go down in a streak across her window:

He was a little emerald bobbin, suspended as always before the opening four-
o'clocks. Metallic and misty together, tangible and intangible, splendid and
fairy-like, the haze of his invisible wings mysterious, like the ring around
the moon—had anyone ever tried to catch him? Not she. Let him be suspended there for a moment each year for a hundred years—incredibly thirsty,
greedy for every drop in every four-o'clock trumpet in the yard, as though
he had them numbered—then dart.

The hummingbird image again appears in the memory of Eugene
while he is sitting in the restaurant with the Spaniard. Through a
process of association and synesthesia, Eugene is reminded by the
sweet, exotic odor of the Spaniard's tobacco of the mimosa flowers
that used to bloom outside the window when as a boy he played a
favorite piece on a hot summer's day and the notes of music were
transformed into drops of light "plopping one, two, three, four,
through sky and trees to earth, to lie there in the pattern opposite to
the shade of the tree. He could feel his forehead bead with drops and
the pleasure run like dripping juice through each plodding finger, at
such an hour, on such a day, in such a place. Mississippi. A hummingbird, like a little fish, a little green fish in the hot air, had hung
for a moment before his gaze, then jerked, vanishing, away." At the
concert the Spaniard's intimate, compelling music of his distant home
sounds like a hummingbird's wings, "so soft as to be almost without
sound, only a beating on the air like a fast wing. . . ."

Once again the hummingbird appears, to Virgie. She is standing
at the bedside of her mother, a moment after her death, when sud-

denly her vision turns to pure image and sensation. "Behind the bed
the window was full of cloudy, pressing flowers and leaves in a heavy
light, like a jar of figs in syrup held up. A hummingbird darted, fed,
darted. Every day he came. He had a ruby throat. The clock jangled
faintly as cymbals struck under water, but did not strike; it couldn't.
Yet a torrent of riches seemed to flow over the room, submerging it
with what was over-sweet."

The suspension of the hummingbird is related to those incidents in
which a character is literally and symbolically suspended in a moment
of felicity. Eugene spread out, flying over the sea like a bird from the
Spaniard's hands, and Virgie spread out, floating like a fish in the
Big Black River, experience moments of pure ecstasy, a freeing from
confining form, weight, destiny, time, and every human burden.
These moments carry with them a suggestion of change in a life pattern which registers as the pause before some actual physical metamorphosis; the state is dreamy or trancelike, the sensations are at once
disembodied and acutely sensuous; the postures, and in Eugene's case
the thoughts, are those of the act of love. Floating is also related to
felicity in other contexts: floating in a boat on Moon Lake is dreamlike enchantment; mist floating on a river or lake in moonlight sus-
pends the viewer in felicity.

Other patterns of symbolism in *The Golden Apples* have to do with
freedom, confinement, and the need for discipline. If fulfillment is to
be achieved, a person must be free. To the characters with family
bonds and internal inhibitions, the state of being, or appearing to be,
completely free, is glorious and enviable: thus Cassie envies Virgie;
Nina envies Easter (in the "beatific state" of being "not answerable to
a soul on earth"); Eugene envies the Spaniard ("There was no one he
loved, to tell him anything, to lay down the law"). But even to the
free ones, walls and barriers are unavoidable. Beating against a wall
may signify the rebel's revolt against rules, as when Virgie as a child
in school is angered because recess is to be held in the basement on
account of rainy weather, and she announces that she is going "to
butt her brains out against the wall." (The teacher says, "Beat them
out, then," and she goes ahead and tries while the children watch admiringly.) To Eugene, the open, free look of San Francisco is decep-
tive; he could tell the Spaniard how the hills and clouds could bank
up, one upon the other: "they were any man's walls still," and a man
could feel closed in there as anywhere.

Walls are also symbolic of separateness, of the barriers between human beings. People may "wall up" against each other, feel so acutely their isolation, the privacy and uniqueness of their experience, the impossibility of being penetrated, that they might as well be dead to others. This kind of inwardly constructed wall is a type of the final cause and result of separateness, death itself. Returning from the cemetery, Virgie thinks about King MacLain's conquest of these and all other walls and barriers to fulfillment:

> Virgie had often felt herself at some moment callous over, go opaque; she had known it to happen to others; not only when her mother changed on the bed while she was fanning her. Virgie had felt a moment in her life after which nobody could see through her, into her—felt it young. But Mr. King MacLain, an old man, had butted like a goat against the wall he wouldn't agree to himself or recognize. What fortress indeed would ever come down, except before hard little horns, a rush and a stampede of the pure wish to live?

If the freedom necessary to fulfillment cannot be attained without a struggle against the confinements and barriers of life, neither can it come to meaningful expression without the exercise of discipline. Music speaks of, and embodies, a type of fulfillment, but it can be achieved only out of a costly control; it is passion made orderly, form imposed on the chaos of feelings. Most of the wanderers are musicians of one sort or another, preeminently Miss Eckhart and Virgie. Cassie, though far less gifted than Virgie, develops her minimal talent enough to give piano lessons to the next generation of Morgana children. Loch has his golden horn, Eugene his favorite piece of music, Easter her plan to be a singer. Miss Eckhart's fierce attachment to her metronome indicates her recognition of the need for control in the life and music of her students as well as in her own life; when she becomes a living metronome at her lover's grave, it is her instinctive way of avoiding an expression of uncontrolled grief or hysteria. The Spaniard guitarist has his moments of looking as wild and fierce as a bull, but while playing his music, even the most tender and passionate love songs, he only looms remotely. When he ends his recital with a formal bow, it seems to Eugene "as though it had been taken for granted by then that passion was the thing he had in hand, love was his servant, and even despair was a little tamed animal trotting about in plain view." Virgie too must learn discipline if she is to achieve expression through love or music. In one remarkable passage images of confinement, work, and the expression of will, sexual desire, and music are combined to show the kind of process she is undergoing during the years of her "apprenticeship" at home:

Her fingers set, after coming back, set half-closed; the strength in her hands she used up to type in the office but most consciously to pull the udders of the succeeding cows, as if she would hunt, hunt, hunt daily for the blindness that lay inside the beast, inside where she could have a real and living wall for beating on, a solid prison to get out of, the most real stupidity of flesh, a mindless and careless and calling body, to respond flesh for flesh, anguish for anguish. And if, as she dreamed one winter night, a new piano she touched had turned, after the one pristine moment, into a calling cow, it was by her own desire.

Paradoxically, it is the art form most dependent on time, existing in a present sequence of moments, that has the greatest power to put the listener outside the ordinary sense of present time. Music enables one to summon the past and imaginatively perceive its meanings. Its effect in *The Golden Apples* reminds one of the effect of the little phrase from the sonata of Vinteuil in Proust's *Remembrance of Things Past;* in Eudora Welty's book music provides insight into the meaning of beauty, love, suffering, and loss, and it has the power to suspend, compress, or protract time and experience. The subtle and poignant *"Für Elise"* theme, in a minor key, perpetually draws thanks from Miss Eckhart when Virgie plays it, and sets off a chain of memory in both Loch and Cassie when they hear it. To Loch it brings unaccountable tears; taking him back "to when his sister was so sweet, to a long time ago," it is "like a signal or greeting—the kind of thing a horn would play out." To Cassie the theme brings tumbling the lines from the Yeats poem, and with them the gathering past which breaks like a wave over her head. Listening to the Spaniard play the subtle love songs of his native land, Eugene experiences "a deep lull in his spirit that was as enfolding as love. . . . He felt a lapse of all knowledge of Emma as his wife, and of comprehending the future, in some visit to a vast present-time. The lapse must have endured for a solid minute or two, . . . as positively there and as defined at the edges as a spot or stain, and its affected him like a secret."

If music suddenly evokes the timeless moment, time's own passing creates the wisdom of attrition in those who have survived many deaths (their own and others') and have witnessed decay and change. The small party assembled at Mrs. Rainey's grave show this wisdom when a cornucopia of flowers spills over and no one bothers to set it

straight: "already, tomorrow's rain pelted the grave with loudness
. . . ; this was the past now." And in the narrator's own withdrawal
from the world of her fiction in the final paragraph of her book, time
is telescoped by the swift evocation of prehistoric or mythical animal
life, even then mysterious, heroic, and beautiful, as it is now. An ancient black woman sits down by Virgie for shelter from the rain. At
first a couple of stray familiar figures pass. "Then she and the old beg-
gar woman, the old black thief, were there alone and together in the
shelter of the big public tree, listening to the magical percussion, the
world beating in their ears. They heard through falling rain the running of the horse and bear, the stroke of the leopard, the dragon's
crusty slither, and the glimmer and the trumpet of the swan."

Passionately and humbly the wanderers have made their way in *The
Golden Apples*. Each of them might have said, with Randall MacLain,
"And all along I knew I rode in the open world and took my bearings
by the stars." And so they rise and set in the reader's imagination,
these stars and constellations of fiction by Eudora Welty. Contem-
plating them from a distance, we perceive a form of internal and external motion, lofty but never static. A dynamic pattern appears in
her presentation of the careers of the wanderers; something is freshly
viewed each time she revisits a character or theme, especially, perhaps, the conception of what heroic action means. It takes Loch's
comic rescue of the metronome in "June Recital"—that little box of
time disciplined to minute regularity—followed by his serious rescue
of Easter in "Moon Lake"—the strict rhythm of his whole body and
breath bringing the dead to life—to show one kind of heroism: concentrated, physical but also intelligent, and sacrificial. This is the
heroism of a Perseus. It takes Miss Eckhart's living through of her
own tragic and frustrated life and Cassie's sympathetic perception of
its meaning in "June Recital"; it takes Miss Eckhart's deep understanding of the relatedness of victor and victim, love and separateness,
the absoprtion of that tragedy in the greatest of music and art, received unconsciously and over resistance by a rebellious young Virgie
Rainey, coming to fruit after a quarter-century's growth in that same
mind and heart—it takes all these long human processes to show the
emotional, spiritual, and artistic aspect of heroism, the heroism of
Beethoven and his music. As the motif of the stars and constellations
points up the *cyclical* structure of the stories, so the musical motif un-
derscores the *dynamics* of that structure, a pattern of continuous development absorbing to follow, deeply enriching to each particular
moment or movement of each story as well as to the finished whole.

It is easy to see why Eudora Welty considered *The Golden Apples* "in a way . . . closest to my heart of all my books." It is deeply human, at once tragic and comic, with the levels of myth and actuality blended in an entirely unobtrusive and natural manner. In years to come readers may also find the book their favorite among her works. It is at least certain to continue to be read as one of her major achievements, as well as a great contribution to the literary form of the short story cycle, of Southern, and all American literature.

Chapter Seven
The Bride of the Innisfallen:
A Collection of Lyrics

The first impression given by the stories collected in *The Bride of the Innisfallen* (1955) is that a number of departures have been made from the patterns of Eudora Welty's earlier fiction. A major change is the predominant shift from her usual regional settings and Southern characters. Four of the seven stories have their settings outside Mississippi. "Circe," set on a legendary island and based on the Circe episode in the *Odyssey,* is Eudora Welty's only explicit use of a Greek myth. The title story depicts a group of chiefly Irish people en route from London to Cork; "Going to Naples," a group of Italian-Americans on a ship headed for Italy; the viewpoint, in both cases, is largely that of an outsider. "No Place for You, My Love" has a Southern setting (the delta country south of New Orleans), but one unfamiliar to Eudora Welty; furthermore, the two principal characters of this story are an open-faced, self-conscious young woman from the Middle West and a sophisticated Eastern businessman.

"Kin" is one of the three stories with a Mississippi setting, but its point of view is that of a girl who at the age of eight moved away from the state to the urban North and is making a return visit. "The Burning" is Eudora Welty's first and only Civil War story. Only in "Ladies in Spring" do we return to something familiar: rural Mississippians in their own setting, in and near a tiny town named Royals.

Experiment, range, and variety are apparent in the stories. Only the initiated may, at first, be able to perceive the continuity with Eudora Welty's earlier stories—the focus on place and on the themes of love and separateness, the human mysteries, vulnerability, the sense of exposure and need for protection, the rarity of genuine communication, the glory of one precious moment of personal insight and fulfillment. Though much happens in the stories, little can be summarized. The climaxes are internal and difficult to locate: they are likely to occur in a series of moments, or realizations, which do not usually effect a turning point in external action or behavior. Brilliant descriptions, pictures, moods, snatches of conversation, epigrammatic summations contribute to the whole, which tends to be a dominant impression rather than a clear rational design.

The differences between the earlier stories and those of *The Bride* emerge more clearly through comparison. "A Worn Path" and the "The Wide Net" are both stories of journey or quest. In each case a journey is taken for a specific purpose: Old Phoenix goes to fetch the "soothing medicine" for her grandson; William Wallace and his entourage drag the river to recover the body of Hazel. In each case episodes, stages, and diversions engage the attention of characters and readers; the journey becomes a progression in which the final purpose is temporarily lost sight of (as when William Wallace dances with the fish in his belt, or Old Phoenix forgets why she made her trip). In each case the trip also takes on a ceremonial significance and becomes a symbol for a whole life, in which processes and rituals carry us, unwitting, to our goals and destinies.

"The Bride of the Innisfallen," "No Place for You, My Love," and "Going to Naples" are also stories of quest or journey. But whose is each journey, why is it taken, what is its significance? In the title story the central character is not, as might be expected, the bride, but the American girl for whom the bride, never identified, seems to represent love at its pristine moment of joy, hope, expectancy. Contrasted with the motivations of Phoenix or William Wallace, her motivation for taking the journey is as obscure as her central "problem." Perhaps recently married herself, she seems to have run from her husband in London in order to rediscover and affirm an inner self, a "primal joy" threatened both by her marriage and by the grayness of London. An excess of hope and joy, an openness to life, expectation and outgoing love of it, have become a burden on her heart because these feelings cannot be shared or acted upon. This motivation is not incomprehensible: it seems to me both credible and moving. But it is somewhat rarified and difficult for the reader to discover, especially outside the context of Eudora Welty's work as a whole; and part of this difficulty is the lack of the immediate, tangible human relationships found in "A Worn Path" or "The Wide Net."

A similar vagueness surrounds the flight of the young woman in "No Place for You, My Love." We know only from the Easterner's point of view, that back home she must be involved in some hopeless love relationship (possibly with a married man), that there may recently have been a "scene," since she has on her temple a bruise which affects her "like an evil star," that her frantic need is for escape and the protection of distance and anonymity, and that her painful obsession is with exposure. But if the heroine's situation is vague, we know from Eudora Welty's account in "Writing and Analyzing a Story,"[1] that it is intended to be; we also know that the point of view was neither the woman's nor her companion's but that of a mysterious third presence:

It was . . . fished alive from the surrounding scene. As I wrote further into the story, something more real, more essential, than the characters were on their own was revealing itself. In effect, . . . there had come to be a sort of third character along on the ride—the presence of a relationship between the two. It was what grew up between them meeting as strangers, went on the excursion with them. . . . I wanted to suggest that its being took shape as the strange, compulsive journey itself, was palpable as its climate and mood, the heat of the day. . . .

I wanted to make seen and believed what was to me, in my story's grip, literally apparent—that secret and shadow are taken away in this country by the merciless light that prevails there, by the river that is like an exposed vein of ore, the road that descends as one with the heat—its nerve (these are all terms in the story), and that the heat is also a visual illusion, shimmering and dancing over the waste that stretches ahead. . . . I was writing of exposure, and the shock of the world; in the end I tried to make the story's inside outside and then leave the shell behind.[2]

Eudora Welty accomplished what she set out to do, but it was a perilous undertaking. She took a human feeling—a panicky, raw-nerved sense of exposure—and invested an entire landscape and journey with that feeling; she rendered a strong emotional effect without supplying much information about its cause. The vivid impressionism of this method is strangely exciting, but the story is not as fully and solidly alive as is a story like "A Worn Path," in which there seems never to have been a shell to leave behind because every part—plot, character, setting, theme—seems essential to every other part.

Experimentation in narrative technique is also evident in "The Burning." The characters in this story are clearly conceived, but monolithic: a pair of genteel maiden sisters, and an obedient young slave, Delilah. The narrator is usually hovering in and around the consciousness of Delilah, recording what is said and done in a language subtly adjusted to the minds, mode of life, relationships, and idiom of the three women. The description is sharply detailed, textural, impressionistic. Frequent gaps in the action have the effect of averted eyes; confusions and ambiguities are abundant.

The action that can be pieced together is sufficiently horrible. Two of Sherman's soldiers, with a white horse, invade the home of the two ladies; though it is not clear how the soldiers attack the women, it is implied that Miss Myra and Delilah are raped, and all three women are put out; the house is looted by soldiers and slaves, then burned with a child named Phinney in it. The three women, who witness the burning, wander toward and through a devastated Jackson; Miss Theo murders her sister by hanging; then, with Delilah's help, she tries to hang herself but apparently succeeds only in breaking her neck and dies by inches in the grass. After a day or two Delilah returns to the blackened ruins of the house, finds and takes Phinney's bones, and is seen, finally, with a "Jubilee cup" set on her head, advancing across the Big Black River.

The effect of all these grim happenings is not what the facts would suggest. It is weirdly diffused, muted, diverted by the variety of irrelevant detail that swamps Delilah's consciousness and by the quaint, ladylike speech, behavior, and "props" of the two old maids. Only the slightest hint notifies the reader of some new horror: "the soldier . . . dropped on top of her" tells us Miss Myra is being raped; "when it came—but it was a bellowing like a bull, that came from inside—Delilah drew close" tells us that Phinney is being burned alive. Then the profuse details come flooding: pictures of the elegant interior of the house, "glimmering with precious, breakable things white ladies are never tired of"; or outdoors, of butterflies and insects and "black-eyed susans, wild to the pricking skin, with many heads nodding." Or there are bits of dainty, playful argument or assertion, which are madly inappropriate to the grim occasion, such as this one of Miss Theo, who is tying the noose for Miss Myra: "I learned as a child how to tie, from a picture book in Papa's library—not that I ever was called on. . . . I guess I was always something of a tomboy." Because the felt reactions often have no correlation with the events, the effect on the reader is ironic almost to the point of perversity.

There are two main reasons for this apparent perversity. The first is that the old style of Southern gentlewoman behaves with faultless consistency, which means, in extreme circumstances (as in Faulkner's "A Rose for Emily"), that she may behave insanely. The proud Miss Theo has the godlike strength that befits her name. Sufficiently warned of the coming destruction, she can't "understand" the message, pulls down the shutters, and goes on living as if nothing is going to happen; attacked, turned out, she retains her dignity and consummates her protest with suicide.

Miss Myra is even more insane. A delicate, childish woman with purple eyes and bright gold hair, she seems a parody of the Lady of Shalott living in a fantasy world of chivalry. When she first sees the mirror image of the intruding soldier on his white horse, she asks, "Will you take me on the horse? Please take me first" as though he were a knight on a rescue mission. She imagines Phinney to be her child by "an officer, no, one of our beaux that used to come out with Benton." But the child is black, and appears, from Miss Theo's comments, to have been their brother Benton's child by a slave—probably Delilah, who thinks of him as "her Jonah, her Phinney."

If Miss Myra's delusions and Miss Theo's strong-willed resistance to outrage and cruelty are a source of confusion, the use of Delilah as a main center of consciousness is another reason for the strange narrative technique. Delilah is innocent and does not understand the meaning of the horror and catastrophe that she witnesses. Her world is shattered into fragments, but she cannot make a tragic shape out of the fragments. Like Little Lee Roy in "Keela, the Outcast Indian Maiden," she is incapable of the moral comprehension of her experience.

The major symbol in "The Burning" is an important container of the story's meaning. In the parlor is a large Venetian mirror, the ornate "roof" of which is supported by two black men (Moors), who stand on either side of it and appear almost to be looking into the glass themselves. When the soldiers and horse invade the house at the beginning of the story, the two ladies raise their eyes to the mirror and regard the intruders reflected there instead of turning to face them directly. While Miss Myra is attacked, Delilah's vision is turned away from the violence and fixed on the mirror; it reflects her, obediently holding the white horse, and the tranquil parlor interior with the "bare yawn" of the hall reaching behind. The elegant mirror is the symbol of a way of life: placid, decorative, sheltered, lived at a remove, out of touch with reality, and supported by slaves.

Returning to the ruins after the burning, Delilah finds the mirror. The black men are now "half-split away, flattened with fire, bearded, noseless as the moss that hung from swamp trees"; the glass is clouded "like the horse-trampled spring." Peering into it, Delilah has a hallucinatory vision in which the mirror's decoration (images of aristocratic Venetian life) are blended with images of "Jackson before Sherman came"; then, "under the flicker of the sun's licks, then under its whole blow and blare, like an unheard scream, like an act of mercy gone, as the wall-less light and July blaze struck through from the opened sky, the mirror felled her flat." And finally, in a phantasmagoria of destructive images, Delilah sees and feels her world violently shattered.

Elaborateness, subtlety, and sophistication are distinguishing marks of the stories in *The Bride of the Innisfallen*. These qualities are visible not only in choice and motivation of character, structure, and narrative technique, but also in style. The changes, though in no way absolute and already visible in some of the stories of *The Wide Net*, may be illustrated by a comparison of the opening sentences of a few stories from *A Curtain of Green* and *The Bride of the Innisfallen*. Following are three from the first-mentioned:

R. J. Bowman, who for fourteen years had traveled for a shoe company through Mississippi, drove his Ford along a rutted dirt path. It was a long day! ["Death of a Traveling Salesman"]

I was getting along fine with Mama, Papa-Daddy and Uncle Rondo until my sister Stella-Rondo just separated from her husband and came back home again. ["Why I Live at the P.O."]

It was December—a bright frozen day in the early morning. Far out in the country there was an old Negro woman with her head tied in a red rag, coming along a path through the pinewoods. Her name was Phoenix Jackson. ["A Worn Path"]

And following are two opening sentences from *The Bride of the Innisfallen*:

They were strangers to each other, both fairly well strangers to the place, now seated side by side at the luncheon—a party combined in a free-and-easy way when the friends he and she were with recognized each other across Galatoire's. ["No Place for You, My Love"]

There was something of the pavilion about one raincoat, the way—for some little time out there in the crowd—it stood flowing in its salmony-pink and yellow stripes down toward the wet floor of the platform, expanding as it went. ["The Bride of the Innisfallen"]

Striking in the first set of opening sentences is directness of style. Characters, setting, time of day or season, the beginnings of situation or action are at once set before the reader purely and plainly in short, simple statements. By comparison, the style of the second pair of opening sentences is oblique and sophisticated. Characters are introduced without their names (in these two stories they never get them). Questions are raised, and the reader knows instinctively that answers may not be immediately forthcoming. The pertinence of each opening to the central action is subtle rather than explicit. The style is that of a storyteller who knows there are a thousand different ways of getting into a story rather than the one of simply beginning with persons, places, and things.

The changes in style in *The Bride of the Innisfallen* must be considered in their relation to character, situation, and point of view. The sophistication of style in "No Place for You, My Love," for example, is fitted to the sophistication of the two main characters and their situation: two self-conscious modern people, briefly whirled together and then apart, whose relationship is determined by the environment they encounter together and by the heat and speed of their journey, as much as by their own natures. The self-consciousness of the relationship pervades the style. Even the metaphors are difficult to interpret, as, for instance, the following, which appears toward the end of the story, just after the couple have returned to New Orleans and are about to leave each other: "Something that must have been with them all along suddenly, then, was not. In a moment, tall as panic, it rose, cried like a human, and dropped back." Without the help of the author's explanation, one might puzzle over that metaphor long and fruitlessly. She says the cry was that of "that doomed relationship—personal, mortal, psychic—admitted in order to be denied, a cry that the characters were first able (and prone) to listen to, and then able in part to ignore. The cry was authentic to my story: the end of a journey *can* set up a cry, the shallowest provocation to sympathy and love does hate to give up the ghost."[3] The metaphor is odd, but it was born legitimately out of an odd story with an odd point of view.

It is, finally, the storyteller who reveals sophistication in the stories of *The Bride of the Innisfallen*: a writer who is far more aware of multiple choices, the varieties of form and technique possible to the creative imagination, than was the writer of *A Curtain of Green*. As an artist, Eudora Welty seems to have gone through the kind of change she has so often described in her fiction: the passage from innocence to experience. What is lost in this process is simplicity, purity, lucidity, immediacy in relation to the materials of fiction, a natural and instinctive grace, an intuitive perception and realization of form, and relative ease and spontaneity of creation. The sophistication that is gained at the expense of the loss of innocence has a compensating value: the stories provide the delight that comes from the experience of an art beautifully and skillfully executed, varied, mature, experimental. And throughout, the power of feeling has never been lost. Indeed, an undercurrent of certain kinds of feeling provides a sort of unity among these seemingly disparate stories.

Michael Kreyling has shown convincingly that the stories of *The Bride of the Innisfallen* are related in several ways. He finds a new, "metaphysical" interest in place—"the lively medium that makes things possible and confers identity." He finds rhythmic motion, patterns recurring in time but leading to an inner form through which is achieved, in T. S. Eliot's phrase, "the stillness, as a Chinese jar still / Moves perpetually in its stillness." He finds "the motifs of pilgrimage" (frequently involving water, images of crossing, meetings and partings, rivers, bridges and separating seas), "passages toward fulfillment of dream, lonely souls in need of response, calls sent out in hope of connecting with other lonely hearts."[4] Except in "Kin," where the pleading call is that of an old man remembering, the call is a woman's, as in "Ladies in Spring"—secret, plaintive, unanswered. A small boy named Dewey, "playing hooky" and gone fishing with his father Blackie, hears him called and feels intuitively the desolation of that lonely girl's cry. Each of the heroines is abandoned by her potential or actual lover: even the powerful Circe, semideity that she is, must endure the departure of the mortal Ulysses. Yet each of the love-burdened heroines retains the virtues of openness to life, the capacity to love, to renew hope and joy, to achieve an inner poise, steadiness, or stillness, even when alone. These resources are costly, for each is troubled not only by the finality of partings, but by the inhibitions of propriety, everything that gnaws and nibbles away at joy and fulfillment.

In "Going to Naples," among the literal and figurative pilgrims on board the *Pomona,* is plump young Gabriella Serto, on her own quest for love and fulfillment. She is given to screams that often seem "endeavors of pure anguish or joy that youth and strength seemed able to put out faster than the steady pounding quiet of the voyage could

ever overtake and heal." Anxiously hovering over Gabriella is a mama
too impressed with her own and everyone's "terrible responsibility,"
running "her loving little finger over the brooches settled here and
there on her bosom like St. Sebastian over his arrows." Precious few
candidates are available even for a "shipboard romance," but there is
one budding musician, a cellist named Aldo, whose courtship begins
with Ping-Pong, and flowers the moment when he buries his face in
Gabriella's blouse. He produces a lifting of the soul in onlookers as
they "contemplate among companions the weakness and the mystery
of the flesh" and feel "something of an old, pure loneliness come back
to them—like a bird sent over the waters long ago, when they were
young. . . ."

Gabriella is abandoned by Aldo on "Gala Night." The sea turns
heavy; and like many others, finally including Mama Serto, Aldo suc-
cumbs to seasickness. But Gabriella enjoys a physical triumph that
turns metaphysical when she dances solo on the heaving ocean against
pitching floors; a few intrepid survivors, "*indisposti* or not," witness
and applaud her triumph:

That great, unrewarding, indestructible daughter of Mrs. Serto, round as an
onion, and tonight deserted, unadvised, unprompted, and unrestrained in
her blue dress, went dancing around this unlikely floor as lightly as an angel.
. . . Some radiant pin through her body had set her spinning like that tonight, and given her the power—not the same thing as permission, but what
was like a memory of how to do it—to be happy all by herself.

This speaks not so much of a *discovery* of her own "primal joy" as her
performance of it, for "how can we know the dancer from the dance?"
In that innermost steadying of her turbulent adolescent passion, the
eye of her storm, the axis of that "radiant pin" through her whirling
body, we have the equivalent of a Chinese jar or Grecian urn—a kin-
esthetic one: the point at which time freezes into no-time and life into
art.

Approached with the set of expectations we bring to the reading of
lyric poetry, the stories of this collection will often yield to the reader
of "willing imagination" experiences of surpassing beauty reminiscent, in their texture and meaning, of great Romantic poetry, most
often that of Keats, but also that of Wordsworth. Surely the "primal
joy," "the kind you were born and began with," related as it so often
is to the act of seeing and the need for telling, "being able to proph-
esy, all of a sudden" ("Kin"), singing, even screaming from sheer in-

tensity ("Going to Naples"), resembles the phenomenon Wordsworth sang of so memorably in his "Ode on Intimations of Immortality": the experience of splendor in the objects of sense, "the glory and the freshness of a dream." Threatened, lost, recoverable by the characters in the stories of *The Bride,* it is recovered by their creator through the lyric feeling captured in those stories.

Even more impressive in the stories are echoes of and parallels with the poetry of Keats: in their nostalgia and ineffable yearning, their questing and questioning, their sensuous texture and richness of imagery, their use of synesthesia, their bitter sweetness through juxtaposition of joy and sorrow, their themes of time and eternity, truth and beauty, life and art. The poet who, "in embalmed darkness," bathed in the myriad springtime odors and pictured images of flowering trees and fragrant blossoms, listens to a bird "pouring forth [his] soul abroad," is not far from Dewey ("Ladies in Spring") roaming in "drenched and sweet" places, and standing quietly, half-buried in fragrant flowers and vines, listening to "the lonesomest sound in creation, an unknown bird singing through the very moment when he was the one that listened to it." Something of Keats's ineffable yearning is what Dicey sees in the portrait of her great-grandmother ("Kin"), her romantically tragic history known from family stories, now viewed in all her openness, vulnerability, and courage, through eloquent eyes. Dicey feels "kin" to this ancestor who had felt "the wildness of the world," and knows the two of them, Dicey and her "divided sister," were "homesick for somewhere that was the same place"—perhaps a place where love is fresh, sweet, and forever, existing now in her old dying Uncle Felix's (happy) fevered nostalgia as he yearns to recover a girl named Daisy, by some nameless river, in a midnight tryst. The whole romantic story is squeezed into the three words scribbled on the note he presses into Dicey's hand—"River—Daisy—Midnight"; the pathos to Dicey, and to us, lies in the fourth word, "Please."

The parallels with Keats's odes are most remarkable in the title story, through the experience of the American girl who comes to Cork with her questing heart and her burden. As the *Innisfallen* sails toward the harbor, church bells ring along the river; time past and present blend as "an older, harsher, more distant bell rang from an inland time: *now.*" Walking the streets of Cork, she feels the spring with the intensity of sense impressions merged, of the metamorphosis of branch and blossom to bird to song, of tree to golden goddess.

"The trees had almost rushed with light and blossom; they nearly had sound, as the bells did. Boughs that rocked on the hill were tipped and weighted as if with birds, which were really their own bursting and almost-bursting leaves. In all Cork today every willow stood with gold-red hair springing and falling about it, like Venus alive. Rhododendrons swam in light, leaves and flowers alike; only a shadow could separate them into colors."

She wants to *tell* this joy, but cannot; she can only see, feel, and finally know:

I see Cork's streets take off from the waterside and rise lifting their houses and towers like note above note on a page of music, with arpeggios running over it of green and galleries and belvederes, and the bright sun raining at the top. Out of the joy I hide for fear it is promiscuous, I may walk for ever at the fall of evening by the river, and find this river street by the red rock, this first, last house, that's perhaps a boarding house now, standing full-face to the tide, and look up to that window—that upper window, from which the mystery will never go. The curtains dyed so many times over are still pulled back and the window looks out open to the evening, the river, the hills, and the sea.

This remarkable sequence of images, in which the horizon of a town becomes the rising and falling of musical notation, and architectural decoration with nature's green becomes arpeggios and light becomes rain, in which what is passing and temporal seems to become eternal, ends with an ordinary window looking out over the sea. But it is filled with mystery. The unheard music of the lifting houses and towers is magical, reminiscent of the eternal bird whose song "Charmed magic casements, opening on the foam / Of perilous seas, in faery lands forlorn." In the story Ireland is made to seem such a faery land opening out on perilous seas.

Briefly, the window has a tenant: the mood of the passage turns realistic, then shifts back to a tempered echo of another of Keats's odes:

For a moment someone—she thought it was a woman—came and stood at the window, then hurled a cigarette with its live coal down into the extinguishing garden. But it was not the impatient tenant, it was the window itself that could tell her all she had come here to know—or all she could bear this evening to know, and that was light and rain, light and rain, dark, light, and rain.

As a mere window, however wonderfully perceived, is to a beautiful Grecian urn, so is the summation of "All ye know on earth, and all ye need to know" of window and urn. Yet the alternations of light and rain, surely suggestive of the weather of the mind, of joy and sorrow, is a simple truth made beautiful by a lyricist in prose.

But comedy defeats high romance, and few scenes in Eudora Welty's fiction are without comic relief. These intrusions are like the sudden "Tweeeet!" of outrageous old Papa's ten-cent whistle into "life's most precious moments" ("Going to Naples"). The title story ends, as it began, with the comedy of colorful Irish characters when the American girl throws away the message to her husband and plunges into a pub. At her entrance "a glad cry [goes] up" and they all call out "something fresh . . . like the signal for a song."

Yet the whole collection, with the closing lines of "Going to Naples," brings together transformations of the "Ode on Melancholy," "Ode to a Nightingale," and "To Autumn." When the *Pomona* reaches Naples it is golden autumn; there are tender reunions and partings, tears are shed. Gabriella knows that Papa, the raucous old whistle-blower, has come home to die; her own Nonna turns out to be a fabulously ancient, tiny lady, bright-eyed with a brown face "creased like a fig-skin." Gabriella feels her long journey, every tumultuous event, every new thing seen and old thing remembered, "caught up and held in something: the golden moment of touch, just given, just taken, in saying good-by. The moment—bright and effortless of making, in the end, as a bubble—seemed to go ahead of them as they walked, to tap without sound across the dust of the emptying courtyard, and alight in grandmother's homely buggy, filling it." Then as the black horse pulling Nonna's buggy tosses its mane and they are about to leave, "the first of the bells in the still-hidden heart of Naples began to strike the hour."

A strangely haunting question ends the book. " 'And the nightingale,' Mama's voice just ahead was beseeching, 'is the nightingale with us yet?' "

The question is rhetorical: the "immortal bird" is, of course, with Mama Serto as it was with the homesick Ruth in Keats's ode. The nightingale's song rises and falls like Gabriella's bright bubble of memory: both end buried, first in valley-glades or buggy, at last in the reader's memory. He may even come to think of the bride of the *Innisfallen,* forever surrounded by the pilgrims' delight in her sweet, shy loveliness as she stands alone by the rail in her white spring hat and dazzling little white fur muff, as Keats's "still unravished bride of quietness, . . . foster child of silence and slow time."

Eudora Welty has said that "the source of the short story is usually lyrical." In the stories of this collection the completed artifact is as close to pure lyricism as she has ever come.

Chapter Eight
Home Truths in a Divided Community

After her explorations in *The Bride of the Innisfallen* of the relationships between people and places in distant settings, Eudora Welty returned her focus exclusively to Mississippi. And a troubled place it was during several of the fifteen years between the publication of *The Bride* (1955) and *Losing Battles* (1970). Inevitably, to a writer both as sensitive and implicitly moral as she, as knowing about and loyal to her Southern community, the division, violence, hatred, breakdown of many of the traditions of Southern life, the intolerable ambiguity of race relations, were causes of a deep wound.

When she published the photographs in *One Time, One Place* in 1971, she subtitled the volume, "Mississippi in the Depression: A Snapshot Album," suggesting her amateur status as photographer; in her introduction she extends the resonance of that subtitle by saying the book is offered "not as a social document but as a family album. . . ."[1]

Roughly two-thirds of the Mississippi family in her album are black. Though the photographs are sufficient testimony, from her introduction we learn with what affection, curiosity, and simple pleasure she viewed her subjects, and how she admired certain "heroic" faces, eloquent in a meaning "more truthful and more terrible and, I think, more noble than any generalization about people could have prepared me for. . . ." This is her explicit tribute to what chiefly black people had taught her about wide zones and vast reaches of human suffering, endurance, courage, joy—"those defiant things of the spirit." She testified to her good fortune in having been "well positioned" to take the photographs, "moving through the scene openly and yet invisibly because I was part of it, born into it, taken for granted." When she asked for a "portrait," permission was given, often, because the person had never been photographed before, and she was able to give her subjects their picture as a souvenir. Writing of the experience some forty years later, she realizes that she was attended by "an angel—a presence of trust . . . that dates the pictures now, more than the vanished years."[2]

As the photographs came out of knowledge, mutual trust, affection, and respect, so also did the stories Eudora Welty's imagination supplied for her black characters. Three of these are among her best—"A Worn Path," "Powerhouse," and "Livvie"—made possible by her "invisibility" as a shy, sympathetic white woman with the power to "slip into" people whose lives and social and economic situations differed greatly from her own. Yet her portraits are always individualzied: those of Powerhouse and the band members nearest him, Livvie and Solomon, old Phoenix Jackson.

Southern manners are, perhaps, never so subtly revealed in Eudora Welty's fiction as in her presentation of relationships between the races. In the 1930s and 1940s when most of her stories were written, these relationships were characterized by the apparent opposites of formality and intimacy. Implicit in the paradox were the structured community's ideals (often violated, like all ideals) of trust, affection, concern, sense of obligation, as well as different kinds of pride or dignity, defensiveness or hostility, elicited by the average white person's assumption of racial superiority. Though Eudora Welty deplored that assumption, her fiction reflects these paradoxes of racial interaction in all their social and moral complexity. In "A Worn Path," for example, old Phoenix Jackson has three separate encounters with white people. At each meeting her driving motive of love for her grandson, her natural dignity, courage, humility, and specific needs, are delicately adjusted to the white person and situation encountered. Together, the three encounters reveal a responsible white community whose "charity" as dispensed both privately and officially to one old poor black woman, though minimal, is sufficient to her need, and not permitted to be demeaning by the indominitable old woman herself.

Such a generally favorable picture of race relationships is characteristic of Eudora Welty's earlier fiction: harmony is more evident than disharmony, and the darker crimes of white against black which so obsessed Faulkner are rarely to be seen. Rather, we find, in *Delta Wedding* and other works, intimate and mutually supportive relationships among members of the black and white community, especially between the servants, cooks, and caretakers of their white mistresses and children. Black superstitions are shown as folklore, or even moral and religious piety, as when Solomon labors to complete his bottle tree to fend off evil spirits in "Livvie." But all this changed in the 1960s.

In her introduction to *Collected Stories* (1980) Eudora Welty explains how, in general, her stories "have reflected their own present time, beginning with the Depression in which *I* began; they came out of my response to it." This is dramatically true of the final two stories, "Where is the Voice Coming From?" (1963) and "The Demonstrators" (1966). "Written in the changing sixties," she says, "they reflect the unease, the ambiguities, the sickness and desperation of those days in Mississippi. . . . They were *part* of my living here, of my long familiarity with the thoughts and feelings of those around me, in their many shadings and variations and contradictions."[3]

"Where is the Voice Coming From?" she describes as unique in conception, rising from her sense that she understood the sort of person who could, one hot August night in 1963, have killed the black Civil Rights leader, Medgar Evans, from behind. She knew "not his identity, but his coming about, in this time and place," and felt, through her "shock and revolt," that she could "make no mistake." The story was completed the night of the shooting and appeared in the next issue of the *New Yorker*.[4]

The title is odd, but suggestive: who asks the question? The *voice* is that of the murderer, speaking from the privacy of his home, where he is somewhat reluctantly in hiding with his TV and guitar. His "confession" seems addressed to Thermopylae (the fictional Jackson)—its white citizens—though the local news has now become national and international. Thermopylae wants to know *where* the voice is coming from in order to find the killer: to publicize, praise, blame, arrest, convict, conceivably even burn him in the electric chair. On the other hand, the voice is also intruding upon the consciousness of the author who writes in her introduction, "The story pushed its way up through a long novel I was in the middle of writing, and was finished on the same night the shooting was taking place." Present time for author was present time for fictional speaker in what must have been an extraordinary act of imaginative concentration. "Where" is more than a physical location: it is also psychic, moral, even metaphysical. The voice is welling up from *out* of the mind of one Mississippi city as well as speaking *to* it.

The story of how and why the man behind the "voice" came to kill

Roland Summers (the name given the black leader) brings to mind
Hannah Arendt's famous observation about "the banality of evil." The
man is no clever conspirator, nor is he diabolically wicked. He is simply an ignorant, complacent man whose sense of racial superiority is
being threatened sufficiently to drive him to murder. His mind is
petty, clogged, obsessed by the heat—ninety-two degrees all night
and this day "so hot, all I did was hope and pray one or the other of
us wouldn't melt before it was over." Running away, he throws down
his gun because "it was scorching." So oppressively does the heat in-
teract with the claustrophobic atmosphere of this racist's mind as to
make reading the story a wringing ordeal not easily repeated. The
tension that arises from the murderer's pride in his crime, the perversity of his own outrage at what he considers the presumptive acts of
his victim and his own "innocence" as killer, translate into some
moral equivalent of heat—suffocated fury, perhaps—in the reader's
mind.

Stopping a human life is no more to the man than turning off the
television: he says to his wife, "You can reach and turn it off. You
don't have to look at a black nigger face no longer than you want to,
or listen to what you don't want to hear. It's still a free country."
Racist attitudes and language pour out of him. He has no trouble
finding "where in Thermopylae that nigger's living that's asking for
equal time. . . . It's where you all go for the thing you want when
you want it the most. Ain't that right?" When he finds Summers's
car gone, he guesses the Civil Rights leader is "out planning still
some other ways to do what we tell 'em they can't." He wants credit
for having acted alone and effectively, like some model of American
self-reliance; though "Old Ross" (Barnett), the governor, owes him
"a pat on the back," he doesn't need it. "I done what I done for my
own pure-D satisfaction."

The euphemism of "pure-D" (elsewhere "dern") is one of many ironies showing the disparity between the "innocent" surface of this man
and the depths to which his prejudices have plunged him. He has
been exposed to fundamentalist preaching: just before he shoots his
victim he describes Summers's back against the house light as "fixed
on me like a preacher's eyeballs when he's yelling 'Are you saved?' "
If this is a momentary twinge of conscience, it disappears as he has
the impression that a mockingbird, singing all night, has been taunting him. After he'd "loosed his load," the killer feels, "I was like
him. I was on top." The pathos of dying briefly affects him as he says

of the dying man, "Something darker than him, like the wings of a bird, spread on his back and pulled him down. He climbed up once, like a man under bad claws, and like just blood could weigh a ton he walked with it on his back to better light. Didn't get no further than his door. And fell to stay." Triumphantly he goes up and addresses the dead man. "I says, 'Roland? There was one way left, for me to be ahead of you and stay ahead of you, by Dad, and I just taken it. Now I'm alive and you ain't.' "

Indications are that the murderer's satisfaction will be short-lived. Already his shrewish wife, who outdoes him in the banality of evil, adding a low-grade wit and a malicious capacity for taunting to her racism, threatens his proud sense of achievement. She points out that his "solution" has long been advocated by many, that Roland Summers will receive all the fresh publicity on television rather than himself. He is almost afraid not to be found and celebrated: he wants a reaction, even a race riot—"hundreds all to smash, like Birmingham. I'm waiting on 'em to bring out them switchblade knives, like Harlem and Chicago." All he has now is the memory of irritatingly peaceful demonstrations: "them new baby face cops loading nothing but nigger children into the paddy wagon and they come marching out of a little parade and into the paddy wagon singing." He editorializes: "Ain't it about time us taxpayers starts to calling the moves? Starts to telling the teachers *and* the preachers *and* the judges of our so-called courts how far they can go?"

He knows he may be found, though he can be elusive, being a country boy with a history of running away. This time is different, for "people are dead now." He reaches for his guitar, which he has held onto over the years through all his roving, and starts to play and sing "a-Down. . . . Sing a-down, down, down, down. Down!" The final, traditional cadence of the song, the close of the story, leaves a question. Does he already guess where his life is headed?

It is in her prize-winning story, "The Demonstrators"—possibly the greatest story to come out of the Civil Rights era—that Eudora Welty most effectively captures the "feel" and essence of that troubled period in the South. The "home" truth presented in "The Demonstrators" is that of Holden, Mississippi, small town in a stricken land. Close to the center of this tightly knit town is Dr. Strickland, whose activity and compassionate nature place him in the best tradition of his humane profession. He is of the middle generation, carrying on his father's vocation, aware of the demands and interests of both the older and the younger generations. He acts quickly and practically, but he also feels, reflects, sorts out. We follow him through a night that does not seem, despite the "freak episode" later headlined by the local *Sentinel,* all that unusual. It finds him, in a way, simply powerless. Violence, disease, and death are his familiar antagonists: they reign as ominously as the dark night, as the racial friction, the personal and social hostilities that make up the restless, murderous life of the modern world. At best, Dr. Strickland's is a holding action.

His night journey begins with a call on Miss Marcia Pope, a pillar of the community, who reigned as teacher for more than forty years. Though she is stricken by some disease of old age, her authority is undiminished, and she calls her former student on the carpet to give an account of his marital difficulties. She is the first of the demonstrators, old style, and her ornery independence prefigures that of most of the demonstrators in this deeply and subtly interdependent community where a trio of deaths diminishes no one, and everyone.

Back in his office Dr. Strickland picks up his newspaper: a young man is making *his* declaration of independence, burning his draft card publicly to show his revolt against the state that makes war. He is another demonstrator, new style.

Then a black child summons the doctor on a nameless but urgent mission over the tracks. He drives into the dark (the street lights have gone out), reaches his destination, walks through a strangely quiet group of men, and enters a room where a wounded black girl lies on an iron bed. For a time the atmosphere is dreamlike—shadowy, vaguely threatening, crowding the senses with vivid and kaleidoscopic impressions. Yet the doctor works efficiently by trained instinct, knowing how to treat his patient and to order the charged information coming in to him; but not without initial mistakes and one total lapse of recognition—the identity of the patient herself.

Witnesses and helpers are secret and suspicious, oddly protective of the girl and her assailant, reluctantly and hostilely carrying out the doctor's orders as though he were an intruder. The patient, too, is uncooperative about her wound, too private to expose, just below her breast, a heart wound; her bleeding is all internal. She rebels against his searching the wound, touching it compulsively with sticky, bloodstained fingers. Finally the doctor identifies the girl as Ruby Gaddy, the maid who cleans his office. She wears a kind of white dress unfamiliar to him, of "skintight satin" with "a banner of some kind crossing it in a crumpled red line from the shoulder"—possibly some part of a choir gown. Ruby lives in a social world unknown to Dr. Strickland's white, middle-class world. Out of her own private life comes her trouble now.

Other identifications follow rapidly. The small girl who fetched the doctor is Ruby's sister, Twosie. Guinea pigs running about were left by Dove, Ruby's man, "just to be in the way." It is an ice-pick wound, inflicted by Dove. The doctor knows Dove Collins: "I've had to sew him up enough times on Sunday morning, you all know that." Given more light, the doctor would know everybody: Oree, legless, an "inherited" care, is among the first. Then there is Ruby's brother, her baby, her mother, and a pipe-smoking matriarch who may be the grandmother.

Everyone in this hot, crowded room is making a private claim to rights and privileges belonging to the self alone by reason of position or authority. Twosie lays claim to Ruby's necklace. Ruby is absorbed with the dignity and privacy of dying: to the doctor her eyes seem filled with "the unresponding gaze of ownership." She rejects her baby, who cries loudly in protest when she ignores him. Ruby's mother rejects both the baby and her daughter, insisting, "I ain't going to raise him." She identifies herself as Lucille, who did the washing for the doctor's mother. Attached to the older generation and their ways, she furiously denies Dr. Strickland's medical competence: "Let me see you do something. . . . You ain't even tied her up! You sure ain't your daddy!" The doctor's retort brings a hush, and when he asks for a drink, it is brought to him in an old china cup.

Seeking out one person in the room with clear authority to watch over Ruby, he fastens on the old pipe-smoking woman in a boiled white apron. He recognizes her as a local "tyrant" who had single-handedly run the railroad station at night: dispensed coffee, "thundered" out instructions to passengers in her baritone voice. She might have been called the Miss Pope of the railroad station: both had been benevolent despots. Now the doctor gives *her* the orders, which she may or may not choose to carry out.

His call over, the doctor steps out into the night, now flooded with moonlight. Driving back into town and waiting for a long freight train to pass, he has time for reflection. So much of the past has sprung out of memory; so many new impressions wait to be sorted out and stored among costly things suffered and loved. And now it is chiefly of relatedness that the doctor becomes aware as the long train of linked cars goes by; "the regular, slow creaking" reminds him of "an old-fashioned porch swing holding lovers in the dark." So also he holds in his mind all Holden's "lovers in the dark," living and dead; lovers aware of themselves and each other, but ignorant, seemingly divided and hostile:

> He had been carried a cup tonight that might have been his own mother's china or his wife's mother's—the rim not a perfect round, a thin, porcelain cup his lips and his fingers had recognized. In that house of murder, comfort had been brought to him at his request. After drinking from it he had all but reeled into a flock of dresses stretched wide-sleeved across the porch of that house like a child's drawing of angels.

He had recognized the dresses as those of his mother, his sister, his wife. Stiffly starched, they are like independent people who can "stand alone," "scratch his forehead," wound, or irritate. They seem disembodied, nobody's property. Yet linked as they are, they make a vision of peace and blessedness, of his whole family linked with this black family, of older generation with younger. All wear the same clothes, drink from a fragile, common cup with an imperfect rim, share the same human joys and griefs; they are linked by society, tradition, common responsibility and service, personal and impersonal forms of love. But they are also separate, and therein lies the tragedy of human life.

With the résumé of Dr. Strickland's past life and experiences, our vision shifts to the causes and symptoms of this tragic separateness and hostility between persons and races. Dr. Strickland and his wife are separated, by her wish. The loss of their only child, more intensely loved and served because she was afflicted, has caused his wife to turn her devotion to "an idea," possibly related to the Civil Rights Movement, though the real reason may be that she resents the fact that the doctor's learning and skills could not save their daughter. In any event, she leaves him, as Dove had left Ruby.

Thinking about everything, the doctor is deeply tired, "so sick and even bored with the bitterness, intractability that divided everybody and everything." Yet he has not forgotten his vision of relatedness; it seemed as if "some old, trusted, half-forgotten family friend that he had lost sight of since youth" had assumed his burden. "Was it the sensation, now returning, that there was still allowed to everybody on earth a *self*—savage, death-defying, private?" Hope affects him like an "assault"—what else to a heart resigned to a burden of hopelessness?

But too futile and costly a feeling to nourish, it ebbs away, "like nausea put down."

Yet when the doctor drives back through town and sees Dove lying in the moonlight, transfigured by cottonseed meal into a golden form, he is the abstract self of Dr. Strickland's imaginings become visible: "savage, death-defying, private." Dove is the last and best of the demonstrators: a strong, violent man, he fights for his very life. "Blood laced his head like a net through which he had broken." His final plea, to the only man in town who might save him, seems less for protection from the law than for privacy: "Hide me." Then his lifeblood spills through his mouth.

The impersonal newspaper report supplies many details, but tells very little. We do learn some of the circumstances of the slaying, and we learn also of the accidental death of Billy Lee Warrum on a motorcycle: he demonstrates the restlessness of a generation that has turned to speed and machines for the thrill of power that hurdles him into an early death.

Reading on and between the lines as though over Dr. Strickland's shoulder, we learn with what apparent self-satisfaction public leaders of the white community wash their hands of the double murder. "No cause was cited for the fracas," the paper reports. But none is needed. It is built into the natures of strong, death-defying people who hate as passionately as they love, two lovers who with sure instinct plunge the weapon alternately into heart and brain, and then walk or run away. Left for dead, they refuse to die. Equally heroic, they are savage, dignified, and above all, *private*. "He offered no statement" is Dr. Strickland's laconic understatement to the press about Dove's last moments; for whatever the doctor has learned on that night of tragedy, he will keep to himself.

The story closes with a brief, poignant elegy, which, like all elegies, ends with hope. It is autumn; the garden is declining, though still bright with color. Sitting on the porch, finishing his morning coffee, Dr. Strickland thinks of his daughter, who used to lie there on her daybed, enjoying the flowers and watching the birds. Then he sees a pair of flickers, the cock in one part of the garden, the hen in another. As he watches, he sees the cock spread a wing, "showy as a zebra's hide," then turn his head and show his red seal—nature's token and stamp of love. The birds are linked with the lovers. Ruby—a gem, deep red. Red for hearts. Ruby had posted her valentine on the wall over her bed. She had also worn a red banner over her breast. Red for violence, for blood. And Dove. The newspaper got that

wrong, calling him Dave. Dove, man of violence—no more Saturday
night scrapes for him. Dove for peace.

Dr. Stickland picks up his bag, reassuming the burden of his own
human care and responsibility. He knows it is not going to be easy.
There is no one in all Holden who does not need help, unless it is
Miss Marcia Pope, "still quite able to take care of herself—or such
was her opinion."

There is one final demonstrator implicit in this story: the author
herself. She has shown the writer's independence and privacy, her refusal to take sides in any current problem, to show the complexities
of all human relationships. The writer cannot be a crusader, she asserted in an article titled "Must the Novelist Crusade?" "Fiction has,
and must keep, a private address. For life is *lived* in a private place;
where it means anything is inside the mind and heart." External incidents change, but the artist's "instruments of perceiving" stay the
same. What is perceived, despite all the changes, is that

there is a relationship in progress between ourselves and other people; this
was the case when the world seemed stable, too. There are relationships of
the blood, of the passions and the affections, of thought and spirit and deed.
There is the relationship between the races. How can one kind of relationship
be set apart from the others? Like the great root system of an old and long-
established growing plant, they are all tangled up together; to separate them
you would have to cleave the plant itself from top to bottom.[6]

"The Demonstrators" is a delicately balanced portrait of one such
intricate root system, part of a long-established growing plant,
Holden, Mississippi. The town is now stricken by hostility and suspicion, and threatened by an old internal blight. It has lost a couple of
vital young branches and is about to lose older ones. But since the
root system reaches deep into the earth, it seems quite possible that
Holden will hold.

Chapter Nine
Losing Battles: Song of the Two Sides of a Fight

The long novel through which the "voice" of a murderer "pushed its way up" that hot August day was *Losing Battles*. The short story could not have been resisted because of the pressure of knowledge and fury that lay behind it. The novel, in its sheer length and development into a complexly organized work of fiction, had at first been resisted for other reasons, chiefly the author's preference for the story and the novella. But she gradually succumbed to the longer form; in the proliferation of its scenes and characters, it even became a pleasurable source of entertainment during a period not only of public but also of private distress. What started out to be short and farcical became, as she grew fonder of her characters, a full-blown novel.

If affection for and the desire to celebrate a variety of characters were her aims, a carefully selected time and place were crucial to her ways and means in the novel. The time was familiar, that of her earliest fiction—the 1930s, the Depression. The place was unfamiliar to her fiction—the hill country of northeast Mississippi, a corner of Appalachia. The choice was tactical because of her decision to write an "outside" story, the near equivalent of a play. She told an interviewer, "I needed that region, that kind of country family, because I wanted that chorus of voices, everybody talking and carrying on at once. I wanted to try something completely vocal and dramatized. Those people are natural talkers and storytellers, in a remote place where there was time for that."[1] The challenge, abundantly met, lay in making the chorus sound not only authentic and united, but also a blend of finely tuned individual voices. The Banner folk are like one of those marvelous choruses in which each singer is an accomplished professional, and from anywhere, at any time, may emerge as a soloist, virtuosic, though unique in timbre and quality. But even within the general harmony (this is comedy), dissonance and cacophony erupt. The sounds of individual voices can be ugly and dissenting as well as pleasant with the concord of family love and loyalty. Furthermore, the idiom of this verbal music is an original blend extending from the sonorous cadences of the King James version of the Bible to the rawest of hillbilly twangs.

It is the author who livens her speakers' tongues, brightening their hill-country dialect, infusing all the folk talk with metaphor, fresh comic turns of phrase, exaggeration, a soft pathos or unexpected lyricism. And she has made these talkers, young and old, delightfully self-conscious and "critical" as storytellers, aware of the joys and responsibilities of their art as narrators and attentive listeners. Though one person may be unofficially "in charge" of a certain segment of story, others may correct, question, encourage, draw out the teller, may even take over the tale, to make it more (or less) truthful, entertaining, shocking, or mysterious, whichever of these alternatives seems called for. The interplay of the characters, what each person says and how others react to his or her words, is the chief means of characterization in the novel. Adults do most of the narrating, but some of the young ones are apt learners. Etoyle, a nine-year-old Renfro daughter, is especially keen, acknowledging, "I love to hear-tell." She is both admired and rebuked for her well-known tendency to "embroider" a tale, the metaphor itself linking the art of narrative with another form of folk art cultivated by Banner women.

Once Aunt Birdie, an in-law of the Beecham clan, speaks admiringly of the family's "power . . . to draw us a picture." This is a tribute to the large visual element in the brilliant narration. As readers of *Losing Battles,* we are immediately aware that we cannot "just think of [the novel] as voices," as the author advised her audience before she read from it in the old state capitol in Jackson on "Eudora Welty Day" in May 1973. The narrator acutely *sees* as well as hears; what is shown is sometimes well "painted," but so little being stationary, her teeming scenes are often a great tumble of action. The farcical element in it reminds Robert Heilman of "old dizzy movie scenes" in "the great two-reelers of the '20's." Heilman also shows that behind the "surface impression . . . of haste, casualness, haphazardness, movement rather than direction, scattershot unselectiveness, of . . . hop-skip-jumping," lies a highly though subtly ordered work of art, the great variety of episodes and tales having been mastered with "an instinctive grasp of their potential coherence."[2]

The novel is divided into six untitled "parts," which may be thought of in this fiction of mixed genres as acts, chapters, books, or cantos, each with an underlying thematic and narrative unity, a sense of "closure," and the expectancy of theatrical suspense. Each "part" is marked by the appearance of a full-page woodcut print of a highly stylized bois d'arc tree, in triplicate (the work of artist Guy Fleming). The overarching tree, according to family legend, had been planted as a mere twig by the original Vaughn pioneer to settle in Banner's hill country, and is known as "Billy Vaughn's switch." Having supernaturally sprouted at once, taken firm root, grown, spread, and sheltered the family, survived many a storm and one massively destructive cyclone, the tree is symbolic of the family itself in its solidity, powers of endurance, and the sheltering and nurturing of fragile life. In the woodcut two of the three trees recede off through perspective into small and smaller gray images, as though trailing into the mists of time and history; they suggest the dead who stand behind the living members of the family tree.

The six major "parts" are subdivided into a number of shorter segments of varying length, not unlike scenes, separated by a printer's decorative design bearing a tiny leaf. In such delicate ways everything in the book is an exquisite wedding of nature and art, of broadly epic or mock-epic action and precious miniatures. Transitions between these "leaves" are varied and graceful. Once, for example, a section opens with Uncle Noah Webster catching a baseball flying in from the pasture. Throwing it back into the game, he says, "So the next thing we knew, there we all was at the trial," thus resuming the game of storytelling after a short break.

The reader of *Losing Battles* is, however, aware of more than the artistic skill of the narrator; one senses a narrative presence through the quiet, lyrical voice that binds all together. Despite the lack of direct interpretation of her characters, this narrator seems to lean over them expectantly, protectively, lovingly. In the beginning it is a hovering presence, brooding with "bright wings" like the Holy Ghost in Hopkins's poem, to bring about her initial act of creation. Dawn comes slowly as the moon goes down "on flushed cheek" and "the distant point of the ridge, like the tongue of a calf, put[s] its red lick on the sky." Then two chinaberry trees light up, caterpillar nets shine, and the new tin roof of the Renfro house seems to come "sliding out of the sky." And finally, after the length of a breath when the world is "shadowless . . . as under a lifting hand," as the sun makes its passage through the open center of the house, and "Sunday light . . . race[s] over the farm," it is as though the creator of this fictional world had said, "Let there be light." Yet human beings are already discovered in it. Even before the moon sets and the sun reveals old granny in her rocker, a baby (Lady Mae Renfro) has "bolted naked out of the house, open-armed, knocking at the walls of flowers, . . . tagging in turn the four big trees that marked off the gatepost, the well-piece, the birdhouse, the bell-post, a log seat, a rope swing, and then, rounding the house," she has pushed over a crate "that let a stream of white Plymouth Rocks loose on the world." Thus swiftly is a fictional universe created, with a new little Eve setting the stage and establishing its boundaries and central "props" with her tagging, her "original sin" that of breaking away from her mother and turning order to chaos by mischievously loosing the hens. Joy and exuberance most characterize the narrator of *Losing Battles,* as she discloses the world in its pristine state and pronounces it "good." Later, the narrator uses other perspectives as her presence broods over a ravaged natural world, the evidences of human greed, pride, envy, ignorance, the finality of death.

The theme of the novel is the paradox suggested by its title, and its central action is the celebration of reunion. Losing battles implies not only fighting them repeatedly without winning, but also dropping them off, emerging from a state of destructive conflict to one of at least temporary reconcilation, peace, union. On the day that the "warring" clan of the Vaughn-Beecham-Renfros come together to celebrate the ninetieth birthday of its most ancient survivor, great-granny Vaughn, old and current battles are revived, refought, and finally "lost"—mostly because charitable human beings are capable of forgiveness, prerequisite to the bonding of enemies. Weddings, rings, and babies are evidences and symbols of union; and even the death of old battler, Miss Julia Mortimer, provides the occasion, at wake and funeral, for reunion. The warrior achieves final rest and peace in death, together with the long-submerged and freshly evoked admiration—in some cases, love—of the living.

Among the varieties of battles fought in the novel, most elemental is that against poverty. Devastating storms, the felling of trees, soil erosion, drought, and widespread economic depression compel these clean, courageous folk to wrest their living from a wasted, resistant soil and endure a mode of existence in which money is too scarce to be a viable medium of exchange. Yet the members of the reunion make thrifty and ingenious use of their limited resources, growing what *can* be grown (apparently watermelon thrives best on hard red clay), "making do" by transforming all varieties of sacks into clothing. A bright new tin roof for the Renfro house shows their defiance of ruin, and the return of Jack Renfro to his family spurs their hope for a better economic future.

In *Losing Battles* clan warfare, in the form of a standing feud between the Beecham-Renfros and Stovalls, is not vicious as it is in *Huckleberry Finn,* though Stovalls are shown as a rapacious breed. The narrative opens with an account of this feud, as told to a new member of the family, Aunt Cleo, from southern Mississippi, recently married to a Beecham brother, Uncle Noah Webster. Cleo's first husband had been a Stovall. The current fight had begun over the attempt of Jack Renfro to rescue his dead grandmother Ellen Beecham's golden wedding ring from libidinous Curly Stovall (who had snatched it from the bosom of Jack's sexually ripening sister, Ella Fay). The outbreak of the feud is thus laced with comic "romance," even "chivalry," as the knight protects his sister's honor. Indeed, the lives and destinies of the two families are so thoroughly intertwined that Mr. Renfro resignedly admits, "Stovalls is with us and bury with us." Curly Stovall is town marshall and owner of the grocery store, formerly Mr. Renfro's; by means fair and foul, Curly manages, while Jack is in the penitentiary, to gain possession of both Jack's truck and his great favorite, a stud named "white Dan."

Hilarious and farcical is the story of Jack's reaction to Curly's "aggravating behavior," his theft of the safe supposedly containing the ring; his arrest and conviction in a trial at which Ludlow's Judge Oscar Moody charges him with having committed "aggravated battery." (A nesting purple martin turns up in the safe at court.) But the result for Jack's family is serious: they are deprived of their eldest and strongest son's labor on the farm, and Jack's wife Gloria and their baby Lady Mae lose husband and father while Jack serves his year and a half term in jail. He escapes a day early in order to attend the reunion, though the family is convinced that its concerted will is bringing him back. Jack's and the family's battle with Judge Moody continues because of the heavy sentence meted out for tomfoolery. Returning home, Jack unwittingly assists the Judge by hauling his car out of a ditch; when he discovers he has assisted his enemy, he leaves the reunion in order to reverse his good deed and put the Judge back in the ditch. His plan is altered when the Judge saves the lives of Gloria and Lady Mae, who have slipped into the road, by veering his car. Momentum drives it up to Banner top, where it comes to rest, precariously near a cliff, wheels still spinning and motor humming, suspended on a sign just posted by the apocalyptic Uncle Nathan Beecham—"Destruction Is At Hand." Jack, now grateful, battles to save the car, which involves the balancing weight, in the back seat, of Jack's sidekick, Aycock Comfort; vast labors on Jack's part during much of Sunday's reunion and Miss Julia's funeral on Monday morning; the attempted use of a mule, a truck, a towline, a human chain, and an old cedar tree uprooted by Mr. Renfro's dynamite. Though Jack finally wins the battle, the Buick emerges looking itself like the result of "aggravated battery."

Because the Judge and Mrs. Moody are invited to join the reunion and spend the night with the Renfros, and have no real alternative, they are subjected to a kind of "trial," a series of amazing revelations of the family history, legends, and attitudes, including their feelings toward the old Banner teacher, Miss Julia Mortimer, whose summons the Judge is attempting to answer by visiting her in nearby Alliance. The presence of the Judge through the disclosure of the most serious conflicts in the novel provides a stable perspective on the revelations. These involve various confessions, defenses, questions regarding the validity of evidence, complex moral dilemmas, legal codes, mysteries, even crimes. Squeezed into the only available chair, a child's desk seat blown from Banner school during the cyclone and caught by the bois d'arc tree, the Judge is largely a silent witness; his reactions are most often expressed in long sighs or groans of exasperation, the clash of comedy and outrage, or pure pity. Seated in the lowly learner's chair, the learned man must be taught the inadequacy of the law to deal with the deepest mysteries of human motivation and action, the "reasons of the heart," and the spiritual innocence to be found in persons legally guilty. He is finally "forgiven" in the name of the family by Brother Bethune, Methodist preacher-orator-exhorter who is invited to stand in for preacher Grandpa Vaughn, recently deceased.

Closely related to family feuding in virulence, relative innocence, and comic irony, is the warring among the various Protestant churches to which all the characters of *Losing Battles* belong. The Vaughn-Beecham-Renfros are loyal Baptists. Grandpa Vaughn's preaching, his piety and lengthy prayers, have left their imprint on the family, which prides itself on being, in Miss Beulah's words, "strict, law-abiding, God-fearing, close-knit." The final epithet is clearly the most significant, however, as Miss Beulah concludes, "we've all just tried to last as long as we can by sticking together."

Denominational loyalties seem related not only to family, but to community, town, county, and state loyalties—all fierce. The competitions seem more social than theological, giving evidence of class-consciousness, even though Grandpa Vaughn had given "heartfelt groans" when, at a Methodist revival meeting, he had witnessed infant baptism. Methodists are regarded vaguely as more "lax" than Baptists, while Presbyterians appear to have more intellect, more rectitude, more "class"—at least, others think, in their own eyes. Miss Julia Mortimer had once been Presbyterian; Mrs. Moody now *is,* and expresses herself as being "gladder every minute" not to be either Methodist or Baptist as she hears of and witnesses their behavior. Aunt Beck seems to enjoy the battles between churches ("Can't you make that church rivalry sound a little stronger?"); she is also an authority when it comes to differences between and within the denominations, wanting to know of Miss Julia's Presbyterianism, "Was she deep-dyed?" since among the "whole lot of different grades of 'em, some of 'em aren't too far off from Baptists." Ironically, the clergyman ordered by Miss Julia to officiate at her funeral, a former student, is Father Stephen McRaven ("he can try praying me into eternity"). A man in skirts is, to Bannerites, not only "deep-dyed," but black with the mystery in which he goes clothed: automatically, they accuse him of pride ("Worshipped himself, didn't he?"). In her death Miss Julia brings together "all sorts and conditions," including a Mr. Ike Goldman of Goldman's Store, who supplies a tray of meats; someone else supplies "the bought kind" of liquor, to which several, including even some of the Presbyterians, help themselves.

The lightly satirical treatment of church rivalry is shown in an episode involving the two chief contenders in Banner, Methodists and Baptists, whose churches stand on opposite sides of the street. The cyclone, an "act of God" in religious and legal parlance, spares the Baptist church (providing Grandpa with a topic for a series of sermons on "Destruction"), but picks up and sets down the Methodist church intact beside the Baptist church. Neither side is content to dwell in such brotherly unity; the Methodists have to "tear their own church down stick by stick" and "carry it back and put it together again on the side of the street where it belonged"—in that original, opposing position. They are assisted in this effort by "a good many Baptists."

Like other forms of friendly rivalry, the battle between churches provides not only a means to group and personal identity, but a kind of raison d'etre. Aunt Cleo, the "outsider" who hails from southern Mississippi, is also the member of a sect alien to Bannerites. When, after hearing much of Cleo's critical commentary, Miss Beulah marches out of her kitchen to demand "the name of the church *you* go to," Cleo responds, "Defeated Creek Church of the Assembly of God. One mile south of Piney." "Never heard of a single piece of it," replies Miss Beulah, and marches back to her kitchen. Rich and subtle indeed are the comic revelations in such an exchange. Cleo's spiel of identification meets with a complete blank: Beulah's "put-down" calls attention both to the absurdity of the spiel and her sense of the total obscurity of Cleo's religious identity. The name of her church lightly echoes the theme of "losing battles" as the name of Banner's Methodist church suggests reunion ("Better Friendship"). Other questions spin off from the name of Cleo's church: did the *creek* suffer defeat by drying up? was it "defeated" (perhaps redirected) by the erection of the church? or did it mark a scene of defeat, as, for example, in some local skirmish in the greatest of Southern "losing battles," the Civil War? A minor mystery surrounds a battle that gave a name, a place, and an identity to what all church congregations presumably are, "assemblies of God."

A far more serious battle is that fought by the Banner teacher, Miss Julia Percival Mortimer, whose death on the day of the reunion is reported by the one who discovered her, jack-of-all-trades Willy Trimble. Though she never appears, Miss Julia is as fully evoked as any living character in the novel. She is remembered by her former students with some hostility as the one who "put an end to good fishing." But she is also remembered with admiration and gratitude for the devotion which sounds through her letters and will, as read to the reunion by Judge Moody. This is how she describes her struggle to the only brilliant, successful pupil who followed her urging and example to use Boone County redemptively, as the arena for exercising his talents as lawyer and judge. Miss Julia writes: "All my life I've fought a hard war with ignorance. Except in those cases that you can count off on your fingers, I lost every battle. . . . But as long as I was still young, I always thought if I could marshal strength enough of body and spirit and push with it, every ounce, I could change the future." In her vision for the future, as critics have pointed out, the idea of progress, change, has been Miss Julia's "historical" commitment.[3] In contrast is the family's mythical or archetypal mode of existence, which is cyclical and repetitive, binding members of the clan together for mutual support rather than encouraging the aspiring, independent spirit which breaks with the pattern.

Granny Vaughn, as head of the clan, is implicitly the teacher's archenemy. Fragile though she is, in her mere survival, so cherished and lovingly attended on her ninetieth birthday while Miss Julia dies abandoned, Granny celebrates her triumph. After her rival's tragic tale has been unwound, Granny dances on the table in what seems a weirdly primitive little victory rite. Yet her position is perilous; she dances herself off the edge and is caught by a watchful and listening Jack, who, unseen from the fringes, has heard and been moved by Miss Julia's story.

Though Miss Julia's dedication seems at times almost fanatical, chiefly when she teaches through the cyclone, she is pragmatic in helping students without the capacity for book learning to master a useful form of employment—sewing for Rachel Sojourner, carpentry for Willie. She tries to improve the whole community by sending out free peach-tree switches, with instructions as to their planting and nurture. It is therefore tragic and ironic that in her closing days Miss Julia is abandoned by the community and made to suffer a good deal of punishing treatment at the hands of Miss Lexie Renfro. This failed teacher, who takes to home nursing, keeps Miss Julia tied to her bed and denied access to pencil and paper: only through wile and heroic effort does Miss Julia manage to set down the written words so infinitely precious to her, mail a letter or two, and thus communicate with Judge Moody. But in her final struggles she seems to experience a kind of victory in defeat—the tragic triumph of insight. She recognizes that the "survival instinct" drives her pupils as well as herself, "but the side that gets licked gets to the truth first. When the battle's over, something may dawn there—with no help from the teacher, no help from the pupil, no help from the book." She is prepared to go on fighting until the end, "ready for all they send me. There's a measure of enjoyment in it."

But what of her final hours? Her last words, as reported by Willy Trimble, are "What was the trip for?" Not so much a sign of defeat, perhaps, as puzzlement, the old Calvinistic conviction pressing up through her clouding consciousness, that one's life is destiny and must have a clear moral purpose.

A major mystery surrounds another serious battle in the novel: and here we are at the center of thematic concerns pervasive in all Eudora Welty's fiction. It is the battle of lovely, red-golden crowned Gloria

Short, to be a living mystery because of her unknown parentage, self-determining, separate, withdrawn from clan solidarity. Initially, in her battle for survival as an orphan, she had been greatly assisted by her friend and mentor Miss Julia, who had in fact chosen Gloria to be her successor. As the new teacher of Banner School, Gloria meets and falls in love with Jack Renfro, returned to school after a six-year gap because of work demands.

In Gloria's person and complex predicament Eudora Welty embodies two of her central themes: the rights and claims of the individual self over against those of the clan and the mystery of human identity. Gloria's battle against Jack's family resembles that of Robbie Fairchild, each young wife striving to protect and salvage her husband from a family that seems all-devouring. Having abandoned her career as a teacher and rejected Miss Julia's noble commitment, Gloria now resists all claims and ties except those binding her to the intimate family group of Jack and her child, Lady Mae, and she asks Jack wistfully during one of the few moments they are alone, "When will we move to ourselves?" That too seems a losing battle, for the family are "piled all over" Jack. Furthermore, they threaten to inundate Gloria completely by putting together a credible story that would make of her not only a member of the Beecham family, but Jack's first cousin, with a much-loved Beecham brother, Sam Dale, killed in World War I, as her father. Granny Vaughn asserts that "fox-headed" Rachel Sojourner is her mother; this seems likely, not only because of Gloria's inherited "crowning glory," but her independent temper and defiance of moral codes in consummating her love and conceiving a child before marriage.

Gloria hotly denies the assumptions about her parentage. She is subjected to a cruel rite of initiation into the family when the women pull her down and ram huge sticky chunks of watermelon down her throat, while laughing and taunting her with "Say who's a Beecham! Then swallow it!" Though physically coerced into submission, Gloria continues to resist identification with the Beechams, insisting that she has lived all her life with mystery, is used to it, was married in it. Now she wishes to be only herself, Mrs. Gloria Renfro, "and have nothing to do with the old dead past."

Gloria's resistance to the Beechams' claims is virulent because it is double-barreled, and the more threatening of the two barrels has been aimed, through Miss Julia's warnings, at herself and her baby. Miss Julia's last act had been wholly characteristic both in its intention of getting at the truth and helping and protecting "the innocent." Apparently all but convinced herself that Sam Dale Beecham was Gloria's father, and knowing and probably having been an original supporter of the state law against intermarriage among close kin, she had summoned Judge Moody to investigate the union of Jack and Gloria. Earlier, she had warned the girl against marrying Jack when a "dark thread in her past" might result in her marriage being declared "null and void," her husband confined to the penitentiary for ten years, her potential child without a name or identity, and in danger of being deaf and dumb. Fearing that Miss Julia might be right, Gloria has kept the secret of her origin anxiously. When her baby is born, she gives the child, who soon develops a little red-golden crest of her own, not only a name but a royal title. Nothing is too good for Lady Mae; Gloria sees her as "the future" for Jack and herself. She has been waiting for her baby to talk before displaying her triumphantly to Miss Julia. The baby's first words, "What you huntin', man?," are spoken on the same day Miss Julia says her last words, and oddly resemble the old teacher's question, "What was the trip for?"

Though in *Losing Battles* the narrator abandons us to versions of the family history that they themselves construct out of fact and legend, the members reveal themselves as much by what they conceal as by what they disclose. There are odd gaps in their narration—we see them trying to protect mystery, prevent confession, the disclosure of dark secrets. Some mysteries are never resolved: why did the parents of the seven Beecham children abandon those children, flee from their home and family one dark stormy night, only to perish in a flood, their bodies discovered not together but far apart? Only Ellen Beecham's wedding ring had been left in the Vaughn Bible; that family treasure, filched by Ellen Fay, is lost forever in the fracas that put Jack in jail. The postcard from Sam Dale, while seeming to resolve a mystery of parentage in his signing himself to Gloria's mother, "Your loving husband," holds another mystery even more tightly, and leads to a further confession. One is joyful and absolving. If Sam Dale is Gloria's father, Miss Beulah is freed from her guilt of being responsible, she thinks, for Sam Dale's emasculation: a live coal from the fire had popped into his lap when he was a baby, and she, supposedly tending him, had not acted quickly enough to save him. But then, as the cryptic Granny later states, giving a "minute nod" at Judge Moody, "Never said Sam Dale was the father. . . . Going to marry

the girl, I said. Think Sam Dale was pulling her out of a pickle."
The pickle would appear to have been Rachael Sojourner's being pregnant by Herman Dearman—"a great big grabber" and "a glorified
Stovall," says Miss Beulah. Dearman had "showed up full-grown
around here, took over some of the country, brought niggers in here,
cut down every tree within forty miles, and run it shrieking though
a saw mill," leaving behind "a nation of stumps." He had taken over
Mr. Renfro's store (now Curley Stovall's), and even his house.

According to Judge Moody, Dearman had "aspired to Miss Julia
Mortimer" when she was young and beautiful, in addition to seducing Rachel Sojourner. This alternate version of Gloria's parentage is
suggested by another of Granny's remarks, that Miss Julia "wasn't
able to put two and two together." But Dearman's career had been
truncated by a loyal friend and protector to Rachel, and a vengeful
brother to Sam Dale—Uncle Nathan Beecham. In response to Jack's
innocent questioning and over Miss Beulah's "prohibitive tones," Nathan blurts out his crime: "I killed Mr. Dearman with a stone to his
head, and let 'em hang a sawmill nigger for it. After that, Jesus had
to hold my hand." In the moonlight he reveals to the awed and horrified company the stump of the hand he had chopped off in reparation
for his double crime, "white and clean with its puckered stitching
like a flour sack's." After that horrible act, the once playful, affectionate Nathan is "lost to the book of Revelation." In voluntary exile,
except for the annual reunion, he becomes a ragged, homeless, penitent, and voiceless lay-preacher, putting his apocalyptic warnings into
signs. So pathetic and anguished is this man that Judge Moody has
to break his code, "take the law in his own hands," and implicitly
pardon Nathan by taking no further action. The Judge is reluctantly
drawn into what he calls "the besetting sin of this house," forgiving.

If Judge Moody seems the rationally moral center of the novel as
the task of judging is thrust upon him in this informal "court," Jack
Renfro is at the core of its generous heart. His sympathies are all-
embracing, which is why his loved ones often get into trouble: Gloria
would not have had to undergo her ordeal of baptism by watermelon
if Jack hadn't been away tending to his buddy Aycock's needs; indeed, he would not have had to go to the penitentiary if he hadn't
got into a fight involving his sister's "honor." Much of this difficulty
Miss Beulah calls "man-foolishness": she and Goria can agree at least
on that. Gloria counters such foolishness with the "common sense"
she does use, though selectively. Jack's task (he does not seem to have

a "battle" unless an internal one with his too-innocent assumption of his own capabilities, his indomitable optimism) is one of reconciliation. More than by his timely reappearance, he "makes" the reunion; more than any other member of the family, in his person he embodies the love within the family circle as all join hands for their parting hymn, "Blest Be the Tie That Binds." Jack feels in some strange way that his having served in the "pen" has "evened up" Uncle Nathan's guilt so that "now the poor old man can rest." He seems, for Granny, the reincarnation of Sam Dale. Though he never knew Miss Julia, he can love her because he has "heard her story"; when Gloria pities her old teacher, Jack corrects, "Don't pity anybody you could love." So hotly and sweetly do these lovers quarrel that the battle of wills appears to dissolve.

It is night; Jack and Gloria are lying together on the porch, their sleeping place, when all are at rest. He pleads with Gloria, who loves him so intensely she "has to hate everybody else" and cannot spare any of her love for his family. He believes, hopefully, that "there's room for everything, and time for everybody, if you take your day the way it comes along and try not to be much later than you can help." He is ashamed that he and Gloria have left Miss Julia out on this reunion day—even suggests they "could go yet, and be back by milking time." Gloria stops him, and the narrator takes her leave of the reunited couple with a bold and appropriate image:

She put her mouth quickly on his, and then she slid in her hand and seized hold of him right at the root. And so she convinced him that there is only one way of depriving the ones you love—taking your living presence away from theirs; that no one alive has ever deserved such punishment, although maybe the dead do; and that no one alive can ever in honor forgive that wrong, which outshines shame, and is not to be forgiven until it has been righted.

In the final sentence of this passage the narrator breaks her own rules and we hear the authorial voice. It is surprising to hear her say that there *is* one unforgivable wrong, and that so often an unavoidable one in actual human life. But happily, it *can* be righted within the comic vision of this novel, by that simplest and most inevitable of actions, the physical union of lovers.

Because of the seemingly random quality of folk speech and the episodic nature of much comic action, *Losing Battles* does not appear to

have the structural coherence of *Delta Wedding*, the unifying symbolism and dimension of classical and Celtic mythology to be found in
The Golden Apples. Yet correspondences may be found, in addition to
the thematic parallels already noted. The biblical Christianity of Bannerites functions in ways similar to those of the mythology in *The
Golden Apples*, a major difference being its living, active state in the
minds of the characters. King MacLain and his lovers do not know
that they resemble Zeus and the mortal women with whom he conducted his amours, nor does Loch Morrison know that he is behaving
like a youthful Perseus. Consciousness of myth, when it occurs, is
mostly "literary": Cassie has read "The Song of the Wandering Aengus"; Miss Eckhart, being a well-educated European, knows all the
myths, including that of Siegfried and the dragon. By contrast, when
Miss Beulah sees Jack about to lift the Judge's Buick single-handedly,
she shouts frantically, "Now watch! Reminds me of Samson exactly!
. . . Only watch my boy show the judgment Samson's lacking. . . ."
Jack is viewed as the Good Samaritan in helping Judge Moody out of
the ditch. With less happy propriety, Brother Bethune sees Grandpa
and Granny Vaughn as "David and Jonathan" (the couple's union had
not immediately been very fruitful—a single daughter had produced
all seven Beechams), Jack as the Prodigal Son, the reunion meal as
"Belshazzar's Feast." The narrator, whose imagery (mostly similes) is
drawn from nature and the staples of the family's daily existence, dips
naturally into the Bible for some of these similes: the school bus is
described as "familiar in shape as Noah's ark"; Mr. Renfro holds two
halves of a watermelon "like the tablets of the Ten Commandments";
a road running between high, wet, threateningly close curved banks
is "like the Red Sea in the act of parting"; dark veins in Granny's
arms are "like long velvet Bible markers"; the lock of Ellen Beecham's
silky blonde hair, all that is left of her since the wedding ring has
been lost, is kept in the book of *Chronicles*—an appropriate place for
a family that dotes on its own history.

Music permeates *Losing Battles* in ways analogous to those in *The
Golden Apples*; but rather than being the heroic art of Beethoven, or
that of the Spaniard's guitar, or even the amateur efforts of Cassie and
Loch Morrison on their piano and trumpet, here it is the folk art of
gospel hymns. The "lyrics" are important—a verbal support to the
art of their storytelling. The two most significant hymns are the pair
that bring the reunion literally together by hand-holding, "Blest Be
the Tie That Binds," and the one that Jack sings at the end, "Bring-

ing in the Sheaves." The harvest in the parable alluded to is one of souls, but as Jack sings so that "all Banner could hear him and know who he was," it prophesies a future peace and plenty consonant with Jack's loving and hopeful, truly redemptive spirit. There is pathos in Uncle Nathan's playing of "Poor Wayfaring Stranger" and "Let the Lower Lights Be Burning" on his cornet ("Some poor sinking struggling seaman / You may rescue, you may save"). When Granny sings to the accompaniment of Uncle Noah Webster's banjo, the lyrics are ambiguous; it sounds like "Frog Went A-Courting" or "Wondrous Love"—half-Christian, half-pagan, like Granny herself. A hymn affords comic juxtaposition when the Moodys, Jack and others, are discussing ways to save the Buick by using a rope, and the Methodists are heard in their Sunday service singing, "Throw out the life line! Someone is sinking today."

Many of the religious allusions are tongue-in-cheek; as with the denominational battles, religious piety is treated with light satire. Brother Bethune, for example, seems more adept at making moonshine than at religious exhortation, and perhaps Grandpa Vaughn has been removed from the scene just in time to spare us (and the author) his long-winded piety. "Home-style" Bible-Belt Christianity and the theme of forgiving are a means, then, of providing a central thread in the novel, binding up the loose ends, while at the same time, paradoxically, leaving them dangling.

Can any of Eudora Welty's works seem either more artlessly artful or more indigenous than the others? Yet this one *does* seem so. Though subtle "literary" allusions to other "mythologies" do appear (the mock-epic-Romance fuss over "the Ring" recalls Wagner's cycle and, more recently, Tolkien's fantasy), even those allusions seem American. Curly Stovall's sheer bulk ("He's great big and has little bitty eyes"; Ella Fay's description makes Aunt Nanny "feel like I can see him coming right this minute") and his smashing into or "stoving" of the Renfro-Beecham clan slyly suggest the destruction of the white whale. Another subtle allusion may be to Hawthorne's story "The Birthmark" (a favorite of Eudora Welty's) in the description of the lovely Gloria, "every visible inch" of whose skin, save for the points of her elbows and inner sides of her arm, is freckled, "as if she'd been sprinkled with nutmeg while she was still dewy and it would never brush off." Later, when Gloria defends the perfection of her baby against the suspicion of any birth defect, she proclaims, "She's speckless," only to discover "the first freckle lying in the hol-

low of the baby's throat, like a spilled drop of honey." Birthmarks
are enhancing rather than fatal blemishes in this novel, which joyfully
celebrates the essential goodness of the characters and their acceptance
of each other. No character suffers from any great tragic flaw: like
Gloria's freckles, their defects are decimated by their loving author-
creator into so many thousands of beauty marks cherished for the way
they contribute to each person's fallible but delightful humanity.

The tale is told, the "song of the two sides of a fight" has been
sung; and if we have submitted ourselves to the world of the Bannerites (it takes some staying power), we are much the richer for having
shared the lives of these poor mountain folk. Once part of experience
and memory, however, the joyful noise of the novel recedes to some
quiet, bright region of the mind and heart: it becomes, oddly
enough, a book remembered visually. And if it then seems more like
a big brown country bucket than a Grecian urn, suited to visual display as a "period piece" of American Literature, one senses that this
novel of children of the Depression may also become a "foster-child
of Silence and slow Time," though ready to resume its bumping clatter the minute anybody picks it up.

Chapter Ten
The Optimist's Daughter:
The Whole Solid Past

The earliest version of *The Optimist's Daughter* appeared as a long story in the *New Yorker* of 15 March 1969, before the publication of *Losing Battles*. At some stages the writing of the two novels overlapped: they came out of the same, personally difficult time of illness and death in the author's family. In many respects the two novels seem almost polar opposites. *Losing Battles* is long, episodic, deeply "textured," objective, dramatic, and epic in narrative method, a kind of literary folk art. Time is the Depression; the characters are poor Mississippi hill-country folk, members of large clans. The lyrical impulse is joyfully celebrative. *The Optimist's Daughter* is short (novella length), tightly structured, spare in style, controlled in pacing. Time is present, setting is mostly small-town Mississippi, the family in focus is upper-class and small—mother, father, child (in manuscript, the novel bears the title "The Only Child"). Though it contains dramatized scenes, usually comic and satirical, the narration is essentially interior: through the character of Laurel McKelva Hand, the narrator is standing squarely inside, looking out.

Despite these contrasts, however, in important respects the novels are alike. Both are generational tales. Their focus is on husbands, wives, and children, community. Both novels are really about losing battles—their eruptions, their deep causes. But the titles are misleading, for *Losing Battles* is essentially comic, and *The Optimist's Daughter* is tragic.

The latter work is divided into four parts, each containing four chapters except for the last, a "finale" undivided. Its careful structure and highly conscious use of the motifs of time and pattern, its packed emotional effect in reading time, suggest the demands of the string quartet. The author's essay, "Some Notes on Time in Fiction," first published in 1973 and collected in *The Eye of the Story,* provides a gloss on her use of time in the novel. Both narrator and characters are fixed on time: scarcely a page is without direct or oblique reference to it. Though time is the essence of every plot, it is of this one in particular. At first the action moves slowly, then swiftly on the arrow of suspense, finding its target in revelation. Time is relentless as the grandfather's clock ticking in the McKelva living room; it is the enemy leading to the death of Laurel's husband and parents. Within her experience and memory, time moves forward and backward, doubles past on present, makes her cast a frightened glance into the future. It loses its destructive fury only in memory, the timeless medium of love's convergence and continuity.

Time begins "on the dot"—the narrator's phrase for the entry of Dr. Courtland, eye specialist, into the room where he will examine seventy-one-year-old Judge Clinton McKelva, accompanied by his daughter Laurel, in her mid-forties, and his forty-year-old second wife, Fay Chisom. Time is nearing its close for the Judge; is somewhere in medias res for Laurel; for Fay, there is only the present, to wait on her pleasure, and the future, ready for her conquest.

"On the dot" argues medical precision, reliability, order. Dr. Courtland has that and more: vast kindness, respect, sensitivity; "his big country hands with the fingers . . . had always looked, to Laurel, as if their mere touch on the crystal of a watch would convey to their skin exactly what time it was." His home had been Mount Salus, Mississippi. (The Latin meaning of *salus* is *health:* moral health is suggested.) This was the home of Judge McKelva, his first wife Becky, and Laurel; before sickness invaded the family with devastating effects, it had seemed sound and solid as the mountains of Becky's West Virginia mountain home in her youth (though she had scorned the notion that Mount Salus could qualify as a "mount"). Affection, generosity, tolerance, wise decisions, and guidance had been Judge McKelva's gifts to his community, which he had at one time served as mayor. The Judge had supported Dr. Courtland's education during the Depression, and the doctor had tended Laurel's mother Becky when she suffered cataracts—a different kind of sight impairment from the Judge's. His malady is a detached retina, near the center of the eye. "It happened to the inside . . . the part he sees with," Dr. Courtland explains to Fay. A slippage of memory in the time for pruning Becky's rose bushes, the "dislocated vision" which had brought him to the New Orleans hospital, are intimations of the Judge's failure of insight and judgment. It had led, ten years after Becky's death and one month after he had found Fay Chisom in a secretary pool at a convention, to his second marriage.

The eye can be repaired by surgery, and *is,* so far as the doctor's skills and prognosis are concerned. The cure is to be the slow healing that nature brings with time. But the inner malady seems to be strangely affecting the Judge's psyche, as, head bandaged, still, and "quenched" looking, he seems to Laurel to be moving backward in time, lying in "a dream of patience." Laurel's presence, so much the revival of her mother's, might help the Judge to heal. Quietly strong and tender in her love, when she works her "shift" in rotation with Fay and the night nurse caring for the Judge, she often reads to him, reviving her parents' cherished custom when she was a child. She "sets her inner chronology" to his. But though the eye appears to be mending, he is not.

In every way Fay contrasts with Laurel. Her reaction to the Judge's illness is, "I don't see why this had to happen to *me.*" She is suspicious of and insulting to Dr. Courtland, opposes the surgery (arguing, ironically, that "Nature's the great healer"), is impatient and selfish in tending her husband. She tries to engage his interest in living (meaning interest in her) with dangling green eardrops and shoes to match, inviting him to go out dancing. "She stood on one foot and held a shoe in the air above his face. It was green, with a stiletto heel. Had the shoe been a written page, some brief she'd concocted on her own, he looked at it in her hands there for long enough to read it through." The message of the heel seems sinister as a dagger poised; the Judge appears to read its meaning. Fay seems capable of anything.

Into the suspenseful first part Eudora Welty introduces the comic relief of a family—that of a blind and nearly deaf, confused old man hospitalized for cancer surgery, who comes to share Judge McKelva's room. Mr. Dalzell is a Mississippian from Fox Hill. "Almost immediately, he convinced himself that Judge McKelva was his long-lost son, Archie Lee."

" 'Archie Lee,' he said, 'I might've known if you ever did come home, you'd come home drunk.' " The Judge does not smile: absurdity is now behind him.

Unmoved by their husband's and father's nearness to death, the Dalzells spread themselves around the waiting room, eating, drinking, and carrying on a steady flow of silly family chatter. Eventually Archie Lee, unrecognized by his father and not at all amusing in the flesh, is present, bottle in hand, drunk. The matriarch comforts Fay as though she were a child; the Dalzells become Fay's surrogate fam-

ily. They are part of "the great interrelated family" who, Laurel
thinks later, "out of all times and future . . . never know the meaning of what has happened to them." The Judge registers Mr. Dalzell's
last comment before his surgery, "Told you rascals not to let the fire
go out," no more than his first.

On the night of Mardi Gras, Fay's birthday, her resentment at
missing the Carnival and her self-centered impatience at the slow pace
of the Judge's healing compel her to seize and attempt to pull him
out of bed. His response is immediate. To Laurel, it seems as though
"his whole, pillowless head went dusky, as if he laid it under the surface of dark, pouring water and held it there." "The renegade," says
Dr. Courtland to the nurse, "I believe he's just plain sneaked out on
us." Both reactions suggest that the Judge subliminally willed his
own death.

Leaving New Orleans, which seems, on Carnival night, to have
achieved some frenzied peak of decadence, disorder, and death, Laurel
is "still gearing herself to the time things took," preparing for the
ordeal of the coming days. Withdrawn in grief as she and Fay are
driven slowly through the streets to the train station, Laurel hears the
crowd noise as "the unmistakable sound of hundreds, of thousands,
of people *blundering*." The word echoes through the novel. To this
woman whose need is for pattern, decorum, order, some ultimate
folly and abuse are being enacted here on a broad human stage. Fay
is sullen, resentful at having missed the ultimate party on her birthday. She looks longingly out of the car window and sees a man
"dressed up like a skeleton and his date . . . in a long white dress,
with snakes for hair, holding up a bunch of lilies!": she recognizes
death no more in its mythical dress than in its reality. She then sees
a man covered wholly with a suit of Spanish moss, vomiting in public, and cries, "Why did I have to be shown that?" as though deserv-
ing of special protection from the loathsomeness of human disorder
and decadence, unaware of how much her own nature and behavior
are part of and contribute to it.

As the train leaves New Orleans, Laurel sees through the window
"filled with a featureless sky over pale smooth water, where a seagull
was hanging with wings fixed, like a stopped clock on a wall." Thus,
her father's time. Long since, the big clock the Judge had always kept
wound in the McKelva living room had stopped. The train passage
marks the end of Book One.

Mount Salus is the "dear, perpetual place" where most of the whole solid past was built and gathered itself, for Laurel, through time. In her homecoming some comfort is provided for her in the embraces and support of her friends: her six bridesmaids, Miss Adele Courtland (the doctor's sister, her former teacher, a wise, firm, and gentle woman who can still provide guidance to Laurel), the family's devoted black maid Missouri, and, more ambiguously, her parents' closest friends, Major and Miss Tennyson Bullock. The community has galvanized itself into readiness for the rites sacred to celebrating the death of its leading citizen.

But nothing can proceed "in decency and good order" for this judge, son of a Presbyterian missionary to China and grandson of a Confederate general. Though his whole solid past has been built with his wife Becky and based on the strength of her character, it is Fay who "runs the show," making a travesty of grief and the dignity due the dead. Fay's direction of the funeral arrangements, through the obsequious undertaker Mr. Pitt, leads to an open coffin. There, ready to be viewed in the family parlor, cosmetically renewed, lies the Judge, bathed in the same "foolish" peach satin that had "smothered the windows and spilled over the bed upstairs"—Becky's conjugal bed, where Laurel had been born and Becky had died, metamorphosed into Fay's marital bed.

Fay delays her entrance until the mourners have arrived. These include—astonishingly to Laurel, since Fay had denied their existence in New Orleans—a pickup truck loaded with Chisoms from Madrid, Texas. (On the bumper a sign reads, "Do Unto Others Before They Do Unto You.") With the exception of a curious seven-year-old boy, Wendell, and a simple, dignified, and generous old grandpa who seems a bit confused, the Chisoms are all too palpably Fay's kin. In concert, their crude voices and tone become loud, critical, and self-congratulatory.

Fay makes her entrance in black satin and puts on a theatrical display of grief and accusation. Outdoing her mother's vaunted performance at her husband's funeral, screaming and crying, Fay challenges the Judge to rise up, and charges him with being "unfair," with "cheating on" her in dying early. Finally, she "show[s] her claws at Laurel," fights free of restraining hands and throws herself forward "across the coffin onto the pillow, driving her lips without aim against the face under hers."

Appalling as this performance is to Laurel, it is as painful to see how the mourners misrepresent her father, appropriating him to their own constructions of what he was. His closest friend, Major Bullock, tipsy on bourbon and smitten by Fay in her "helpless grief," invents stories in which the Judge plays roles such as that of daring a gang of armed "White Caps" to shoot him, unarmed, before the courthouse. Laurel objects: her father "had no patience for show." Her father has reached "some danger point in his life" in such tales, she feels, and she resents hearing him made out to be "a humorist," "crusader," and "angel." In quiet response to the whole parade of mourners, including some odd, comic types who put in an appearance, Laurel declares the truth: "He loved my mother."

Indignities to her father are carried with him right to his final resting place. Instead of being buried in the beautiful old section of the cemetery next to Becky, by Fay's authority he is put in an ugly, unfinished, "new part" overlooking the new interstate highway, where the graves are decorated with artificial flowers.

After the funeral Fay decides to return to Texas for a few days with her family. Clearly outnumbered in Mount Salus, she wants to be with people who "speak her language"—chiefly an absent brother, De Witt, who has sunk into a "sull" since Fay's marriage and retired behind a front yard full of broken appliances he has declined to fix.

Most of Part Two of *The Optimist's Daughter* is given over to scenes transpiring on the day of the funeral. Though the action is largely comic, it is not felt to be so by the reader because time unfolds a series of assaults on Laurel's feelings. Only during the funeral service and at the graveside while the preacher is holding forth is Laurel permitted to retreat into her private grief. The parade of mourners behaves altogether like the pallbearers, seven members of the Bar or their sons and Bubba Chisom in his windbreaker, bringing up the high church steps "the thundering weight of Judge McKelva in his coffin"—and "blundering." The funeral day is a parade of blunders.

The structure of Part Three is contrapuntal: the first chapter scenic (external), with "communal" voices speaking, the second internal, the third scenic, the fourth internal. The two internal chapters contain their own scenes: Laurel's memories of the past; the actors in these dramas are the cherished dead.

Chapter One of Part Three is a kind of chorus, a quartet of the interweaving voices of elderly ladies who visit Laurel and interpret the funeral and its implications while she works among the garden flowers and listens silently. Miss Adele and Miss Tennyson are joined by Mrs. Pease, a next-door neighbor, and the minister's wife, Mrs. Bolt. Central to their commentary is the memory of their friend Becky, the conviction that the Judge "doted on [Fay] exactly as a man will," and the question put by Miss Tennyson: "What happened to his judgment?" All agree that the day of the funeral "left something to be desired"; all but Miss Adele are critical of the Chisoms. Her voice mingling with that of a mockingbird singing, she defends Fay in "giving a sad occasion its due," "emulating her own mother," and providing "a lonely old man something to live for." Laurel's only comment is, "I hope I never see her again." Miss Adele's defense of Fay seems to be a way of providing a "rounded" view of Fay. The old schoolteacher suggests tolerantly that Laurel is taking her father's second marriage too seriously. "Oh, it's all a game, isn't it?", Miss Adele says of the play of cardinals, rival cocks, flying at their reflections on the bird-frighteners which supposedly protect the figs (here, as in *The Golden Apples,* suggestive of sexual pleasure). It is surely the kind of opinion that would be necessary to a fine woman Clinton McKelva had overlooked when he felt he needed a second wife and might have found her right next door (though *teacher* might still have meant *spinster* to a man of the Judge's generation). Miss Adele's comments are not designed to make Laurel's view of Fay appear unbalanced or vindictive. She has, after all, spoken to no one about Fay's behavior during her father's illness and before his death in order to protect his memory. How can such things be said of a man of great "delicacy"? There are also moments when Laurel acts with instinctive sympathy for Fay, whenever she seems vulnerable. When awakening her on the morning of the funeral, Laurel wonders, "Is there any sleeping person you can be entirely sure you have not misjudged?" Then she notices Fay's green shoes with the stiletto heels on top of the mantelshelf. Miss Adele does not know that Fay's selfishness can lead to vicious acts; Laurel does.

The second part of Book Three takes place in the library where, surrounded by her father's earthly effects, Laurel begins her probing of the past: here, her father's relationship with her mother and his role in the community. The books themselves bring memories of her parents' voices reading: "it was the breath of life flowing between them, and the words of the moment riding on it that held them in delight. Between some two people every word is beautiful, or might

as well be beautiful." The papers in his office cabinet testify to his
work on flood control—the drudgery of it, forgotten by the town.
His desk drawers are empty; documents are now in Major Bullock's
charge. The one reminder of the alien presence is the track of vermil-
ion drops on the desk—Fay's nail polish. Laurel works hard at remov-
ing all traces of it.

In the third chapter of Part Three, Sunday evening, Laurel is with
the six bridesmaids for dinner. They are the middle generation, and
the focus seems to be on contrasts in generations: there are fond memories and gentle criticism of their parents (to which Laurel reacts sensitively—she does not want her parents to be the subjects of knowing
winks over good stories told about them); there are baffled reactions
to the odd "courting" behavior of the young. Differences between
Laurel's parents emerge. The Judge had made Laurel's wedding an ex-
travagant affair; her mother had not wanted the display. Laurel comments, protectively, that her mother's "superstitious streak" might
have made her think "it was unlucky to make too much of your happiness."

Major Bullock escorts Laurel home, still concerned about "that
poor little girl," Fay; he is already "recovering his good spirits" and
sings a disparaging little song—"he rambled . . . in and out of town
. . . till we had to cut him down." The scene closes with Laurel en-
tering the house and discovering, with alarm, that a chimney swift is
inside. She runs to trap or escape it, and ends trapped with it.

Chapter Four of Part Three presents Laurel's inward journey as she
moves deeper and deeper into the rooms that form the most congenial, and painful, surroundings for her probing. The night is stormy;
the presence of the bird "making free of the house" fills her with
dread. The old supersition is that "bird in the house means death."
A free, flying thing trapped, it becomes panicky and destructive and
induces panic in Laurel. Listening to the wind and rain and "the
blundering, frantic bird," she wants to cry out "Abuse! Abuse!" as
the nurse had about Fay's action. "Enough is enough!" Fay had
screamed to her father before seizing him: yet if Laurel confronted her
with what she had done, Fay would not acknowledge her fault—she
had only "been making a little scene." But Laurel *must* unburden her
knowledge to someone.

She suffers the first lightning flash of self-revelation this long night
when she realizes that for the sake of relief she would have been will-

ing to tell her mother of Fay's crimes, produce the "damnable evidence," in order to be herself consoled. Then the drumming of the bird on the door and Laurel's growing fear drive her into a little adjoining sewing room, which contains her mother's secretary and her own study table, an old slipper chair, a trunk, the sewing machine. She had slept in this room as a child, securely close to her parents. The room is a retreat: "Firelight and warmth—that was what her memory gave her." Here, when her mother or the sewing woman had worked, Laurel had made scraps of cloth fallen on the floor "into patterns, families, on the sweet-smelling matting, with the shine of firelight, or the summer light, moving over mother and child and what they were both making." It is as hushed and softly bright a memory as the mind can conceive of this child and her mother, their hands and imaginations busy, making patterns, with the double benediction of love and light hovering over them—a Vermeer painting.

Memory moves back now, first tenderly and nostalgically, then with increasing tough-mindedness, putting together the patterns of her own family. In her mother's desk, stored in pigeonholes, Laurel finds her mother's letters, including many from her father ("My darling sweetheart . . ."), and a little boat, carved from slatey stone by her father, and given to her mother when they were courting. In a snapshot album she finds pictures of her parents, and remembers her mother's description of the most beautiful blouse she'd ever had, cloth spun by her mother, dyed a deep, rich American Beauty color with pokeberries, designed and sewn by herself. The passages devoted to memories—Laurel's, her mother's, and grandmother's—collected from family stories and her own recollections of summer visits when her mother went "up home," are purely lyrical. They celebrate the strength and daring of the "darling and vain" girl her mother had been in her West Virginia home: at fifteen, traveling to Baltimore by river raft and train with her dying father and returning with his body in a coffin, running back into their burning house to retrieve her father's complete set of Dickens, riding miles on horseback each day to her teaching post.

Insight comes to Laurel by way of remembered "outsight": images, incidents, scenes with resonance, many of them involving birds—horrible and frightening up close or out of place, beautiful at a distance. Grandma's pigeons had come under her close scrutiny as a child. She was expected to feed them and enjoy it; they frightened her badly, she

hated them, and never told anybody. "Laurel . . . had already seen a
pair of them sticking their beaks down each other's throats, gagging
each other, eating out of each other's craws, swallowing down all over
again what had been swallowed before: they were taking turns. . . .
the other pigeons copied them. They convinced her that they could
not escape each other and could not themselves be escaped from." Her
grandmother had reassured her, "They're just hungry, like we are."

Laurel had not resigned herself to that analogy, her sense of human
privacy, dignity, inviolability being as strong as that of the child in
"A Memory." To Laurel as adult, the aggressive behavior, the crude
forms of family solidarity and individual selfishness revealed by the
Chisoms and Dalzells, are fresh evidence not so much of the "humanity" of pigeon behavior as its obverse. But she cannot fence off her
abhorrence of suffocating family "closeness" by limiting it to the offensive behavior of those who have no sense of pattern, of the meaning
of their own experience or the life and death of loved ones. Even as a
child, she knew how all "parents and children take turns back and
forth, changing places, protecting and protesting each other," and as
an adult she knows how husbands and wives repeat the process. She
knows further what damaging forms both the protecting and the protesting may take when love goes very deep, when sensibilities are
fine, and will is strong.

Her mother had been unable to save her father in Baltimore or her
own mother, who died unexpectedly and alone when Becky was happily married in Mount Salus. She had blamed herself; the Judge had
protested, protectingly, "You are not to blame yourself, Becky, do
you hear me?" Her mother had protested back, "You can't make me
lie to myself, Clinton!" Laurel "did not any longer believe that anyone could be saved, anyone at all. Not from others."

Though at first confident of recovery when her vision failed, Becky
had slowly turned hopeless, yielding to "the storms that began coming to her out of her darkness," and to despair, not only for herself,
but for her loved ones. To Laurel the Judge had seemed helpless
against his wife's illness, had not "passionately enough grieved at the
changes in her," had "needed guidance in order to see the tragic."
Unable or unwilling to follow her in the tortuous ways of protracted
suffering, he had started being "what he scowlingly called an optimist," promised Becky recovery, said he'd carry her back to her
mountain home. "Lucifer! . . . Liar!" Becky had cried. His betrayal
had been his refusal to take her desperation seriously. Lying in dark-

ness, waiting for death, Becky's time had run into the future. She had "predicted" Fay, knowing where her husband's weakness might at any time and finally did lead.

And yet Laurel's most vivid memory is of "her mother holding and holding onto their hands, her own and her father's holding onto her mother's long after there was nothing more to be said." Even fore-knowledge of betrayal cannot break the strong bonds of love nor the memory of those bonds in desperate moments.

The terrors of Laurel's vigil are not over. If loved ones cannot be "saved" from each other, Laurel cannot be safe, even from her dead husband. At the end of the stormy night of revelation he calls back to her across the distance of years and death, "his eyes wild with craving for his unlived life, with mouth open like a funnel's." Like an exceptionally complacent pigeon, Laurel has been chewing and swallowing for a long time, content to leave him in his secure, static place (Chicago) far from home, and in the distant past—part of a brief wedded life of "magical ease," ideal and idealized, perfected to Philip's own high architect's standards in memory, never subjected to the hazards of a living, continuing relationship. However beautiful in its beginnings, it might have ended like her parents' in tragic misunderstanding and an alienation terminated only by death. While she listens, through the wind, to Philip's voice crying for life, "wanting it," demanding it of her now, she weeps "for what happened to life."

Exhausted from so much seeing ("Humankind cannot bear very much reality," says T. S. Eliot), Laurel falls asleep in the chair. Part Four begins with her awake, feeling strangely rested and restored. She has dreamed of an actual incident when, riding on a train with Phil to be married in Mount Salus, they had at dawn seen from a high point a grand pattern of confluence in motion, the beautiful merging of the Ohio and the Mississippi rivers. Far above, Philip had noticed "the long, ragged, pencil-faint line of birds within the crystal of the zenith, flying in a V of their own, following the same course down. All they could see was sky, water, birds, light, and confluence. It was the whole morning world." Laurel had felt that "they themselves were part of the confluence. Their own joint act of faith had brought them here at the very moment and matched its occurrence, and proceeded as it proceeded. Direction itself was made beautiful, momentous. They were riding as one with it, right up front. It's our turn! she'd thought exultantly. And we're going to live forever."

It *had* been their turn—briefly, but perfectly; they had discovered their complementary polarities in a marriage "without a single blunder." But it can be *nobody's* turn for a *perfect* confluence of faith, hope, and love, for very long. Set in motion by living and by time's passing, marriages and families are destroyed from within and without. Phil had been killed soon afterward in World War II combat. "Left bodiless and graveless of a death made of water and fire in a year long gone, Phil could still tell her of her life. For her life, any life, she had to believe, was nothing but the continuity of its love."

A few last trials await Laurel: getting rid of the intruders—the chimney swift ("all birds got to fly, even them no-count dirty ones" says Missouri, reminding one of Grandma's comment on the offensive pigeons); the crass, snooping Mr. Cheek; finally Fay, desecrater of the house. Fay returns early, just as Laurel discovers, in a kitchen cupboard, a breadboard Philip had made for her mother. It had been beautifully planed and crafted, "made on the true," a "labor of love"; Phil had loved the bread her mother made on it. Over the breadboard Laurel confronts Fay with what she did in laying hands on her father while he was dying, with desecrating the house; Fay angrily, jeeringly, denies not only guilt, but any knowledge of what Laurel is talking about. Laurel holds the breadboard tightly, and raises it, then lowers it, remembering Wendell (Fay's lost innnocence and vulnerability as a child). When Fay asks, "What do you see in that thing?" Laurel answers, "The whole story, Fay. The whole solid past." But the past is nothing to Fay, who knows no feeling, no love nor the respect for the dead, and flings back, "I belong to the future, didn't you know that?"

If the past is solid, actual, unchanging, and, for Laurel, supporting, she knows that it is also "impervious." The dead can no longer be either hurt or helped—mercifully, when it comes to people like Fay. Neither can she herself protest or affect the past in any way. Yet memory, "the somnambulist," keeps it alive; memory, always vulnerable, is yet merciful; "it lives for us, and while it lives, and while we are able, we can give it up its due."

Having burned all her mother's letters and all but one of her keepsakes, Laurel refuses now to take even the cherished breadboard. "Memory lived not in initial possession but in the free hands, pardoned and freed, and in the heart that can empty but fill again, in the patterns restored by dreams." Emptied of feeling the preceding night by awareness of her parents' and her own complicity in the kind

of selfishness more comfortably assigned to vulgar and insensitive people or rapacious pigeons, Laurel's night dream of an actual event, a
time of hope and expectations, refills her heart with love. Emptied
once again by her confrontation with Fay, Laurel's heart fills once
again as she thinks of the durability of memory and the power of
dreams to restore the internal harmony of patterns—the lives of loved
ones and her own in relation to them, seen, interpreted, understood
with a changed and enriched perspective.

Like no other work since a few of Eudora Welty's early stories, *The
Optimist's Daughter* comes shrouded in what I have earlier called the
dark or "sorrowful" mysteries of life and death, finally impenetrable.
The weighting of terrible ambiguities and contraries in the novel has
left many readers moved by its depth and beauty as by no other of
Eudora Welty's works, and yet strangely baffled and saddened, as if
the revelations heaped on Laurel, the understanding won by this intelligent, sensitive, truthful, and loving woman were not the final
truth of the novel. From somewhere over and behind the vision of an
entirely "reliable" central intelligence, the reader must seek to discover the patterns of meaning in this intricately woven work.

Laurel Hand is a professional designer of fabrics in Chicago, a creator of designs and figures on material suited to their functions. She
is no "decorator" but a genuine artist: she works in a studio, on
"commission." She *thinks* like an artist, has always done so, even
played like one as a child, making patterns of the fallen scraps of
cloth from her mother's sewing. As always, Eudora Welty suits her
metaphors to the specific consciousness of her character, and creates
some beautiful images for her heroine's kind of artistic sensibility.
Here, for example, is Laurel's memory of the sound of her parents'
reading: "She was sent to sleep under a velvety cloak of words, richly
patterned and stitched with gold, straight out of a fairy tale, while
they went reading on into her dreams." Her architect husband Philip
had "taught her to draw, to work toward and into her pattern, not
to sketch peripheries." Good design for Laurel is a matter of integrity, order, value, and it had been so for Philip, who was *not* an optimist, knowing that houses designed with care and devotion to *last*
"could equally well be built of cards."

Laurel is always aware of the inner dimension of pattern as it is
made visible, by light, through its creation and discovery in time and
space. On the Carnival night of her father's death, as she is impelled

by a sense of foreboding back to the hospital and walks down the corridor, she has an experience of mystery and ambiguity externalized in images of light and pattern:

A strange milky radiance shone in a hospital corridor at night, like moonlight on some deserted street. The whitened floor, the whitened walls and ceiling, were set with narrow bands of black receding into the distance, along which the spaced-out doors, graduated from large to small, were all closed. Laurel had never noticed the design in the tiling before, like some clue she would need to follow to get to the right place. But of course the last door on the right of the corridor, the one standing partway open as usual, was still her father's.

The "clue . . . to the right place" in the novel might be the discovery of the pattern of ambiguity symbolized by receding black bands on white in a design difficult to *visualize*. A "milky raidance" is beautiful, but cloudy; the mystery of closed doors suggests impenetrability in human character, relationships, or meaning in the universe; the door standing partway open leads to the most ambiguous character in the novel, Judge McKelva, engaged in one of the most ambiguous acts of his life, dying.

Who and what is he? Before his surgery Laurel had looked at him searchingly. "In the limelight glare of New Orleans, waiting for the ambulance without questioning the need for it, he seemed for the first time in her memory a man admitting to a little uncertainty in his bearings." When Laurel is outraged at the "falsifying" (her mother's word) of him before his open coffin, she reflects that "the mystery in how little we know of other people is no greater than the mystery of how much. . . ." Despite her certain knowledge of his modesty, his dislike of "theatrics," his incapacity for heroic action, his love of her mother, she knows him no better than he knows himself. Did Becky know him—herself the daring, heroic one who at fifteen had traveled to Baltimore by raft and train with her dying father and astonished the doctors because she didn't know anyone in that big city? But Becky hadn't needed to because "she had known herself." How could the Judge have "doted on" and "spoiled" Fay after so many years of love and intimacy with the extraordinary Becky? How, for that matter, could the lightweight Major Bullock have been his best, most trusted friend?

In "predicting" Fay, Becky had perceived the fault in the design and fabric of his character—the need to protect and indulge a woman.

It becomes, finally, a form of self-indulgence. Becky had herself indulged that need until her illness made it no more possible for him to give her what she *didn't* want (such as the heavy beaded crepe dress that had to be kept in a bucket) than what she did (a return to health, a visit "up home").

In marrying Fay the Judge had yielded to his need to indulge, find solace in, a woman perceived as in need of protection. Sexual indulgence is implicit in this pattern. Becky's genuinely passionate nature, symbolized by the true American Beauty red of her hand-dyed and home-woven-and-sewn blouse, had given way to the sexy "foolish" pink satin of Fay's marital bed and the Judge's coffin. A wearer of the panama hat, the Judge appears to have had a streak of Uncle Daniel Ponder in him, compromising his dignity, making him slightly absurd, like another of those gallant Southern hat-wearers, King MacLain. But if the Judge has the Ponder heart, its object, Fay, is more dangerous than Bonnie Dee Peacock, even though she resembles her in slightness, a fluffy woman with curly blonde hair of "tow texture" which looks as if, "well rubbed between the fingers, those curls might have gone to powder." Empowered by "nature" and her unthinking, rapacious family, Fay desecrates his home and destroys the beautiful, valuable patterns of his life with Becky.

Yet Laurel remains herself indulgent to her father's memory, as though recognizing in his defect the excess of his virtues—affection, delicacy, gentleness. She sees him as dying "worn out with both wives," being caught between "too much love and too little." The Judge remains an ambiguous though chiefly sympathetic character with an amiable weakness that led to a cheapening of his character, a kind of "comic flaw."

Nor is Becky "perfect" from the same perspective, though hers is more like a "tragic flaw." She had lived her early life as a series of tests or trials more or less successfully met by her answering courage, loyalty, truth. She had been brave to the point of recklessness where duty or loved persons or things were concerned (the two converged when she saved her father's set of Dickens from their burning house). Throughout her life she had judged everything and everyone by her own high standards; had been unable to see what the pigeons were doing to each other because when she looked closely it was "to verify something—the truth or a mistake; hers or another's." But she was helpless against the supreme antagonist, death, and all its harbingers: weakness, disease, blindness, the confusion of old age. As a girl she

could not save her father, but she had tried. Later she judged herself
severely for not having been present to save her mother when she was
alone and ill.

Tested by the long years of waiting in her own physical weakness
and blindness, Becky shows none of the Judge's capacity for gentleness and patience. If the Judge is too vapid in his optimism, Becky
is too virulent in her despair, inconsolable, suspicious, bent on preserving her blind misery intact, incapable of anything like resignation. She accuses her husband of being a coward, allowing her to be
punished. To him and Laurel she says, " 'All you do is hurt me. I
wish I might know what it is I've done. Why is it necessary to punish
me like this and not tell me why?' And still she held fast to their
hands, to Laurel's too. Her cry was not complaint; it was anger at
wanting to know and being denied knowledge; it was love's deep
anger."

From out of her torment, Becky calls for "spiritual guidance"; the
Presbyterian minister is summoned, but his visit is "not well taken."
Becky outcites him in Scripture reading. Her feats of memory had
been part of her very courage and resourcefulness as she had recited
poetry while riding on horseback to her teaching post. Blind, she recited "The Cataract of Lodore" as though the better she recalled it,
"the better she could defend her case in some trial that seemed to be
going on against her life." She counters Dr. Bolt's question whether
God intends her to return to her mountain home "with a barb," defy-
ing him to find anything "as delicate, as fragrant" as the wild white
strawberries growing in a hidden spot in the mountains, asking to be
eaten at once. She seems to be challenging religious piety to offer anything to match the wonders of nature "up home," the seat of her joy.

This intrepid soul has all her life tried to *be* God in saving and
protecting her loved ones. And she summons herself and everyone to
judgment as though she *were* God, finds everyone guilty, and is outraged to find them so. But in this novel God is not justice, love,
mercy, but time, chance, fate—blind, as in classical myth. In wrestling with such an antagonist, the blind Becky is fighting a losing
battle. Finally disoriented from a stroke, she believes herself to be in
some strange place among aliens, dying "in exile and humiliation."
Her last remark to Laurel is deeply wounding: "You could have saved
your mother's life. But you stood by and wouldn't intervene. I despair for you."

The accusation of abandonment of her mother had been a deranged

"falsifying" when it came to Laurel; but the judgment glances off
ironically on Laurel's relationship to her father. She might well have
"saved" him from Fay had she allowed her father the privilege of in-
dulging *her,* his and Becky's only child. She might have gone to Eu-
rope with him when he invited her shortly before he met and quickly
married Fay. She is openly blamed for her non-involvement at home
by an old neighbor. By the time her father has set himself in patience
toward dying, Laurel no longer believes that people can save or be
saved from each other, but that is a truth only partially tested in relation to her father. Once her mother died, she had let go her hands
from the strong triangle of support and dependence that kept the
three of them together, when hope was gone.

Yet Laurel's integrity is her finest quality and keeps the pattern of
her own values clear, their structure solid. She rejects all cheap,
shoddy forms of motive and behavior in herself and others, just as
Philip would have nothing to do, as an architect, with an assignment
to Camouflage in World War II. She rejects the lies told about her
father, but also the ways of consoling herself that might be hurtful
to others. She listens in silence to Miss Adele's defense of Fay without
producing the "damning evidence" of Fay's role in her father's early
death: she protects her father's memory at the expense of being herself
justified in the eyes of her best friends. She rejects the use of physical
force on Fay, though Miss Tennyson, who had slapped Fay after her
hysterical display before the funeral, thinks Fay needs "a crowning
. . . over the head with a good solid piece of something." As a symbol of "the whole solid past," the breadboard would have broken like
air over Fay's head had its story been told. As an actual plank, the
breadboard could have inflicted serious physical injury, but that could
only have turned back on Laurel, reducing her to the size of the spit-
ting, biting, clawing feist that Fay, embattled, becomes.

The pattern of ambiguity, plural truths contained, enables the
reader to see Laurel's withdrawal from conflict as a moral triumph,
while perceiving that her values have suffered immediate defeat. Left
in charge is Fay, who will destroy everything truly valuable in the
house, starting with "that old striking clock" she had always hated.
Her challenge, "I belong to the future, didn't you know that?" is om-
inous: one thinks of the end of Chekhov's *Cherry Orchard.* "Gentle"
folk do not inherit the earth, nor even spirited and courageous mountain folk.

The implications of Laurel's defeat to the future of the Mount Salus community are also, however, ambiguous. Should the Chisoms move on into it with their wrecking business after finishing with Madrid, and Mrs. Chisom make a boarding house out of the McKelva home as she threatens to do, there would be no stopping them. The deep freeze of social hostility would pass them by as surely as death had. But class is no true indicator of value in the novel. As Miss Adele perceives, the Chisoms and the McKelvas' closest friends are engaged in "rivalry" at the funeral, and on that occasion neither side appears much better than the other. Major Bullock's partiality to Fay inclines him toward the Chisom side of the conflict: it was he who invited the Chisoms, to Fay's surprise and irritation, until she becomes aware that without them she would have had no fit audience for her fine performance and favorable judgment on the obviously costly funeral she had ordered.

But the more underlying battle in *The Optimist's Daughter* is between two great interrelated families of persons: those who know how to feel, love, honor, and practice the truth, understand the importance of life and death, live fully and passionately to create value and meaning in their own and others' lives—and those who do not. Those who do not create, destroy. The creators' existence has little if anything to do with wealth, class, race. The Courtlands were once poor, but not "trash": Laurel sees in the "experienced face" of the doctor an expression "utterly guileless. The Mississsippi country that lay behind him was all in it." The black servant Missouri, whom the Judge had helped in a trial, is part of the family of spiritual artistocrats. Robbie Reid of *Delta Wedding,* a "poor white," socioeconomic sister of Bonnie Dee Peacock and Wanda Fay Chisom, is rightfully married to George Fairchild, since like him she belongs to the family of people who love.

In doing battle, members of the self-ignorant, uncaring family fight, just as they think, simplistically, to protect themselves and their clans. Fay fights like an animal. The men fight with guns, in the pioneer tradition. In the hospital waiting room where the Dalzells are spread out, on a television screen "a pale-blue group of Westerners silently shot it out with one another." Little Texan Wendell arrives at the funeral dressed in a cowboy suit and hat and double pistol-holders—somebody's idea of suitable garb for what is to be the learning experience of his first funeral. When Major Bullock pronounces the Judge "goodness itself" and Fay screams in protest, "Why did he do me so *bad?*" Wendell pipes up, "Don't cry! I'll shoot the bad man

for you." He knows that you shoot the bad guys and protect the
women of your family. Riding away from Mount Salus, he shoots his
gun at everybody from the back of the truck crying, "Pow! Pow!
Pow!" in his "thin, wistful voice." If he is to retain his tender spirit
in that family, he may have to take the course of an older brother, a
suicide by oven-gas inhalation.

The future lies with children. The novel closes with Miss Adele
and her first graders waving goodbye: the "twinkling" of "the many
small hands" is the last sight empty-handed, full-hearted Laurel
Hand has of Mount Salus. These children have a more auspicious beginning than Wendell's, but this is no guarantee of what will become
of them, nor which of the two great interrelated families each child
will eventually belong to. Most of them will probably discover what
Ellen Fairchild (of *Delta Wedding*) found: that "the real fight is *in* us
already, . . . *in* people on earth, not *between* us. . . . It's over things
like the truth, and what you owe people." Eudora Welty shows the
field of combat to be as small as a single person's mind and heart, as
wide as international combat. The *kamikaze* (Japanese fighters) had
come close enough for Philip to shake their hands—then killed
him—from a distance with a planted mine. His work as a communi-
cations officer had been in a battle for freedom forcing everyone to
choose up sides. Years later, when the Judge needs eye surgery, Dr.
Courtland suggests that a Dr. Kunomoto perform the operation since
he has "a more radical method" of dealing with a detached retina.
With time, enemy races turn friends in the healing arts. And it is
time Dr. Courtland fights against, trying to save the Judge's eye, since
the other eye is afflicted with a growing cataract. The doctor fights
for the Judge's *sight* in his old age. But against "the universal cataract
of death" (Robert Frost's phrase) there is no prevention.

Throughout Eudora Welty's fiction, the battle between right and
wrong is joined most clearly within the single human heart. In that
battle Laurel attains her spiritual freedom. It is she who finally sets
free the imprisoned, menacing bird; with a blow of air, it ascends and
becomes a crescent against the sky, harmless and beautiful back in its
natural element. Laurel takes nothing with her as a keepsake of the
past, unless it is the little river soapstone boat her father had made
for her mother in their courting days "up home." When Laurel tries
to give it to Miss Adele, her old friend presses it in her hand as something she must "cling to." The little stone boat—the love between
her parents—is the one thing she may cling to out of the house which

lies, after the storm, "like a ship that has tossed all night and come to harbor."

The season of the novel is spring, season of flowers; their beauty permeates the work. Becky had loved them, named her daughter after the West Virginia state flower, a spring blossomer; planted, pruned, and tended each plant and species in her large garden like so many persons and families. On the day of the Judge's funeral the house is overflowing with them, and they are named, evoked—the catalog of flowers in this elegiac novel. The Judge has had his favorite camellia, "the old-fashioned Chandlerii Elegans," planted on his wife's grave; on the day of his funeral Laurel finds it in bloom, "big as a pony," like the ones she rode "up home," "saddled with unplucked bloom living and dead standing on a fading carpet of its own flowers." The following day Laurel works in her mother's garden as a memorial act, and while tending to "Becky's Climber," she thinks, "Memory returned like spring . . . had the character of spring. In some cases it was the old wood that did the blooming." That climber had been old, with roots "utterly strong": Becky had judged it to be "maybe a hundred years old." The rose bush becomes "the great rooted blossomer" of the McKelva family just as the bois d'arc tree is of the Vaughn-Beecham clan in *Losing Battles*. But it is as fated to be cut down as Chekhov's cherry orchard. Fay will see to it, as she has seen to the Judge's burial where graves are decorated with fake, out-of-season poinsettias, without the life or fragrance of memory.

The specific job to which Laurel will return in Chicago is the design of a theater curtain for a repertory company. This detail too opens out suggestively as literary art (drama) and visual art (design) converge, the functions of a curtain are pondered, and the design of this particular life drama becomes clear. The infinite value of what imagination holds, in *life* on the stage of memory, lies partly in its tenuous nature, its vulnerability. In the novel we are shown how the curtain can fall at any moment. Advancing age and disease cause slippages of memory, confusion, absolute loss of large chunks of what is precious in life. Death stops memory, along with life. The survivor of the death of loved ones is left with ambiguous feelings of guilt, questions about the *nature* of the reality that once was, the story that survives as indelible and treasured to the survivor. The state or condition of being alive or dead becomes blurred; dreams, fantasies, and hallucinations become their dim or vivid meeting ground, the mind of the somnabulist. "What's happening isn't real," says Laurel to herself at the funeral. Philip appears to her as an apparition, Lazarus from the dead: a ghost so furious and demanding as to make her own existence seem ghostly. The dead of Mount Salus, fixed in their graves, appear as travelers in another realm. "The top of the hill ahead was crowded with winged angels and life-sized effigies of bygone citizens in old-fashioned dress, standing as if by count among the columns and shafts and conifers like a familiar set of passengers collected on deck of a ship, on which they all knew each other—bonafide members of a small local excursion, embarked on a voyage that is always returning in dreams." At one point Laurel thinks, "The fantasies of the dying could be no stranger than the fantasies of the living. Surviving is perhaps the strangest fantasy of them all."

Laurel shows no more hope nor confidence in a divine "surround" than had her parents or husband. For all his churchgoing, her father, when alive, had seemed unable to get much beyond the awareness of Dr. Bolt's opening prayer at the funeral: "Heavenly father, may this serve to remind us that we have each and every one of us been fearfully and wonderfully made." Laurel seems to recall her father's using the words in his table blessing.

The vision of the novel is not that of *Hamlet*: "There's a divinity that shapes our ends / Rough-hew them how we will." Rather, it is that of *The Tempest*: "We are such stuff / As dreams are made on, and our little life / Is rounded with a sleep." In *The Optimist's Daughter*, "the whole solid past" narrowly misses dissipation into the insubstantial "stuff" of dreams. For all its ambiguity, it takes on substance and solidity because the author, through imagination, has transformed memory into story, into art, which is long, though life is short.

Chapter Eleven
A Continuous Thread of Revelation

"The events of our lives happen in a sequence in time, but in their significance to ourselves they find their own order, a timetable not necessarily—perhaps not possibly—chronological. The time as we know it subjectively is often the chronology that stories and novels follow: it is the continuous thread of revelation." Thus Eudora Welty summarizes the method of her autobiography, *One Writer's Beginnings*. The voice of memory speaks with an artlessly rambling progress, revealing, celebrating—mostly her beloved parents, to whom the book is dedicated. Personal experience and family history are blended with observations about her development and practice as a fiction writer.

Much is achieved in the hundred pages of this book. Though the comparison may seem absurd for a work so brief and modest in its claims, it is a private odyssey, an inward journey or quest for the self as writer, of the same nature as Wordsworth's *Prelude* or Joyce's *Portrait of the Artist as a Young Man*. It is a compendium of private human insight and wisdom flexible in tone—playful, sorrowful, satirical. It is also something more public, wholly justifying its original sponsorship as a series of three lectures in the History of American Civilization program at Harvard University: a vivid re-creation, over more than a century of places, persons, and experiences remembered and tales told, of the physical settings, manners, customs, values, and beliefs of three independent though, in the writer's life, convergent American types: the educated Appalachian "pioneer" (her mother's roots), the midwestern farmer (her father's roots), and the small-town "New South" Mississippian (her own and her brothers' roots).

Wonderful is her evocation of early twentieth-century American character types. Miss Duling, big brass bell in hand, ringing and summoning all vagrant, unruly children to march to their learning, is the Ur-teacher-principal: self-denying, stern, dedicated, omniscient, controlling the town, "a lifelong subscriber to perfection," the most "whole-souled figure of authority" Eudora Welty ever knew. Other teachers, and there are many, are variants on the type which came to be the most usual "heroine" of her fiction. Miss Calloway, she of the "dragon eye," "a witch," is the Ur-librarian, bastion of petty public morality, insistent on SILENCE except for her own "commanding voice," strict enforcer of rules intended to prevent books and readers, like lovers, from achieving their joyful unions. A friend of her mother's (nameless) is the Ur-Southern storyteller, garrulous monologist, gifted with the power to create scenes and dialogue, locate the drama in any situation ("the crisis had come!"), above all, *invent*. Nearer to home and more lovingly described are the types represented by her grandparents: many-talented Edward ("Ned") Andrews, energetic, forward-looking, flamboyant, legend-making mountain lawyer; Eudora Carden Andrews, "fine-grained," gracious, large-spirited, resourceful, whose lifelong exercise of courage, independence, and tolerance became the "mountain strain" in her daughter and granddaughter (namesake); Jefferson Welty, the pious, gentle, saturnine, hardworking farmer. As the direct descendent of these people who embodied the American character at its best, Eudora Welty has always shown in her life and work how truly she inherited their native virtues.

The first two sections ("Listening" and "Learning to See") are concerned chiefly with the writer's preparation; the last ("Finding a Voice"), her performance; but the progression is not chronological. It is spiraling, with overlapping time periods, sense impressions, themes. She proceeds always from the particular to the general, stressing that connections can be made only by the use of hindsight, and that patterns are discovered through memory: to use Richard Wilbur's phrase, only as they are "wrought . . . in the tapestries of afterthought." She speaks of how, in writing about her parents, new connections in their lives became evident to her—perhaps because she is a fiction writer—making her perceive them "as even greater mysteries" than she knew. Writing fiction has given her "an abiding respect for the unknown in a human lifetime and a sense of where to look for the threads, how to follow, how to connect, find in the thick of the tangle what clear line persists." While retaining my own abiding respect for the mysteries of Eudora Welty's life and fiction, I have attempted in this final chapter to weave some threads, newly visible to me since reading the autobiography, into patterns, through which runs "the continuous thread of revelation."

The chief revelation to me of *One Writer's Beginnings* is the importance of lyricism to *all* of Eudora Welty's fiction—something I first
perceived in *The Bride of the Innisfallen*. Bringing to her stories the
emotional, aesthetic, and even logical expectations that we bring to
the experience of music, song, poetry, I am convinced, results in the
best reading of them.[1] This begins with awareness of the celebrative
impulse that she says is the source of her fiction—the desire "to
praise, to love, to call up into view." The reader should be prepared
for something "more felt than seen ahead like prophecy" (to borrow
Robert Frost's words about poetry), a certain "wildness of logic" to
be found in lyrical works—the surprise and delight of choices made
from an abundance of possibilities supplied by imagination. Lyricism
affects form, language, subjects, themes, tone, and sound in Eudora
Welty's fiction, and it is evident from the first in her autobiography.
    She opens with a kind of prose poem, epigraph, or musical pre-
lude, which appears by itself on the first page, italicized:

When I was young enough to still spend a long time buttoning my shoes in
the morning, I'd listen toward the hall: Daddy upstairs was shaving in the
bathroom and Mother downstairs was frying the bacon. They would begin
whistling back and forth to each other up and down the stairwell. My father
would whistle his phrase, my mother would try to whistle, then hum hers
back. It was their duet. I drew my buttonhook in and out and listened to
it—I knew it was "The Merry Widow." The difference was, their song almost floated with laughter: how different from the record, which growled
from the beginning, as if the Victrola were only slowly being wound up.
They kept it running between them, up and down the stairs where I was
now just about ready to run clattering down and show them my shoes.

    The child "tunes in" to her parents' lovely way of making their
own habitual morning tasks light; for the song, whistled and
hummed up and down, back and forth, while the buttonhook is
rhythmically drawn in and out, seems to take on corporal existence
in her. Readers who know "The Merry Widow" waltz (as is true of
any musical reference) will have a sharpened perception of this musical love exchange: the short phrases are antiphonal, a dialogue of
identical phrases slowly lifts on the musical scale, the tune is fluid on
the musical "stairs"; it ends as the little girl stands ready to run "clattering" down them. The "live" music's human imperfection (her
mother's failed attempt to whistle), countered by its human perfection (their song floats with laughter while the Victrola growls) is part

of the transformation of what's commonplace or necessary (their morning tasks) to something delightful. The child's containment, through listening, of an overflowing pleasure in what's heard; her sense of inclusion, expectancy, confidence in loving approval to follow, and the promise of the new day to be lived excitedly within the shelter of parental love—all these feelings are packed into the small buttonshoed listener who is to become the writer and lift her own song, decades later, in praise of the beloved parents. The lyrical prelude, utterly simple and pure in language, becomes not only a tribute, but also an invocation to the muses of her fiction.

The pattern of lyricism continues throughout the book, for the writer's memories seem almost literally to be strung on song and rhythm.[2] "Listening" begins with clocks striking, answering each other through the house, ticking in rhythm to her mother's rocker as she reads stories to Eudora before the fire, the cuckoo clock ending the story with "Cuckoo." Her earliest memories of listening include the sound of her mother's song, coming out "just a little bit in the minor key," making "Wee Willie Winkie" seem "wonderfully sad." Next comes the Victrola, offering opportunities for lullabies, marches, and musical comedy hits at her pleasure, with movement (especially dancing) as part of it, for movement is "at the very heart of listening." The observation leads the writer to reflect that from the time of her own earliest reading, she *heard* whatever was on the page, as though a silent voice, "human, but inward," were speaking—"the voice of the story or the poem itself." "The cadence, whatever it is that asks you to believe, the feeling that resides in the printed word, reaches me through the reader-voice." Her awareness of this voice, especially in its unique rhythm and movement within any particular story or poem, seems to be part of the lyrical impulse informing her work—something *heard*, almost musically, the sound and flow of the sentences testing their truth, reflecting the various moods of her fiction.

Some songs are gregarious, uproarious, made for family and group singing: the Methodist hymns learned in Sunday School, often juxtaposing dire content with cheerful ("Throw out the lifeline! Throw out the lifeline! Someone is sinking today!"); the rousing folk songs, ballads, and hymns sung a cappella or with banjos or other instruments by her mother's five entertaining brothers in West Virginia, inheritors of their father's "strong need of music." This is the robust lyricism of *Losing Battles*. The strange "chimelike" sound of a music box at her grandfather Welty's—one of the few sounds to break the "solid stillness" of the farmhouse, "faint and unearthly" with its metal discs, a "sparse" and "remote" music—induces a mood of inescapable loneliness as she thinks of her father's lonely boyhood, so different from her mother's joyfully crowded girlhood. This is a music for lonely children like Jenny Lockhart and Joel Mayes, or adults like Clytie and Livvie.

Away at the Mississippi State Woman's College the developing writer mingles in her thoughts the sound of a piano played by an enviably solitary music student, in an overcrowded school ("Pale Hands I Loved Beside the Shalimar") with a romantic poem of yearning ("I have a need of silence and of stars"). Her intense longing is not so much for the "Home" of the poem's title, but the elusive, distant place and condition. "In the beautiful spring night, I was dedicated to *wanting* a beautiful spring night." She wanted to be *"transported"*— the essence of romantic longing conveyed in song and verse. This is the music of all the dreaming, yearning people in, for instance, the overcrowded house of Shellmound, through which Mary Lamar Lakey's piano music drifts constantly in *Delta Wedding*. A couple of years later at the University of Wisconsin Eudora Welty is smitten by the poetry of Yeats, especially "The Song of the Wandering Aengus," which would become the lyric poem running through *The Golden Apples*. It was *passion* she discovered there—the passion of the wanderer on a romantic quest for love and adventure—and fed into her fictional characters.

From all her work, she selects the character of the German-speaking music teacher from "June Recital" as the one in whose *making* she achieved the essence of her own fictional voice. The life and identity of this music teacher in no way resembled her own, and yet she realized that "Miss Eckhart came from me. . . . What I have put into her is my passion for my own life work, my own art. Exposing yourself to risk is a truth Miss Eckhart and I had in common. What animates and possesses me is what drives Miss Eckhart, the love of her art and the desire to give it until there is no more left." In *creating* this character she found her most "inward and deeply feeling self." Miss Eckhart's passion is viewed from a distance, the emotional remove of the child Cassie, an observer, who feels, in response to the music teacher's wild sonata playing during a sudden morning storm, that "something had burst out, unwanted, exciting, from the wrong person's life." Cassie looks for an escape. Only the mature Virgie

Rainey begins to comprehend her old teacher after the remove of time. She had offered Virgie *"the* Beethoven"—the great Romantic composer who had absorbed the hero and the victim and had *that* passion to give. Yet the Beethoven who seems closer in feeling to the author's in "June Recital," as to Cassie's, is the composer of *"Für Elise"*—that tender, affecting tune in a minor key.

The lyrical impulse seems closely related to Eudora Welty's often expressed preference for the short story of indeterminate length as a fictional form. The form permits—indeed requires—a writer to select a single situation, raise feeling to a high level and maintain its tension, carry its mood, achieve its wholeness and intensity, as though conveyed straight from writer's to reader's mind. The time period of a single reading should be the felt time of composition, for writer and reader are "caught up" by the same intensity, as in a song or a poem. The time period of writing nearly *was* the same as reading time for some of Eudora Welty's early stories.

It seems no chance that "Powerhouse," written directly after she heard Fats Waller and his group perform, precisely catches up the sound and feel of the great black jazz performer's music—its improvisation, syncopation, verbal and instrumental "conversations," wide and fluid range of feeling, color and texture of human and instrumental voices. That story may well have been one of the greatest risks in fiction writing the author ever took, an experiment brilliantly carried off. It must be the story she has read most often in public. (The power that entertainers exerted upon her, not always musicians but always travelers, is something she speaks of in *One Writer's Beginnings*.) Freedom, authority, risk-taking, passion, discipline, and gift-giving are what Eudora Welty has in common with Miss Eckhart, Powerhouse, and every traveling entertainer-artist she ever saw or imagined or wrote about.

The lyric voice in Eudora Welty's stories is as various as are the stories themselves, but a few patterns may be distinguished within stories making use of some pure or modified "outside" (dramatic) or "inside" (interior) point of view. In dramatic monologues the lyricism seems to be carried by the Southern conversational or tale-telling voice. In such works as *The Ponder Heart,* "Why I Live at the P.O.," and "Shower of Gold," the teller seems at one with the tale, and has an equal claim on our amused attention (for these are largely comic stories). There are notable exceptions: "The Whole World Knows" is a lament, and "Where Is the Voice Coming From?" defies categories,

though it seems both complaint and boast. This last-named story creates a disturbing split in the reader's response as pleasure in the murderer's lyrical Mississippi country dialect is defeated by revulsion and
horror at his action and his trivial motives and preoccupations. In
"Petrified Man" a hidden and detached observer-narrator defers to the
speaking voices of the denizens of Leota's beauty parlor, whose conversation proves there can be such a thing as a lyricism of vulgarity
that all but overwhelms disgust at moral freakishness. *Losing Battles*
is lyrical throughout, for the narrator matches her hovering descriptive voice to her characters' speech, actions, and feelings; and once,
when all are sleeping, she matches the thoughts and feelings of the
sensitive, roused, and wandering boy Vaughn to the eloquence of the
silent night in a beautiful third-person soliloquy.

In the largely interior stories the purest expression of Eudora
Welty's fictional lyricism is to be found. It is here that one of the
most important resources of a lyricist in fiction—figurative language—offers its greatest opportunities. My fresh awareness of the
auditory side of Eudora Welty's lyricism does not imply any oversight
of her gifts as a descriptive writer and her imaginative use of imagery:
I take these gifts for granted. They seem related to earlier evidences
of her visual powers and interests as an amateur painter and a photographer of proven sensitivity and talent. I also count her use of symbols
and myth in "functional" ways as part of her lyricism: she uses both
as lyric poets do—Yeats, for instance.

The achievement of lyricism in its fullness is, in most of her stories, a process. In *One Writer's Beginnings* she describes how she usually
begins "writing from a distance," sometimes of things seen from a
traveler's perspective: pictures, scenes, situations, persons viewed
from the window of a train or car, or sometimes met with "the
pounding heart" of one who arrives at a destination, or approaching
on foot, perhaps with a camera for protection. The narrator seems to
be led on by a sympathetic curiosity, interest, the desire to bring the
outer world into her inner life (for her work, she says, "is as dearly
matched to the world as its secret sharer"). The narrator is waiting
for the still moment of revelation into which there breaks, at last, the
cri de coeur. For the daydreaming inner self then seems to rush out,
meet, and give lyrical utterance to what she creates from imaginative
penetration of her characters' secret life.

How often, like "The Song of the Wandering Aengus," it is the
cry of the traveler or wanderer, lonely, passionate, and in search of

love. Here is Bowman's unspoken cry in Eudora Welty's first published story, "Death of a Traveling Salesman":

I have been sick and I found out then, only then, how lonely I am. Is it too late? My heart puts up a struggle inside me, and you may have heard it, protesting against emptiness. . . . It should be full, he would rush on to tell her, thinking of his heart now as a deep lake, it should be holding love like other hearts. It should be flooded with love. There would be a warm spring day. . . . Come and stand in my . . . heart, whoever you are, and a whole river would cover your feet and rise higher and take your knees in whirlpools, and draw you down to itself, your whole body, your heart too.

The language is simple, repetitive; the cadence is surging; the imagery—of spring, warmth, rising water, drowning, love-making—is natural, eloquent.

In "First Love" (is there a more lyrical subject?) Eudora Welty makes the tongue of the dumb to sing. She does this almost entirely through third-person descriptive writing and soliloquy as the deaf-mute Joel Mayes, who hears no sound but that of a violin playing, with limited sense perceptions and limitless intuitions and feelings, is given an internal voice. The words he cannot speak orally are one night transmuted into touch, into his hands and fingers, which after the long month of his love's growth have "some wisdom" in them, and know "with what gentleness to hold the burning hand" of Burr. "With the gravity of his very soul he received the furious pressure of this man's dream."

The passage I have already quoted and discussed at the end of chapter eight illustrates the more sophisticated lyrical style that Eudora Welty uses in the stories collected in *The Bride of the Innisfallen*. The young American wife of the title story cannot tell her husband her secret of joy, but finds its release and expression in a kinetic and rococo rapture as she sees the streets of Cork "rise lifting their towers like note above note on a page of music, with arpeggios running over it of green and galleries and belvederes and the bright sun raining at the top." Her lyrical cry is as much in contrast to Bowman's utterance as the red clay Mississippi country cabin is to the elaborate multileveled facades and climbing greenery of the charming Irish city waterside. Viewed together, the passages show the range of this author's lyrical style.

Her lyricism may be oblique or direct, dreaming or earthbound, satiric or sober, revelatory or reticent, exaggerated or understated: all these polarities appear in *One Writer's Beginnings* as much as in the fiction. The reticence is most apparent in a passage describing what must have been one of the most devastating experiences of her life, witnessing her father's death when her mother attempted to save his life by giving her blood in a transfusion. The two parents are lying on adjoining cots; her mother looks at her father with a "fervent face" as she hopes to do for him what he once did for her in helping to save her life:

> All at once his face turned dusky red all over. The doctor made a disparaging sound with his lips, the kind a woman knitting makes when she drops a stitch. What the doctor meant by it was that my father had died.
> My mother never recovered emotionally.

The brief visual description followed by an account of the doctor's reaction with a homely comparison of sounds (almost trivializing the great event to his experienced perception), and finally the childlike simplicity of the witness-narrator's interpretation of the sound, is gratefully numbing in its reticence, as though the reader's heart were caught in a still moment of hiatus before the comprehension that brings its soundless shock. Such passages are beyond praise. This lyricism of reserve, of withholding, could not be in greater contrast to the lyricism that is overflowing, as where the sound of "The Merry Widow" running up and down the staircase opens the autobiography.

As has often been noted in this study, the vision of life offered in Eudora Welty's fiction is one of double truths, paradoxes, polarities, contradictions contained and often subsumed in a mystery that is part revelation and part concealment. *One Writer's Beginnings* shows the patterns in her life that made for the polarities. Central to these is the polarity of love and separateness: to Virgie Rainey's mature reflection, separateness is "a horror in life, that was at once the horror in love. . . ."

The lives of Eudora Welty's parents reveal the pattern in its extremes; for just as there was an ideal quality to their love, bolstered as it was by truth, goodness, hope, industry, generosity, so there seemed a special absurdity, unpredictability, cruelty in the separateness death brought into their lives again and again. It had started early for her father, whose mother died when he was at the vulnerable age of seven. She had left in his keepsake book a note written on the day of her death: "My dearest Webbie, I want you to be a good boy and to meet me in heaven. Your loving Mother." Early loss of a parent was a grief he had in common with his wife—a tragedy no less hurtful to the fifteen-year-old Chessie, though shared with her large family and perhaps relieved by the tales and legends surrounding his memory.

Another early loss of Eudora Welty's parents involves love and separateness with a double reticence. She describes how as a child she had been entreating her mother to tell her where babies came from: like other mothers of her place and time, she could not speak of this. "Not being able to bring herself to open that door to reveal its secret, one of those days, she opened another door." The door left closed— the one to the bedroom—was also kept closed in her daughter's fiction; the door opened—on death—remained so in her fiction. It was a baby brother who had died, neglected, her mother told her, because she herself had almost died when he was born. These shocks of death had left their marks on her parents differently. Her father, especially aware of the mortality of a parent, had taken great precautions to protect his family. His faith in economic progress, insurance, preventive measures taken, made an energetic optimist of him. Her mother, always a pessimist, tried bravely to avert disaster, and too often, when it fell, blamed herself.

Then the Depression came and, in 1931, the personal affliction of leukemia, which caused her father's death at the age of fifty-two. The double blow to Eudora Welty of her father's death in suffering her own and her mother's more complicated loss, fell before she did any serious fiction writing. Could the shock of grief have shaken the beginning writer, then in her early twenties, into writing some of her earliest and most poignant stories? She does not make the connection in her autobiography, but it is certain that there are many sudden and unexpected deaths, catastrophes, accidents (or near-accidents) recorded in her stories, and the reaction of a passionately loving young woman's heart to such a loss is the exclusive concern of the title story of her first collection, "A Curtain of Green." Mrs. Larkin, the young widow whose husband is killed by a falling chinaberry tree, finds it was "accident that was incredible when her love for her husband was keeping him safe . . . so helpless was she, too helpless to defy the workings of accident, of life and death, of unaccountability." There is "no prevention" against the death that seizes a loved one, no reason to protest because nothing to protest against. Chance is blind and irrational.

The curtain of green, as a symbol of nature in all its myriad life, is never drawn back in Eudora Welty's fiction. No transcendental knowledge nor religious vision or hope appears to comfort her characters, a pattern which reflects the resistance, within her family, of the influences of a "religious-minded society."

In her autobiography Eudora Welty states that she believes "the guiding emotion" in her mother's life was that of a pity that "encompassed the world." It is abundantly clear that this trait was inherited by the writer as much as her mother's independence. Her fiction shows her to be large-spirited, compassionate, quick to sympathy, slow to blame. Tragedy in her stories is rarely seen as the result of personal or social evil, though Fay Chisom is exceedingly selfish, and the murderer in "Where Is the Voice Coming From?" has an invincible racial prejudice. The characters in her stories are usually just *seen*, inside and out, with a vision that does not judge, and may so closely relate polarized experiences that they become identical. In "The Wide Net" the philosophical Doc says, "The excursion is the same when you go looking for your sorrow as when you go looking for your joy."

In many of her stories Eudora Welty shows what she discovered in her life: how interfused and how juxtaposed joy and sorrow may be, or comedy and tragedy, or hope and despair, or the world of dream and the world of fantasy. In "A Memory" and "At the Landing" the two worlds seem in contrast; in "Old Mr. Marblehall," "The Winds," and *The Golden Apples* they are mostly fused. In her autobiography she says: "Other sorts of vision, dream, illusion, hallucination, obsesssion, and that most wonderful interior vision which is memory, have all gone to make up my stories." But memory is "the treasure most dearly regarded" by her. That treasure is opened and shared most fully in *One Writer's Beginnings,* and through many fictional transmutations in *The Optimist's Daughter.* Both works reveal the living confluence, in memory, of "the old and the young, the past and the present, the living and the dead."

Eudora Welty's autobiography shows her view of her *own* life, and life in general, to be all-affirmative. The child so excited and filled with suspense that she had to be put to bed for prolonged rest with a strange illness called "fast-beating heart," the curious and enthralled listener to family stories and local gossip, the hedonistic reader, the rapt dreamer, the mesmerized traveler, the acute observer and sensitive responder to the outside world, the family comic (with her older brother), the devoted daughter, struggling successfully to achieve her independence against unusually protective and self-sacrificial parents—all these speak of an abundant *vitality* and *joy* in existence, which overflows in her fiction. No wonder she chose a musician to convey the passion and intensity she feels for her work and expresses in it. Mystery rushes through this art, or opens slowly as a night-flower, shedding beauty. Or it is caught in a still, rapt moment of revelation.

The great variety of Eudora Welty's fiction means there must be at least one story or novel for every reader. The luckiest readers will have discovered how many there will be; those who are prepared for contemplation will perceive great depth in many of the stories, psychological complexity, artistic subtlety. The best readers will have learned how many of these stories may please, or intrigue. Imagination can make a reader as virtuosic as the writer.

Yet many, including the most seasoned and discriminating among her readers, will go on preferring some of those earliest and undoubtedly great, durable stories—"Death of a Traveling Salesman," "A Worn Path," "A Memory," "Powerhouse," "A Curtain of Green," "A Still Moment," "Livvie," "The Wide Net," "Why I Live at the P.O.," "Petrified Man," "June Recital"—to any of her later works. Because the early stories are the work of a young writer, they are charged with the shock and surprise of the world—its cruelty, horror, and absurdity as well as its beauty and delight. They have an eternal freshness and spontaneity about them, however rich and complex these "simple" characters may be, however elusive their motives and actions. If there is less wisdom and all-embracing tolerance in the early stories than in the later fiction, less evidence of a mature technical command of the craft of fiction, there is always an instinctive "rightness" in her style. This is a "born writer," we feel. Even the occasional story, or aspect of a novel, that doesn't "come off"—a risk taken unsuccessfully—seems to me like the kitten that falls by accident: after some mid-air scrambling, it always lands on its feet.

Eudora Welty has extended the range and potential of fiction by the variety of her experiments in length, subject matter, theme, form, and feeling. Only when the totality of her work is known does one begin to see the whole as possibly greater than the sum of its parts. All she has hoped is to give us each work bright and new, like

a surprise. She has wished no more than that we should see each particular story solitary—as a "little world in space, just as we can isolate one star in the sky by a concentrated vision." But after we have
gazed for a long time at each of these little solitary worlds, some of
them brighter, some dimmer, we begin to perceive the outlines of a
new constellation of great depth and beauty, created by her vision,
lifted to the timeless world of art—"far out and endless, a constellation which the heart may read over many a night."

Notes and References

Chronology

1. A chronology that included all of Eudora Welty's honors, awards, and major activities would run to several pages, and very quickly become dated. Accordingly, by some imprecisely working law of a diminishing number of entries for increasing numbers of honors and events worthy of mention, I have listed many of the early awards and activities, and relatively few of the more recent ones. I have omitted all but a couple of earliest honorary degrees and other awards by universities, colleges, and other institutions, and included only a few of the most prestigious of recent honors and awards.

Chapter One

1. Much of the material in this biographical chapter Eudora Welty generously supplied me in conversations, beginning in March 1961 and continuing through the years. Most of it is now part of "the public record," repeated in many interviews and biographical sketches. The best source for information about her literary career is obviously her autobiography, *One Writer's Beginnings* (Cambridge: Harvard University Press, 1984). Of immense value also are the interviews collected in *Conversations with Eudora Welty* (Peggy W. Prenshaw, ed., Jackson: University Press of Mississippi, 1985), and the autobiographical sketches (particularly "The Little Store") collected in *The Eye of the Story: Selected Essays and Reviews* (New York: Random House, 1983). In the interests of economy and an imperfect consistency, I have omitted page references to Eudora Welty's fiction and autobiography (*One Writer's Beginnings*) while including references for her essays, articles, and interviews. My hope is to make a lure of quotations to the texts from which they ideally cannot be removed, as though they were adages from Emerson. Quotations from Eudora Welty's work are best discovered or rediscovered in context.

2. *The Eye of the Story,* 326–35.

3. The essay titled "Place in Fiction" (in *The Eye of the Story,* 116–33) provides the author's most fully developed statement on this important subject.

4. "Writing and Analyzing a Story," in *The Eye of the Story,* 108–9.

5. *Conversations with Eudora Welty,* 319.

6. Ibid., 255.

Chaper Two

1. "Writing and Analyzing a Story," in *The Eye of the Story,* 108–10.
2. "Looking at Short Stories," in *The Eye of the Story,* 105.
3. "How I Write," *Understanding Fiction,* Cleanth Brooks and Robert Penn Warren ed. (New York: Appleton-Century-Crofts, 1959), 548.
4. Ibid., 552.
5. "Writing and Analyzing a Story," 114.
6. Robert Penn Warren, "Love and Separateness in Miss Welty," *Kenyon Review* 6 (Spring 1944). 247.
7. "Writing and Analyzing a Story," 114.
8. "Place in Fiction," 121–22.

Chapter Three

1. William C. Seitz, *Claude Monet, Seasons and Moments* (New York: Museum of Modern Art, 1960), 8–9.
2. Warren, "Love and Separateness in Miss Welty," 254.
3. Ibid.

Chapter Four

1. Review of William Faulkner's *Intruder in the Dust,* in *The Eye of the Story,* 208–9.
2. Included in *The Eye of the Story,* 300–14.
3. Ibid., 305–7.
4. Ibid., 309.
5. Ibid., 311.
6. Wylie Sypher, *Comedy* (New York: Doubleday Anchor, 1956), 235.
7. Review of *A Curtain of Green, Time* 38 (24 November 1941): 111.
8. Sypher, *Comedy,* 193–95.

Chapter Five

1. *The Eye of the Story,* 120.
2. "Delta Fiction," *Kenyon Review* 8 (Summer 1946): 507.
3. To the present writer in an interview on 15 March 1961.

Chapter Six

1. *Conversations with Eudora Welty,* 88.
2. Thomas L. McHaney, "Eudora Welty and the Multitudinous Golden Apples," *Mississippi Quarterly* 26 (Fall 1973): 622.

Chapter Seven

1. *The Eye of the Story,* 107–15.
2. Ibid., 111–13.

3. Ibid., 114.

4. Michael Kreyling, *Eudora Welty's Achievement of Order* (Baton Rouge: Louisiana State University Press, 1980), 128–29.

Chapter Eight

1. Collected in *The Eye of the Story,* 349–55.

2. Ibid., 352, 354, 352–53.

3. *The Collected Stories of Eudora Welty* (New York: Harcourt Brace Jovanovich, 1980), x.

4. Ibid., xi.

5. Originally published in *Atlantic* 216 (October 1965): 104–8. Collected in *The Eye of the Story,* 146–58.

6. Ibid., 154–55.

Chapter Nine

1. *Conversations with Eudora Welty,* 31.

2. Robert B. Heilman, "Losing Battles and Winning the War," *Eudora Welty: Collected Essays,* (Peggy W. Prenshaw, ed., Jackson: University Press of Mississippi, 1979), 270.

3. See, for example, Michael Kreyling's discussion in his chapter "Myth and History: The Foes of *Losing Battles,*" in *Eudora Welty's Achievement of Order,* 140–52.

Chapter Eleven

1. My discovery is not original. Michael Kreyling, for instance, states that "Welty's fiction is more lyrical than narrative; one must read it with 'an ear for song,' " in *Eudora Welty's Achievement of Order,* xv.

2. Elizabeth Evans explores Eudora Welty's use of musical metaphors, images, and allusions in "Eudora Welty: The Metaphor of Music," *Southern Quarterly* 20 (Summer 1982); 92–100.

Selected Bibliography

PRIMARY SOURCES

1. Novels
Delta Wedding. New York: Harcourt, Brace & Co., 1946.
Losing Battles. New York: Random House, 1970.
The Optimist's Daughter. New York: Random House, 1972.
The Ponder Heart. New York: Harcourt, Brace & Co., 1954.
The Robber Bridegroom. New York: Doubleday, Doran & Co., 1942.

2. Short Story Collections
The Bride of the Innisfallen. New York: Harcourt, Brace & Co., 1955.
A Curtain of Green and Other Stories. New York: Doubleday, Doran & Co.,
     1941.
The Collected Stories of Eudora Welty. New York: Harcourt Brace Jovanovich,
     1980.
The Golden Apples. New York: Harcourt, Brace & Co., 1949.
The Wide Net and Other Stories. New York: Harcourt, Brace & Co., 1943.

3. Essays
The Eye of the Story: Selected Essays and Reviews. New York: Random House,
     1978.

4. Autobiography
One Time, One Place: Mississippi in the Depression. New York: Random House,
     1971. Photographs with an introduction by the author.
One Writer's Beginnings. Cambridge: Harvard University Press, 1984.

SECONDARY SOURCES

1. Bibliographies
McDonald, W. U., Jr., ed. *Eudora Welty Newsletter.* Toledo, Ohio: Univer-
     sity of Toledo, Winter 1977 to the present. Published bi-annually, the
     Newsletter includes a continuing bibliography of Welty's works, criti-
     cism and scholarship, editions, information about manuscripts, revi-
     sions, news stories, interviews, and foreign language publications.

————. "An Unworn Path: Bibliographical and Textual Scholarship on Eudora Welty." *Southern Quarterly* 20 (Summer 1982); 101–8. A good discursive account of the state of Welty scholarship up to 1982, indicating areas needing attention.

Polk, Noel. "A Eudora Welty Checklist." *Mississippi Quarterly* 26 (Fall 1973): 663–93. The most complete listing of works by Eudora Welty up to 1973, followed by a selected but comprehensive checklist of secondary material. According to Polk, "a complete descriptive bibliography" is soon to appear.

Prenshaw, Peggy W. "Eudora Welty." In *American Women Writers: Bibliographical Essays,* edited by Maurice Duke, Jackson R. Bryer, and M. Thomas Inge, 233–67. Westport, Conn.: Greenwood Press, 1983. Excellent descriptive bibliography of Welty's works up to 1983, containing substantive and discriminating evaluations of bibliography, editions, manuscripts and letters, biography, interviews, criticism ("general estimates," special topics, and individual works). Indispensable to Welty scholars; useful as well to the general reader.

Swearingen, Bethany C. *Eudora Welty, a Critical Bibliography, 1936–1958.* Jackson: University Press of Mississippi, 1984. A complete annotated listing of primary and secondary sources for the period, useful in tracing Welty's early reputation.

Thompson, Victor H. *Eudora Welty: A Reference Guide.* Boston: G. K. Hall & Co., 1976. A comprehensive listing of secondary material on Welty's fiction and biography, including reviews and newspaper clippings, compiled annually from 1936 to 1975. Also lists Welty's nonfiction, exclusive of reviews. Useful for its introduction on Welty's reputation and its brief summaries of items listed.

2. Books and Monographs

Appel, Alfred, Jr. *A Season of Dreams: The Fiction of Eudora Welty.* Baton Rouge: Louisiana State University Press, 1965. A comprehensive treatment of Welty's fiction through *The Bride of the Innisfallen.* Unfortunately, use is made of the 1962 edition of this now revised and updated study without proper acknowledgment.

Bryant, J. A., Jr. *Eudora Welty.* Minnesota American Writers Series. Minneapolis: University of Minnesota Press, 1968. A brief introduction to Welty's fiction and criticism, stressing her evocation of perplexities through the stories, her visual imagination, use of place, and other topics.

Devlin, Albert J. *Eudora Welty's Chronicle: A Story of Mississippi Life.* Jackson: University Press of Mississippi, 1983. This study argues thoughtfully that Welty's work displays a structure of the historical imagination, the time span extending from the territorial era to the present. Selected works (such as *Delta Wedding*) receive detailed attention and insightful readings.

Evans, Elizabeth. *Eudora Welty*. Modern Literature Series. New York: Frederick Ungar, 1981. Sympathetic, reliable study of Welty's career, her fiction and nonfiction. Introduces new material (such as Welty's correspondence with her publishers), and covers important aspects of Welty's fiction with economy.

Howard, Zelma Turner. *The Rhetoric of Eudora Welty's Short Stories*. Jackson: University and College Press of Mississippi, 1973. Applies Wayne Booth's critical vocabulary in *The Rhetoric of Fiction* to an analysis of Welty's stories.

Issacs, Neil D. *Eudora Welty*. Steck-Vaughn Southern Writers Series. Austin, Tex.: Steck-Vaughn, 1969. Good treatment of Welty's first-person narratives; somewhat forced imposition of a central myth or archetype of renewal on most of Welty's fiction.

Kreyling, Michael. *Eudora Welty's Achievement of Order*. Baton Rouge: Louisiana State University Press, 1980. A sensitive and intelligent reading of Welty's fiction which manages, by its flexibility of approach, to trace a pattern of development in Welty's growing control over fictional technique, while appreciating its overall excellence and variety. Kreyling's use of manuscript and early versions of Welty's fiction, and his comparisons with the work of other writers, are illuminating.

Manning, Carol Sue. *Ears Opening Like Morning Glories: Eudora Welty and the Love of Story Telling*. Westport, Conn.: Greenwood Press, 1985. Study arguing that the Southern oral tradition and Welty's early delight in storytelling shaped every aspect of her art and provided her with a rich social vision of the South.

Manz-Kung, Marie Antoinette. *Eudora Welty: Aspects of Reality in Her Fiction*. Bern: Francke Verlag, 1971. Most valuable for its discussion of Welty's use of an experience of rhythm as a means to evoking reality.

Vande Kieft, Ruth M. *Eudora Welty*. New York: Twayne Publishers, 1962. The first edition of the present book, contains an evaluative final chapter on Welty's work through 1955, placing it among Southern and world writers. A second edition (1973) updates chronology and bibliography, the latter, extensive and annotated, up to 1973.

3. Special Issues and Symposia Devoted to Welty Criticism

Boatwright, James, ed. *Shenandoah* 20 (Spring 1969). Includes brief tributes by such important writers as Reynolds Price, Robert Heilman, Malcolm Crowley, Walker Percy, Allen Tate, Robert Penn Warren, and Joyce Carol Oates.

Desmond, John F., ed. *A Still Moment: Essays on the Art of Eudora Welty*. Metuchen, N.J.: Scarecrow Press, 1978. Interesting collection of ten essays, original and reprinted, on topics relating to Welty's fiction.

Devlin, Albert J., ed. *Mississippi Quarterly* 39 (Fall 1986). Important essays by leading Welty critics on occasion of fiftieth-year celebration of publication of her first story.

Dollarhide, Louis, and Ann J. Abadie, eds. *Eudora Welty: A Form of Thanks*. Jackson: University Press of Mississippi, 1979. Fine essays on various topics contributed by Cleanth Brooks, Peggy W. Prenshaw, William J. Smith, and others.

Prenshaw, Peggy W., ed. *Eudora Welty: Critical Essays*. Jackson: University Press of Mississippi, 1979. Most inclusive of the symposia, the collection includes twenty-five essays, contributions by leading Welty critics. Nine essays are "general studies," the rest being devoted to special topics or individual Welty works. Selections from this volume appear in *Eudora Welty: Thirteen Essays*, Peggy W. Prenshaw, ed. (Jackson: University Press of Mississippi, 1983).

————. *Southern Quarterly* 20 (Summer 1982). Critical essays, a bibliographical article, an interview, photographs, and an article on Welty's Jackson.

Simpson, Lewis P., ed. *Mississippi Quarterly* 26 (Fall 1973). Fine essays by many hands; a Welty essay (on time in fiction); an interview with Walker Percy and William F. Buckley; and Noel Polk's useful bibliography.

4. Interviews

Prenshaw, Peggy W., ed. *Conversations with Eudora Welty*. Jackson: University Press of Mississippi, 1984. An invaluable collection of twenty-six interviews spanning forty years, providing a variety of information about Welty's life and literary career, her attitudes toward her art, other writers, the South, and other subjects. Thoroughly and usefully indexed.

5. Films

Haines, Frank. "An Interview with Eudora Welty." Filmed for the Mississippi Authority for Educational Television, 26 October, 1971.

Moore, Richard R. "Eudora Welty." The Writer in America Series. Sausalito, Calif., 1971.

————. "Four Women Artists." Memphis, Tenn., Center for Southern Folklore, 1977.

Index